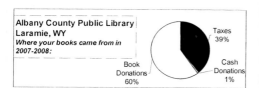

ALSO BY RICH COHEN

Tough Jews: Fathers, Sons, and Gangster Dreams

The Avengers: A Jewish War Story

Lake Effect

The Record Men: The Chess Brothers and the Birth of Rock & Roll

SWEET AND LOW

RICH COHEN

SWEET AND LOW

A FAMILY STORY

FARRAR, STRAUS AND GIROUX

NEW YORK

Farrar, Straus and Giroux
19 Union Square West, New York 10003

Grateful acknowledgment is made for permission to reprint the following previously published material:

"Benjamin Eisenstadt, 89, a Sweetener of Lives," by Robert McG. Thomas, copyright © 1996 by The New York Times Company. Reprinted with permission.

"Lawyer Doubles in Cafeteria Job" copyright © 1935 by The New York Times Company. Reprinted with permission.

James Wright's translation of "Toussaint L'ouverture," by Pablo Neruda, appears courtesy of Anne Wright.

The excerpt from "Gerontion," by T. S. Eliot, is reprinted by permission of Faber and Faber, Ltd., and Harcourt Brace.

Library of Congress Cataloging-in-Publication Data
Cohen, Rich.
  Sweet and low : a family story / Rich Cohen.— 1st ed.
    p.   cm.
  ISBN-13: 978-0-374-27229-6 (hardcover : alk. paper)
  ISBN-10: 0-374-27229-8 (hardcover : alk. paper)
  1. Eisenstadt family.   2. Eisenstadt, Benjamin—Family.   3. Cohen family.
4. Cohen, Rich—Family   5. Cumberland Packing Corporation.   6. Sweet'N Low
(Trademark)   7. Businessmen—United States—Biography.   8. Brooklyn (New
York, N.Y.)—Biography.   I. Title.

  CT274.E375C64   2006
  929'.2'0973—dc22

                                                              2005015730

Designed by Abby Kagan

www.fsgbooks.com

1   3   5   7   9   10   8   6   4   2

TO ELLEN AND HER ISSUE

Benjamin Eisenstadt, 89, a Sweetener of Lives

By ROBERT McG. THOMAS Jr.

Benjamin Eisenstadt, the innovative Brooklyn businessman who set Americans to shaking their sugar before sweetening their coffee and then shook up the entire sweetener industry as the developer of Sweet 'N Low, died on Monday at New York Hospital-Cornell Medical Center. He was 89 and a major benefactor of Maimonides Medical Center in Brooklyn.

The cause was complications of bypass surgery, his son Marvin said.

Considering the scope of his eventual philanthropy, Mr. Eisenstadt, a Brooklyn resident who gave millions to Maimonides, followed a circuitous path to business success.

Mr. Eisenstadt, who was born on the Lower East Side of Manhattan, seemed headed for a brilliant career as a lawyer, but his timing was off. He graduated first in his class from St. John's University law school in 1929 — just in time for the Depression. Taking a job at a cafeteria his father-in-law operated in Brooklyn, Mr. Eisenstadt later ran a couple of cafeterias of his own, eventually finding a measure of success by opening one in 1940 on Cumberland Street, in the Fort Greene section, just across from the Brooklyn Navy Yard, which became a boom town in World War II.

When the end of the war turned the Navy Yard into a ghost town and left him bereft of customers, Mr. Eisenstadt, recalling that his uncle had once operated a company that filled tea bags, turned the Cumberland Cafeteria into the Cumberland Packing Company, transforming it into a tea bag factory, one that was never a threat to Tetley or Lipton, and which limped toward oblivion in 1947.

Faced with yet another business failure, Mr. Eisenstadt had the brainstorm that changed the way Americans dispense sugar. The

Benjamin Eisenstadt

same equipment that injected tea into tea bags, he realized, could be used to put sugar into little paper packets.

At a time when restaurants had never used anything but open sugar bowls or heavy glass dispensers, the idea of individual sanitary sugar packets was so revolutionary — and Mr. Eisenstadt was so naïve — that when he proudly showed his operation to executives of giant sugar companies, his son said, they simply set up their own sugar-packet operations.

A contract with the little Jack Frost sugar company kept Cumberland alive, but without a branded line of its own it was little more than a marginal operation.

That changed in 1957 when Mr. Eisenstadt and his son Marvin, who had studied chemistry at the University of Vermont, began fooling around with saccharin. The low-calorie sweetener had been around since the 19th century (Teddy Roosevelt used it), but until then it had been available only as a liquid or in pill form, and its use was restricted to diabetics and the obese.

When the Eisenstadts mixed saccharin with dextrose and other ingredients to make a granulated low-calorie sugar substitute, another coffee revolution was at hand. Taking care to obtain a patent for the use of saccharin as a sugar substitute, Mr. Eisenstadt, recalling a Tennyson poem that had been made into a song, came up with the name Sweet 'N Low. The treble-clef musical logo on a pink packet set Sweet 'N Low apart from the white sugar packets on restaurant tables.

This time, his timing was perfect. The man who had made spooning sugar obsolete and created millions of sugar-pack shakers rode the crest of the health craze of the 1960's.

In time, an even lower-calorie sugar substitute, aspartame, marketed in blue packets under the brand name Equal, would challenge Sweet 'N Low. Even so, the company, which also makes a butter substitute, Butter Buds, and a salt substitute, Nu-Salt, still derives the bulk of its revenues from Sweet 'N Low.

With sales of about $100 million a year, the company, which employs 400 people, turns out 50 million Sweet 'N Low packets a day in what used to be a cafeteria.

You just can't buy a cup of coffee there anymore.

In addition to his son, who lives in Neponsit, Queens, Mr. Eisenstadt is survived by his wife, Betty; another son, Ira, of Manhattan; two daughters, Ellen Cohen of Washington and Gladys Eisenstadt of Brooklyn, seven grandchildren and six great-grandchildren.

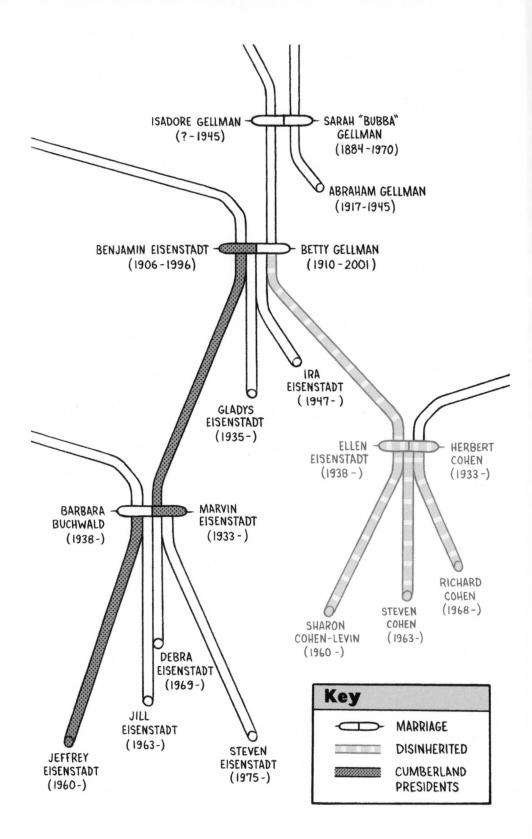

THE EXTENDED FAMILY GATHERED MOSTLY FOR
WEDDINGS AND FUNERALS. HERE, AT MY SISTER, SHARON'S,
WEDDING, IN 1990, ARE MY EISENSTADT GRANDPARENTS,
PARENTS, SIBLINGS, UNCLE, AUNT, AND COUSINS.

Everyone in my family tells this story, but everyone starts it in a different way. My mother starts it in the diner across from the Brooklyn Navy Yard, where my grandfather Benjamin Eisenstadt, a short-order cook, invented the sugar packet and Sweet'N Low, and with them built the fortune that would be the cause of all the trouble. My sister starts it with his wife, Betty, the power behind the throne, the woman who, in this version, found in Ben a vehicle for her dreams. Whenever anyone asks what Betty was like, I say, "Betty had her name legally changed to Betty from Bessie."

My father starts the story in downtown Brooklyn, in the courtroom where my Uncle Marvin, the first son of the patriarch, a handsome, curly-haired man who insists on being called Uncle Marvelous, is facing off against federal prosecutors. After assuming control of the Cumberland Packing Company, which makes Sweet'N Low, Sugar in the Raw, Nu-Salt, and Butter Buds, Marvin, among other things that caused a scandal, put a criminal on the payroll, a reputed associate of the Bonanno crime family. That criminal made illegal campaign contributions to Senator Alfonse D'Amato, who sponsored legislation that kept saccharin on the market. Saccharin, a key ingredient of Sweet'N Low, had been found to cause cancer. In the end, Marvin cut a deal with prosecutors, testifying for the government and keeping himself out of prison.

In other words, Uncle Marvelous turned rat.

I start this story at the Metropolitan Club, on Manhattan's Upper East Side, where my cousin Jeffrey, the oldest son of the oldest son, the scion of the third generation, is getting married for the second time. Jeffrey, a burned-out surfer, a bloodshot member of the high school class of '78 whose yearbook picture still tells the story, is earmarked to inherit the empire. If Jeffrey read more widely, he would know that he is fated to screw the pooch, lose his grip, open his hands and let the money blast back into the whirlwind.

Or I start with Uncle Ira, the youngest son of Ben and Betty, a vice president of the company, who controls 49 percent of the stock. Ira, who has always struck me as an extreme eccentric, is years younger than his siblings, a pampered, interesting kid who grew into a genuine nut, a man who carries a purse, wears sandals, follows whims, sports an unruly red beard, and lives in an East Side town house with his wife and many cats. Ira has been to his office at the factory just twice in the last ten years. (Though he says he works many hours a day from home via phone and fax.) He is the trick that fate played on empire, the inscrutable brother who has to be watched.

At Jeff's wedding, he approached me in the bathroom. Standing next to me at the urinal, he said, "What is the last thing you want your crazy uncle to say to you in the bathroom?"

"What?"

"Nice dick."

My brother starts the story in Flatbush, in the icebox chill room of my aunt Gladys, a woman who, for mysterious reasons, had not been out of the house—her childhood home, where she still lived with Ben and Betty—in almost thirty years. I once heard a politician describe a rival's tax scheme as "the crazy aunt hiding in the attic," and I said to myself, "She actually lives on the ground floor." Whenever I asked what was wrong with Aunt Gladys, why she never left her room, words were muttered about arthritis, psoriasis, lack of confidence. Even though she is the least physically active of the Eisenstadt siblings, Gladys, with her telephone, drives the action of this story. In a way I am still trying to fathom, Gladys is its protagonist. When I was briefing my brother-in-law on his new family and told him that Gladys had not left the house since the Nixon administration, he said, "You mean mostly she stays in the house but now and then she leaves the house to go to the store?" I said, "I mean mostly she stays in her room but now and then she leaves her room to go to the bathroom."

As I mentioned, my aunt's room, for reasons I still do not understand, is kept as cold as a meat locker. To this day, if we are in a movie theater or a mall where the AC is really cranking, my brother will say, "It's like Aunt Gladys's room, it's so cold in here." By which we know him to mean more than just the temperature: Gladys's room is where my brother, Steven, learned the nature of things. Once a week, before I was born, my brother and sister were taken to Flatbush to visit their grandparents, aunt, and cousins.

There was an ancient form of primogeniture at play in the family; as the son of the oldest son, Cousin Jeffrey was golden. One week, Grandma Betty decided that a grandchild would, for no particular reason, have a party thrown in his or her honor, complete with cake and gifts. While standing in my aunt's room, Betty wrote the names on a slip of paper and dropped the slips in a hat. A winner was drawn: Jeffrey. Since Jeffrey seemed to win many such contests, my brother grew suspicious. When he picked up the hat, Betty said, "Don't look!" Unfolding the slips, he had the great early shock of his life. Every ballot was marked "Jeffrey." Later, when my brother refused to follow some instruction, Ben led him upstairs and spanked him—a grandfather who spanks!—ending, for my brother, the sweet ignorance of childhood.

In 1995, when my grandfather collapsed in the hospital, the first relative on the scene was my brother. In a nice twist of fate, Steven found himself charged with making life-and-death decisions for the man who had helped him recognize the unfairness of the world. And the winner is? Jeffrey! In the months following Ben's collapse, the family battle moved into its titanic phase, with Ben shuffling from doctor to doctor and everything up for grabs: the money, the legacy, and the story itself. When Grandma Betty died, I found out that my mother had lost this battle and that she and all of her children had been written out of the will—the factory and assets of the company are worth an estimated several hundred million dollars. Betty's last words came in a legal document: "I hereby record that I have made no provision under this WILL for my daughter ELLEN and any of ELLEN'S issue for reasons I deem sufficient." Her issue? It was like being called discharge, or refuse, or excrement. She swallowed a dime but it came out in the issue. So fate has placed me in the ideal storytelling position: the youngest son of the once-favorite daughter. Outside but inside, with just enough of a grudge to sharpen my sensibility. I am Napoleon staring at Paris from Corsica. All they have left me is this story. To be disinherited is to be set free.

PART ONE

WHEN GRANDPA BEN BEGAN TO COME UP IN THE WORLD,
HE BOUGHT A HOUSE IN FLATBUSH, WHERE MY MOTHER AND
HER SIBLINGS WERE RAISED AND WHERE MY AUNT GLADYS
STILL LIVES. THE HOUSE HAS WITNESSED ALL THE ACTION.
AS THE REVIEWERS SAY, IT'S ANOTHER CHARACTER IN THE STORY.

1.

Cumberland Packing, the company that manufactures Sweet'N Low, occupies a boxy building across the street from the Brooklyn Navy Yard. It sits amid the factories of Fort Greene, the last of the city's vanishing industrial base. The neighborhood is ringed by housing projects, dark windows looking out on the long skies over Williamsburg.

In the summer of 2003, I drove to the factory to talk to my uncle Marvin, the president of the company. I had not seen much of him since my grandmother died. I gave my name at the door and was told to go around the side of the building, where my uncle was waiting.

To me, Marvin is always forty-five, blond, thin-hipped, and handsome, the kind of uncle who fixes things. When I was a kid, he took me on tours of the plant and had an ID made that showed my face in front of Cumberland's pink musical logo. He always had the newest gadgets and the biggest televisions. When he was a block from his car, he'd press a button and the trunk would pop open. It was a convertible. I would sit in back as the storefronts of Brooklyn whistled by. Even into his sixties, Marvin was as peppy as a camp counselor. Now, as I shook his hand and followed him inside, he seemed slower and sadder. He had a tremor in his voice and a shuffle in his step. Uncle Marvelous had gotten old! It's like this: young, young, young, young, young, OLD. Like the sun going down and down and down and bang, you're in the dark. It reminded me of something a journeyman baseball player once told me: "Some guys go on and on, but other guys just fall off the table."

Marvin led me to his office. It's cramped, with the kind of drop ceiling you can fling pencils into. One wall is covered with photographs. By following these, you can watch Marvin age—face fill out, eyes deepen, children arrive. Some of the pictures go back to the 1950s—Marvin in sepia tone, trim and tan, like a memory of Coney Island. He smiles in others, puts his arm around his wife, my beautiful aunt Barbara, or holds his kids on his back. None of the pictures was taken less than five or ten years ago, maybe when the scandal broke. It's as if he just shut off the camera and stopped recording. Most were taken on vacation, tropical beaches on Caribbean islands—the triumph of the Jews, across the Jordan at last. My family had been along on some of these trips, but there was no hint of us—why should there have been? It made me blanch to see the familiar settings with his sister Ellen and her issue so neatly excised.

Marvin wore a sleeveless fleece coat—an "alpine wife-beater" or a "muscle fleece"—over an Izod shirt. His face was florid, as if one of those Caribbean tans had recurred like a fever. He said he had been prescribed a pill for failing memory, but told me he forgets to take it. He does remember that he forgets, which struck me as suspicious. An aquarium is built into one of his walls. It was once a saltwater tank, schools of tropical fish as gaudy as muscle cars amid a world of colored gravel and faux seaweed, a vibrant seascape that has degraded into an acid pond.

The fish died in the course of a single season some years ago, one of those strange kills that can decimate a closed system. I learned about it while reading the court papers. (A defense attorney wanted to know why Marvin had asked Cumberland's controller and chief financial officer, Gil Mederos, to clean out the tank.) "Unfortunately, yes, there was one incident where there were saltwater fish, which are very delicate, and all the fish were dying," Marvin testified. "I felt so terrible. I remember telling Gil to cover the tank so I couldn't see the fish die."

Marvin asked why I had come. I told him about the book I wanted to write: It would be about Ben and Betty and the factory; and Brooklyn; and the waterfront; and the Second World War; and Betty's brother Abraham, who died in the Philippines and won the Purple Heart and the Silver Star; and Bubba, Betty's mother, who tried to jump off the roof of her Brooklyn apartment house; and the diner where Ben first worked; and the diner across from the Navy Yard, where Ben invented the sugar packet and Sweet'N Low. And it would be about the history of sugar, which is the history of the West, and how Sweet'N Low is part of that history; and about dieting, and fat people; and packing, and the saccharin ban that almost wiped out the company; and Equal and Splenda; the whole epic of uncles and aunts, Gladys in her bed; and my father and mother, and Ira, and the will, and the lawsuit my parents threatened to bring, and how my brother went with a lawyer and a stenographer and a videographer into the house in Flatbush to depose my aunt, and how, during a break in that testimony, my brother asked Gladys if the pizza place where he used to eat as a kid, where the pizza was so greasy and delicious, was still in business; and the scandal, and the kickbacks, and the raid by the Feds; and always the factory sitting on the waterfront, smoke rising from its chimneys, millions and millions of pink packets pouring off its belts.

That is, I got carried away and threw my arms around and made boasts for the book, and if Marvin would help me, great, and if not, not; and as I spoke, he grew more and more florid; then, at last, he spoke. It was a shout that had collapsed on itself, what might be left of a Bobby Knight harangue after that harangue had passed through a black hole.

He said, "You do what you want, I just don't want you to make my mother and father look bad."

He said, "Your mother wanted to get the money away from Gladys."

He said, "I don't know what your father has against me."

He said, "I agreed to talk to you only because it was you, and Barbara and I always liked you, but if your brother or father had called, forget it."

I said, "My brother or father would never have called."

He said, "I will help you, but I want you to let me proofread whatever you write."

I said, "No."

I said, "Look, Uncle Marvin, I did not come to make you look bad, or look good. I just want to figure out the truth."

I said, "For all I know, my parents have been the biggest assholes in the world."

I said, "You know, when you are young, you accept things as you are told they are, but when you get older, you look around and wonder and you want to know: Is that really how it was?"

He said, "My father was a great man."

I said, "I think so, too."

He had a way of speaking about his father and mother, and about his siblings, even my own mother, as if they were people whom I had never met. It was as if, to deal with this situation, he had convinced himself I was just some local newspaper reporter working on a human-interest story.

He said, "That lawsuit your brother brought almost killed me."

He said, "Gladys follows your career, Richard. She reads everything you write."

He said, "If there is a heaven and a hell, your brother is not going to heaven."

When Marvin spoke about my mother, his eyes filled with tears.

He said, "The thing you've got understand is this: Betty hated Gladys. She was trapped with her in that house. Betty hated Gladys and she loved your mother."

He said this again: "Betty hated Gladys and she loved your mother."

It was like the big reveal in act three, but it made no sense.

"Well, if that's true," I asked. "Why did Betty disinherit my mother?"

He said, "Well, I don't know what you mean by 'disinherit.' Because if you think that your mother was disinherited, then I was disinherited, and Ira was disinherited. The only one who was really left anything in that will was Gladys. To be perfectly candid, the only people that were disinherited were you and your brother and your sister. Because my mother left my kids fifty thousand dollars apiece. I paid my kids that money. Gladys could not afford to give up the money from the estate. So it came from

Marvin Ernest Eisenstadt. Period. So my mother's will actually *cost* me fifty thousand dollars times four. I mean three. One, two—how many kids have I got? Fifty thousand dollars times four. That's what the will cost me. And here I am paying off the lawyers because your mother's contested the will."

I told Uncle Marvin that I wanted to call Gladys and talk to her the way I was talking to him, and he said, "Okay, but I don't want you to tell her that we had this visit."

I said, "Fine. I will just call her on my own."

He said, "But she'll wonder why you're calling."

I said, "I'll tell her about the book. I'll tell her I'm getting older. I'll tell her I'm having a kid. I want to know the story."

"You're having a kid?"

"Yes."

"Congratulations, Richard."

He said, "Don't ask Gladys for anything. Tell her you just wanted to give her a call. Say whatever you want. Just keep me out of it."

I said, "Fine."

He said, "Don't tell her you came here to see me."

I said, "Fine."*

He said, "I don't think you should tell your father about this visit either."

I said, "Fine."

He said, "Your father gave instructions. He said I was never to talk to your mother again. It wasn't good for her health."

"He said that?"

"Yes, but that's between us."

I said, "Fine."

He said, "This is not easy for me. You children were always a big part of us. And yet it's not so unusual either, this kind of split in a family."

I said, "I guess it's why so few people know their second cousins."

---

*I did call Gladys, and I did go to see her, and I did keep Marvin out of it. A few weeks later, when I called my aunt again, she was angry with me. "I spoke to Marvin," she said. "I know you went to see him at the factory. Why did you keep that a secret?"

He said, "That's right. And basically it's all because your mother and father wanted the money. And the only one who suffered because of it was me."

I said, "I don't think it was all about money for my mother."

He said, "Then what was it about?"

I said, "Well, it was about . . . love."

He said, "Well, when you contest a will, you are not asking for love. You are asking for money."

Here's what I wanted to say: You are a momma's boy, Marvin, and you never grew up, and never left home, and never took that cover off the fish tank, and maybe got beat up but never learned from it, and you were given the company and the product itself, which generates over sixty million dollars a year in sales,* and all the property and rights, and I know because I've seen the papers; you've been handed everything you own, so for you to say you know what it means to be cut off and told that you do not count and to have your mother say, with her last words on earth, *to my daughter and her issue I leave nothing*, well, it's like the man sitting on a pile of doubloons telling the man cadging for a cup of coffee, "You care only about money."

That's what I wanted to say.

Here's what I did say: "I could be wrong Uncle Marvin . . . but it's my sense . . . if in the will my mom had been left . . . something of symbolic value . . ."

He said, "I told my mother that. I told her, 'Give Ellen some little thing,' but she said no. I said give her some little thing just so she won't come back and complain. But she wouldn't do it. My mother was a stubborn woman. Toward the end she was even more stubborn."

I said, "If she had just left her a brooch or something."

---

*Because Cumberland Packing is privately owned, it's extremely hard to establish its net worth. You can only extrapolate from raw numbers. According to Information Resources, a market research group based in Chicago, Cumberland products generated $66.5 million in sales during the twelve months ending March 2005—a 19 percent share of the artificial sweetener market. The property alone (the company owns the land occupied by its thirteen thousand-square-foot factory) is believed to be worth many millions of dollars.

I don't know why I said a brooch. Maybe because my grandma Betty was always wearing a brooch. She was one of those old women with a gold tarantula with ruby eyes pinned just below her shoulder.

He said, "Your mother should think of the people she's hurting."

I said, "I don't think anybody's happy about this."

He said, "I agree. But that's just between us."

And then we settled down and talked, for one hour, or two or three—a long time, anyway—about the factory, Ben, everything. When I asked about the scandal, Marvin said he had been the victim of a surfeit of trust. He spoke so much about ethics and doing the right thing because the right thing needs doing that it made me nervous. If you call the factory and get his voice mail, the message ends (or used to), "Have a nice day, and make it an even nicer day for someone else."

Then he took me on a tour of the factory. Out of his office, through an anteroom, onto the factory floor. The plant that began here as a cafeteria in the 1940s has since spread across the street into the Navy Yard and across the world, with facilities in North America, South America, and Europe. To me, Cumberland, with its antiquated packing machines and mixing rooms, is a perfect example of the vanishing urban factory, the behemoth that swallows up workers and forests and spits out product and smoke. To most people, the factory is more concept than actual locale, a place of misfortune, whistles, boredom, and injury. The factory owner is out of Dickens, the evil grandfather, Scrooge. But for a boy, the factory still carries a nineteenth-century sense of awe. It's an erector set. It's amazing machines. In *Charlie and the Chocolate Factory* by Roald Dahl, the boss is not the fat cat exploiter of lore. He is the tinkerer, the visionary whose vision has remade the world. At the end of that book, Willy Wonka fears only for his legacy, finding his successor in Charlie, but you just know the kid will never be up to the task. Within five years, Charlie will go public, sell to Hershey, or get indicted.

During peak hours at Cumberland, the packing machines rattle and the building vibrates and the workers shout over the racket, and all of this builds into a roar. As the packets are filled, saccharin dust drifts into the air, and you breathe it into your lungs. It flavors everything sickly sweet. To make Sweet'N Low, Cumberland uses tons of cream of tartar, dextrose, and saccharin each day. The ingredients are combined in a mixing room on the second floor, a lab where workers wear bathing caps and booties. You see them behind glass, stirring the premix. This product is fed into tremendous whirling, Sheeleresque machines, which cut and load it into packets and dump it onto a conveyor belt that winds through the factory like a river. Every packet is tested and weighed. On the factory floor, the conveyor belt breaks into tributaries, each headed for a different machine. Ladies in hairnets direct this flow into boxes, which totter off to the shipping bay, where they are loaded onto trucks that carry them all over the region.

As Marvin walks across the floor, he shouts, "Hola!"

The women at the machines shout, "Hola!" right back.

This is meant to show Marvin as a man of the people, a regular guy. But because it's so theatrical and because I've read so many newspaper articles in which my uncle executes the same trick, it makes him seem less like a regular guy than like the boss of a sugar plantation walking the fields at harvest time.

Hola, workers!

Hola, Marvin!

But I was less interested in the workers than I was in the machines. Cumberland started with the machines. With these machines, Ben took the chaos and diversity of Brooklyn, all those neighborhoods with all those appetites and all that merchandise, and stacked it and packed it and readied it for sale. Ben packed sugar in the early years, but he also packed soy sauce, perfume, and Sea-Monkeys. Ben had dozens of patents. Marvin has still more. Marvin started on the machines. In his first years at the factory, he came to work in coveralls, a grease monkey with tools on his belt. He is a genius with his hands. You can see evidence of this all over the factory.

He led me up a short flight of steps into a wreck of a room. The floor was covered with debris, the windows were boarded, and sunlight streamed through the cracks making Jacob's ladders in the dust. This was the site of the old cafeteria that was the beginning of it all. It's not hard to picture the room as it was during the Second World War, when it was like

Katz's on Houston Street, a big cafeteria on the waterfront, sailors and factory workers loading steel trays with chicken and fish and getting their order cards punched. Ben worked the counter, refilled the coffee cups, watered the whiskey, and dragged out the drunks.

Marvin then took me to see my cousin Little Steven. I've always called him Little Steven to distinguish him from my brother. It's a nickname that goes back to a vacation when Steven was the youngest and the smallest in the family and spoke in grunts and groans because Chewbacca was his favorite character in the movie *Star Wars*. Little Steven is a name my cousin has outgrown. He is big and beefy in a way that, in our family, has no precedent. His skin is freckled. On that day, his short blond hair was combed forward into a Caesar. He was waiting at his desk, smiling. If the rift between our families is ever healed, it will be because of Little Steven, who does not know or care to know all the facts. He is untroubled by the past.

Marvin introduced us as if we were strangers. He said, "This is my son, Steven Eisenstadt."

The three of us continued through the factory. Marvin showed me the first machine Ben bought more than fifty years ago, the tea bagger he converted into the original sugar packer. It was as stately as a Chinese junk. It's still in operation, used for runs too small for the new machines, which cannot turn out less than twenty thousand packets at a clip. It was on this machine that Ben made the special Sweet'N Low packets for my sister's bat mitzvah: a pink pack with a drawing of a triple-scoop ice cream cone over the words THE COHENS.

In a room filled with boxes, we saw a man asleep in a chair, legs out, cap over his eyes. Little Steven wanted to take a picture of the man with the camera in his cell phone; he'd probably bought the phone for just such occasions. Marvin said, "Let's not embarrass the man." And we crept out.

In the stairwell, Steven's phone rang. He answered it, looked at me, then spoke quickly in a low voice. I heard him say, "Don't worry. It's fine. It's not going down like that."

Handing the phone to Marvin, he said, "It's Jeff."

Steven and I talked, but I kept an eye on my uncle. He was saying, "No, no. It's fine. He's not asking about that. What should I do? No, you tell me! Fine!"

He gave the phone back to Little Steven and said to me, "Come on, let's hurry. I don't have all day."

We went into the parking lot and got into Little Steven's car and drove across the street into the Navy Yard. In 1966, the federal government closed the yard and sold it for twenty-four million dollars to the City of New York, which has since leased it out to industry. There is a jewelry manufacturer and a sign engraver and a printer, but Cumberland is among the biggest tenants. We drove in and out of warehouses, the water at the end of each street, the towers of Manhattan beyond. We parked and walked through the Cumberland buildings. In one, we saw the ghostly rails of a vanished train. In another, we saw giant hooks, relics of the golden age of shipbuilding now deputized in America's never-ending war on fat. One machine seemed to replicate the workings of an angry God: Boxes packed with Sweet'N Low raced across a scale; if a box was even one ounce too light, a mechanical arm did a Heil Hitler, throwing it with great force off the belt and into the ash heap of history.

We got back in the car and drove around—past the ruins of barracks and weed-choked parade grounds; uphill to the Victorian mansion where the commandant of the Yard once lived, with the harbor and the harbor islands stretching below; through the streets of Vinegar Hill, a neighborhood once filled with the Irish immigrants who worked in the Yard, but now a windy ruin, like a ghost town in the West, with creaky storefronts and vacant houses shadowed by a buzzing power plant; then back into the Yard, through the vast construction site where part of this landscape was being turned into a film studio.

We parked near the water and looked back at the buildings above the harbor. We could see the tops of tenements and church steeples. The bridges were at our back. The river was broad and dark. There were tugs and ferries on the water. Down the shore were converted factories and abandoned machine shops. Brooklyn had once been the largest sugar producer in the world, with the biggest refineries on the East River. The last of these, Domino Sugar, shut its doors in 2004. And looking at this, I suddenly realized that Cumberland Packing, and Grandpa Ben, and Grandma Betty, and Uncle Marvin, and my parents, and my aunt, and the sugar packet, and Sweet'N Low, all of it, is really the story of Brooklyn. The money and the product and the people all come from Brooklyn, but it's more than that. It's the longing of the borough, the collective energy of the millions of immigrants who flooded Brooklyn at the beginning of the twentieth century. The diet craze that turned Sweet'N Low into a household name is a concrete manifestation of this longing. Diet cola, the bathroom scale,* Sweet'N Low—it all comes from Brooklyn, the cradle of a new culture, the culture of the body, with its quest for complete freedom: freedom from history, freedom from exclusion, freedom from fat, freedom from the bad bodies of our ancestors. It's the longing that created the fortune and destroyed the family.

---

*Invented in the early 1900s by the Jacobs brothers, who made commercial scales for the kosher butchers and pushcart operators in Brooklyn, then stumbled onto a vast reserve of stout Jewish lady immigrants who had gone on crash diets in hopes of remaking their bodies in keeping with the Anglo-Saxon ideal.

2.

Brooklyn has always been defined by its proximity to Manhattan, a near-miss sort of place, across the river and a light year away. It's a quality that defined the thousands of kids who, from the aughts to the 1950s, poured out of its schools and filled its candy shops and elevated trains. Provincials dreaming of the big city. My father says if he ever writes a memoir, it will be called *I Never Made Manhattan*. To me, the strange insularity of Brooklyn is captured by the image of Grandma Betty shopping for fur coats on Avenue M. Brooklyn is the wilderness and Brooklyn is the sea, as it must have been even for the Dutch merchants who occupied the first houses in Manhattan, employees of the Dutch West India Company, the corporation that built New Amsterdam. They must have stood on the piers in their tall hats and colorful pants, with the painted taverns of Wall Street at their backs, staring at the immensity of Brooklyn, its carpeted hills and inky lakes.

This is the ancient landscape beneath the concrete and steel, the green Eden that American writers have always grown dizzy over. It's the wilderness at the end of *The Great Gatsby* ("The inessential houses began to melt away until gradually I became aware of the old island here that flowered once for Dutch sailors' eyes") and it's all over Mark Twain. It's the land before we wrecked it, the blue vistas that, even when not mentioned, riddle American literature, the meadows and short-grass prairies and plains. American books should always begin with a geological history of the land, the ice floes that carved the lakes and rivers, and the forests, and the mastodons, and the Indians. And the arrival of the first European explorer, Giovanni da Verrazano, who, in 1524, sailed through the Narrows, that sliver of sea that runs between Brooklyn and Staten Island, and by so doing put a claim on the land the way, at camp, we would spit on the piece of steak we wanted. Verrazano sent a dinghy ashore, touched Indians, and traveled on. A few years later, cruising the coast of Brazil, he was killed and eaten by Caribs, a lesson for all wayward New Yorkers.*

Verrazano was followed by dozens of others, including Henry Hudson, who saw Manhattan as a paradise. In his diaries, Hudson notes the quality of the air, the swell of the land, the little ponds and streams, the breeze that arrives in May and blows all summer. The forests were oak, elm, pine. An early hunter listed the game: whitetail deer, fox, black bears, wolves, weasels, ducks, geese, bobcats, mountain lions, wild turkey, and mink. In the first years of settlement, Dutch children kept squirrels as pets, causing much jealousy among the dogs brought from the old country.†

*Many sources were helpful in researching the history of New York, notably: *Gotham: A History of New York City to 1898*, by Edwin G. Burrows and Mike Wallace (New York: Oxford University Press, 1999); *The Epic of New York City*, by Edward Robb Ellis (New York: Coward-McCann, 1966); *The WPA Guide to New York City: The Federal Writers Project Guide to 1930s New York*, with a new introduction by William H. Whyte (New York: Pantheon Books, 1982), originally published as *New York City Guide* (New York: Random House, 1939); *The Encyclopedia of New York City*, edited by Kenneth T. Jackson (New Haven: Yale University Press, 1995). Also a guide published in 1912, which gives the flavor of the time: *Brooklyn: The Home Borough of New York*, prepared by the Municipal Club of Brooklyn.

†This jealousy is memorialized in a painting on display at The New-York Historical Society, which shows a boy in lowland clothes feeding a leashed squirrel as a hound looks mournfully on.

And so civilization pursued its relentless course: The explorers were followed by the trappers, who were followed by the traders, who were followed by the merchants, who sent for their families, and so built the first towns, which they raised armies to protect. From the beginning, New York was noted for its deepwater port, considered among the best natural harbors in the world, a fact that ensured settlement. Brooklyn was colonized by the Dutch in 1634. A few acres cut from the wilderness, corn farms, a feed shop, a church, a blacksmith, and a general store surrounded by woods and called Mid-Wouth, or "middle of the woods," the meaning mostly forgotten three hundred or so years later, when my mother was a freshman at Midwood High School. The greater area was called Vlack Busch, the "wooded plain." In 1643, Lady Deborah Moody, a British aristocrat who used to ride the forest trails alone, bought much of the land along the coast, including what would become Bensonhurst, where my father grew up. Though it was a less famous bargain than the purchase of Manhattan Island, Moody still got a very good deal from the Canarsee Indians: a kettle of wine, some wampum, three guns, and three pounds of gunpowder, in exchange for Gravesend Bay, with its long watery views through the Narrows to the open sea.

In the summer of 1776, soon after the colonies declared their independence from King George, fifteen thousand British soldiers, stationed on Staten Island, crossed the Narrows and invaded Bensonhurst, though it was not yet called that. Boats covered the Narrows from shore to shore. There were no rebels to meet the invaders, no minutemen, no Brooklyn boys. The shore was deserted and forlorn. For a soldier from Manchester or Leeds, it must have been spooky. There were groves of wild fruit trees. Some of the soldiers stripped off their coats and climbed into the branches. Weeks before their first battle, on what today is the Belt Parkway, the British Army had a terrific apple fight.

Manhattan became the financial capital of the new country and grew like a weed, and Brooklyn tacked right along behind it, the fields and farms making way for parks and avenues, then tenements and subway stops. Parts of the borough, like the swamps of Canarsie, where the Mafia dumped its victims, remained wilderness into the 1960s. Brooklyn's East River shore became one of the world's great ports, as bustling as Antwerp or Cherbourg, the masts of the tall ships swaying against hard skies, teams of men unloading corn and cotton and cane. There were waterfront refineries for sugar and beer and a lucrative trade in molasses, a sugar by-product that was distilled into rum. The bridge that connected the borough to Manhattan opened in May 1883, designed by John Augustus Roebling, one of our true visionary engineers. As construction was beginning, Roebling shattered his foot and soon died of tetanus. His son, Washington Roebling, took over, but was struck down by the bends as he emerged too quickly from the caissons, the large airtight chambers used to penetrate the riverbed. He turned the project over to his wife and retired to his apartment in Brooklyn Heights, where, from a wheelchair, he spent his last months watching through a telescope as the bridge was completed. Brooklyn was incorporated into New York in 1898. Within a few years, the Dutch wilderness had been stitched to the city by bridges, tunnels, and wires. It became an annex. Manhattan is neon light and champagne and the party that never ends. Brooklyn is where you sleep it off, where the subway terminates, where your grandparents came from.

Benjamin Eisenstadt was born in New York in 1906. He had an older sister named Bertha and a younger brother named Robert. His parents had emigrated to America from a *god-awful* Polish town. When the tanks rolled east, such towns left not even a stain on the map. Ben is the only thing I know about his parents. To me, their desires are as mysterious as the desires of the ancient Hebrews. Ben's mother's name was Rose. I know that because I'm named after her.* Ben's father was named Morris Eisenstadt and he worked on the waterfront, amid that army of men who dressed before first light and walked in great crowds through the streets to the docks, who climbed on cranes and yardarms, and lifted and carried and hefted and hauled. He was a figure of the air, an immigrant eating lunch on a beam, coaxing the city into the sky. To me, Ben's father is the

*In naming their children, it's the custom of Eastern European Jews to use the first letter of the first name of a beloved dead relative. If I had been a girl, my name would have been Rachel.

man who built the big architecture. When he died, *The New York Times* took no notice, because he was a working man and did nothing that could not have been done by someone else.

When Ben was seven years old, his father tripped off a scaffold and fell several stories, but was saved when a hook caught him by the seat of his pants. (It's unbelievable, but that's how they tell it.) When Ben was eight years old, his father, just thirty-two, was rushed to the hospital with chest pains. The next morning, Ben was sent to the hospital to bring his father a change of clothes. The room was empty when he got there. A nun led Ben into the hall and said, "Your father is with Jesus."

Who is Jesus?

The man who fixed the boiler, is that Jesus?

Or is Jesus the man who turns on the lights during the Sabbath?

Ben walked home. He stood in the doorway holding the bag of clothes. His mother said, "Well, Bennie, did you give your father his shirt and pants?"

"No," said Ben. "Pop is with Jesus."

So begins the actual childhood of Ben, the city as a maze of charity wards and relief agencies. His mother did not have the resources to raise three children. Because Ben was the oldest boy, he was sent to live with his uncles. He moved from apartment to apartment. He slept on floors and couches. He lived mostly in the industrial wastes of northern New Jersey. At the end of his life, Ben told one story again and again—his mind kept returning to it. "We had Christmas dinner at Christian Relief. We had to stand for hours with the bums and drunks, listening to the prayers. Then, at the end of all that, we were finally given Christmas dinner. It was a single piece of desiccated chicken."

This word, *desiccated*, and the way Ben said it, seemed to sum up his entire childhood.

Ben's brother, Robert, who was living with his mother and sister in South Orange, New Jersey, got into a fight with a local gang of Italians. "It was some fight," Marvin told me. "They were going to kill him." So, in a panic, what remained of Ben's family (mother, brother, sister) fled to California. It makes for a tidy narrative. Just like that, Ben is cut off. Ben is set free. He is now part of that special breed of Americans—orphans, mongrels, mutts—responsible for no one but himself. He went to school. He worked for his uncle, who owned a tea bag factory. He walked home in the dark, past the stoops and rum shops. Boys who worked in the factories took on adult mannerisms. They wore slouch-brim hats and chewed toothpicks. Ben worked hard and never had fun and never complained and instead internalized a smoldering anger. I used to sit with Ben while he watched his favorite TV show, *Popeye*. Whenever Popeye— so much like the sailors from the Brooklyn docks, with his tattoos and tobacco and forearms—would take it, and take it, then swallow his spinach and *take it no more*, laying waste to the bearded bully, Ben would slap his leg and roar in a way that, even when I was a kid, struck me as desperate and insane.

In his last year of high school, because he was a credit short on his Regents or something, Ben was told he would not graduate. Because the state was in error and because Ben was determined, he decided to plead his case in person. Because he had no car, or droshky, or train or bus fare, he decided to walk—Brooklyn to Albany on foot—through the Hudson Valley, the wilderness of Washington Irving, with its headless horsemen and its lost Dutchmen playing ninepins, and Rip Van Winkle awake from his second nap on that endless afternoon, unable to recognize the rusty mill towns and factories, and confused by this wandering Jew boy with antecedents in Poland and Russia, a toothpick in his mouth, off to plead his case before the czar.

I've always found this story (Ben walks to Albany, pleads his case, gets his credits and the notion to become a lawyer) unbelievable. It's the *five-mile-walk-to-school-uphill-both-ways* story that your grandfather tells to make you feel weak and lazy. In the Eisenstadt family, it's the cornerstone of a religion. It was even told by the rabbi at Ben's funeral—it had reached the pulpit at last! I sometimes think a family is no more than a collection of such stories, a chronicle that locks you down like the safety bar that crosses your lap before the roller-coaster leaves the platform, without which you would fly away in the turns.

In 1927, Ben was hired as an apprentice to a lawyer in Manhattan. Soon after, he enrolled in St. John's University School of Law. He finished first in his class. He was the valedictorian. He gave a speech about man and law. He rented an office on Broadway. He hung out his shingle. There were no clients. No work. He sat for hours, days, weeks. It was the Depression. He walked about the city. He followed the streets. In these years before Betty and the hassle and complications of family, Ben was a question mark. No parents, no siblings, no friends. Like the best Americans, he was free to invent himself.

3.

The first Jew in New York was named Jacob Bar-Simon. He arrived in the city on August 22, 1654, a step ahead of the Inquisition. He'd fled Spain for Brazil, then, when Brazil went from Dutch to Portuguese, fled Brazil for Manhattan. Peter Stuyvesant, the governor of New Amsterdam, a corporate concern of the Dutch West India Company, wrote his bosses in Old Amsterdam, asking that "none of the Jewish nation be permitted to infest New Netherland."

The bosses said that as Jews such as Bar-Simon were shareholders in the corporation, they must be allowed to settle in the colony. Stuyvesant ignored the board and continued to persecute Jews as well as Quakers, drawing an angry response from some of the locals. The Flushing Remonstrance, addressed to Peter Stuyvesant from the farmers of Flushing, Queens, has been called America's first Declaration of Independence. It says the "law of love, peace and liberty in the states must extend to Jews, Turks and Egyptians, as they are considered the sons of Adam, which is the glory of the outward state of Holland . . . which condemns hatred and war and bondage."

The city's earliest Rosh Hashanah service was held in secret in September 1654, above a shop on Pearl Street in Manhattan, at the charter meeting of the Spanish and Portuguese Synagogue, the oldest Jewish congregation in North America.

Jews continued to arrive—from Brazil, from Holland, from Syria, from Germany—each community escaping its own disaster. The most successful came from Germany, a Jewish community that, by the mid-1800s, had assimilated into the upper ranks of New York society. German Jews worked on Wall Street, owned newspapers and banks. As a result, they felt uniquely threatened by the flood of uneducated dirt-poor Jews who poured into the city from Poland and Russia at the end of the nineteenth century. In 1836, there were just ten thousand Jews in New York. By 1910, more than half a million lived on the Lower East Side alone. Whole towns dropped off the map of Eastern Europe and reappeared on Ludlow and Delancey and Orchard streets, a sea of prayer shawls, the biggest Jewish slum in the world. In *The Epic of New York City*, Edward Robb Ellis gives this community a great backhanded compliment: "Unlike the profligate Irish, the Jews saved their money. According to an immigrant guidebook of that era, a Jew who earned fifty cents a day spent only ten cents for coffee and bagels and saved the other forty cents."

German Jews invented an epithet for their shabby cousins: Because so many had names that ended with the *k-i* of the Russian and Polish peasantry (e.g., Konicki, Jabotinski) they called them kikes.

Perhaps more than any other ethnic group, the Jews who came to America from Eastern Europe lived the dream. A few decades into the twentieth century, they had come to dominate the professions in New York, which had been remade as Hymietown. The statistics are unbelievable. By 1937, 65 percent of the lawyers and judges in New York were Jewish; 64 percent of the dentists were Jewish; 58 percent of the musicians were Jewish; 55 percent of the doctors were Jewish; 50 percent of the artists and sculptors were Jewish; 43 percent of the actors were Jewish; 38 percent of the writers were Jewish; 30 percent of the architects were Jewish; 30 percent of the teachers were Jewish; 29 percent of the engineers were Jewish; 28 percent of the chemists were Jewish; and 11 percent of the college professors were Jewish.*

It's as if these immigrants had anticipated the Holocaust, but of course they were just fleeing the persecutions of their own time. For the Russian Jews, it was the wrath of the czars. After the assassination of Alexander II by an anarchist cell, his son, Czar Alexander III, decided to finally deal with Russia's "Jewish problem." In 1902, twenty thousand Jews were expelled from Moscow. The rest were confined to certain towns and cities, an area known as the Pale of Settlement. Alexander unleashed a wave of pogroms, anti-Jewish riots that ripped through two hundred towns, with Cossack regiments riding through villages, beating and killing inhabitants. The Kishinev Pogrom, in which hundreds of Jews were killed in 1903, made headlines around the world. But the most hated of all the new measures dealt with conscription. In an effort to assimilate the Jewish community out of existence, Jewish boys were taken into the Russian Army at age fourteen and kept in the service for decades. If a Jew was over six feet tall, he was drafted into the cavalry and discharged only when he was forty, by which time his identity as a Jew, or so it was hoped, would be bleached out like a stain.

This is how my family came to America.

In 1901, Isadore Gellman, Betty's father, received notice to report to the Russian Cavalry. In family lore, this man is painted in vague detail, a photo that has been left in the sun. He was tall with red hair and washed-out blue eyes, a description that so perfectly fits my cousin Jeffrey that it opens a wormhole from the past to the present. Rather than report for service, Isadore ran away, paying a peasant to hide him under the hay of an oxcart and carry him across the Russian frontier. He continued west, working until he had earned passage to New York. And so this red-haired ghost hovers over the family tree, a symbol of what was left behind. We

---

*The source for these statistics, and a good source on the great influx of Jews into New York, is *In The Golden Land: A Century of Russian and Soviet Jewish Immigration in America*, by Rita J. Simon (Westport, Conn: Praeger, 1997). Also, *Jewish Immigration to The United States: From 1881 to 1910*, by Joseph Samuel (New York: Arno Press and The New York Times, 1969).

are encouraged to think of him as our link to the past.* And yet if you research such men, you soon realize that they did not think of themselves as links to the past, or as remnants, or as symbols, or as reminders. They thought of themselves as modern people. They, too, knew the story of some distant patriarch, an old man from two or three generations earlier whom they, too, had seen as a remnant of the Old World. No matter how far back you go, in fact, the true patriarch slips away, a generation or two beyond your grasp: the progenitor, the founder, the Jew you can chase clear back to Abraham, the old man from Ur. Perhaps even Abraham carried the legend of a patriarch, a father's father's father, a bearded antecedent who tells you the world is fallen and the old wisdom is lost.

In Eisenstadt family lore, the tall red-haired ancestor is a myth, a man who, like Paul Bunyan or Mose—the Bowery gangster who, before each fight, would hand his cigar to an underling and say, "Hold da butt"— exists in the eternal present, forever crossing the frontier at night. At some point, this man ages into just another nondescript relative, Betty's tired old father feeding pigeons in the park. His red hair, a trademark as distinct as the pink packet of Sweet'N Low, has turned white. By the time Betty was born, he had moved his family to Brownsville, which, with the completion of the subway, replaced the Lower East Side as the biggest Jewish slum in the world.

Because Brownsville was the last stop on the train line, the rents were cheap. In the years before the First World War, the area grew into a great bazaar. The corner of Pitkin and Livonia avenues was like a crossroads on the steppe. There were kosher butchers and dairy-only diners and storefront synagogues. The market stalls were piled high with bluefish and sturgeon. There was a fleet of pushcarts awaiting the morning rush, and flickering neon and crowds outside the candy stores. Women hung laundry between the fire escapes, which, waving in the salty breeze, looked like the flags of forgotten nations. The word used to describe such neighborhoods is *teeming,* with its implications of vermin and infestation. To many people, such immigrant blocks were not America at all. They were

*In my father's family, a similar figure is seen in a single family picture: Noah Cohen, my great-grandfather, a bearded old man in a skullcap.

a foreign colony, a cancer. To me, Brownsville was not merely part of the country, but its essence.

Betty's family lived in a brick apartment house. The ground floor was occupied by the diner, a breakfast-rush sort of place, where working men had a quick meal before catching the train to the factories. The Gellmans were defined by diners, a succession of dirty spoons scattered across Brooklyn. Betty's father bused tables, took orders, and worked the grill. He was sickly. He had his first heart attack the day he was engaged. His wife was named Sarah. She would later become Bubba, our great-grandmother, the gray-haired lady in the photo on the mantel. She wore her long white hair in a bun and was a figure of sad-eyed melancholy. She worked alongside her husband in the diner, a shadow in the kitchen, built like a teakettle, trailed by the smell of mothballs and cabbage.

Young Betty's life was filled with shocks, the first coming when her brother was born and the attention and energy and love of her parents swung away. She was seven years old. In immigrant families, the place of pride was reserved for the boy. (Brownsville was like China, where the peasants bury the newborn girls in the flower bed.) When a boy was born to such parents, it was regarded as a miracle. They named him Abraham. Abe Gellman. Uncle Abie. He was the boy in the lap of the Virgin Mary, the baby Buddha, the fat ball of love, the turkey greased for the oven, the pig with the apple in its mouth served on a bed of greens, smiling and cooing, surrounded by haloes and spectacles of light. And off in the corner, with the gossiping old ladies, the wind sucked right out of her, is gloomy red-haired Betty. Abie's birth taught Betty lessons she would follow for the rest of her life: that boys are better than girls, that love is finite, that love is coal, and there is a shortage, and there will never be enough to go around.

By the time Betty was old enough for school, the family had moved to Red Hook. From the bottom of Atlantic Avenue, you could see Manhattan across the water. In the summer, the doorways and stoops were filled with Irish kids. It was a world of truckers and assembly-line workers and seamstresses and janitors. As a child, Betty suffered from a condition my mother calls, "The only Jew present." The only Jew in her class, in her grade. When school started, she could speak only Yiddish. There was no

English as a Second Language, no tutors. She was simply told to sit and listen until the mechanism in her brain clicked on and the English poured out. Betty was reliving the history of the Jews, or some part of it, and so she learned the old rules: keep your eyes open, keep your mouth shut, don't attract attention, don't be too Jewy.

Even now, my mother seems to struggle with Betty, as if, after all these years, she still cannot get the lady in focus. "Betty was the kind of woman who wanted you to think she never went to the bathroom," my mother told me. "She was afraid if she gave away pieces of herself she would lose everything. She believed a person who loved her shouldn't really be able to love anybody else."

When Betty started school, her name was Pessie. She later changed her named to Bessie, then to Betty. Going from name to name, Betty reminds me of the old illustration of the evolutionary process, the homo habilis rising from the swamps, standing ever more erect, until he is modern man. Pessie, Bessie, Betty. A creature of tremendous will, trying on and discarding identities. She was a great woman long before a woman was allowed to be great in the marketplace. She had to use her talents at home. Her power base would be her family, who existed in her mind in platonic form. The script was written, only the parts had to be cast. When she was eighteen, she saw Ben Eisenstadt on a streetcar, a mode of transport fittingly gone. He was in the window of the car, handsome in his suit. Betty went home and told Bubba, "I have seen the man I am going to marry."

Two years passed before Betty saw Ben again. This time, it was on the subway, in the evening. Ben was coming home from his office. Betty was returning from New York University, where she was studying English literature. Not wanting Ben to slip away a second time, Betty got next to him, smiled, and tugged and brayed. They were married on October 24, 1931. Ben gave up his first dream, which had been to write stories and books. In 1933, because he was now a husband and had to think of more than just himself, he began splitting his time between his law office and the Gellman diner, where he became a regular behind the counter.

What did Betty see in Ben? What got him cast in the big show? Was it because he was a lawyer and wore a suit and carried a briefcase? Or was it the void in him, the emptiness of the orphan? He had no compass, no direction. Betty could guide him. Betty could teach him. Betty was Lady Macbethstein, plotting and planning, not among the Scottish royals on the bluffs and the moors, but among the Jewish proletariat, in the steamy walk-ups and Sabbath dinners of immigrant Brooklyn. Fear was the fire at her back, fogging the windows and burning in the rearview. No matter how fast or far she drove, she could never get clear of it. Betty wanted a pile of money to protect her from shame and disaster. She called this "a lump sum." She said, "If I just had a lump sum . . ." She was the squirrel that cannot stop hoarding, that gathers beyond what it can ever consume. Jewelry and furs, the coats she wore only once. With a lump sum, she would finally have enough to pay the border guards when it came time to flee.

4.

Family members talk about a newspaper article that ran in one of the old New York dailies, *The Herald* or *The Brooklyn Daily Eagle,* a Runyonesque story about young Ben Eisenstadt, a short-order cook who dished out legal advice. When I searched for this article, I could not find it, so I began to think it had never existed. Maybe it was just a fantasy conjured by the collective imagination of the family, the dream of a prehistoric skeleton that will explain everything. Then, one morning, while looking for something else in the New York Public Library, a headline blinked out at me from the microfilm: "Lawyer Doubles in Cafeteria Job." My heart pounded. I had come across the story by accident, and not in some defunct daily but in *The New York Times,* of May 1, 1935. In its depiction of a New York I thought existed only in James Cagney movies, the article confirmed for me the reality of the past. Ben appears in it as a brash go-getter. Long before he had his big idea, my grandfather had made an impression on the city.

LAWYER DOUBLES
IN CAFETERIA JOB

Gets a Client as He Overhears
Conversation of Three Men
While He Serves Food.

'SIDE RACKET,' HE REVEALS

Youth Doffs White Jacket and
Goes to Court to Plead for
Man Accused of Fraud

The versatility of Benjamin Eisenstadt, a young attorney, became known in the Tombs Court yesterday when it was related that only a few hours before he had doffed his white linen coat as a counterman in a Flatbush cafeteria to become counsel for a man accused of forgery.

"This counterman matter is just a side racket," Eisenstadt explained to reporters in the presence of Detective James McDonnell of the Old Slip station and the client, Louis Barash, 24 years old, the detective's prisoner. "You see, I have a law office at 1,440 Broadway, but I have been filling in as counterman at the Flatbush Cafeteria at 1,016 Nostrand Avenue because I am practically the owner of the place now, although it is in the name of my father-in-law."

Then Eisenstadt entered a not-guilty plea for Barash and waived examination for a grand jury inquiry on the charge of David Wallace, secretary of the Hall Jewelers, Inc., 35 Maiden Lane, that Barash had defrauded his company of a watch worth $42.50 through forging a name as that of a buyer.

McDonnell had arrested Barash shortly before 9 A. M. in his home at 467 Empire Boulevard, Brooklyn. Mr. Wallace was with him to make certain that the right man was arrested.

As they started for the Tombs Court, Barash complained that he had not had time to eat breakfast, and the detective agreed to go into the near-by Flatbush Cafeteria with him.

Eisenstadt served the three men at the counter and immediately became engrossed in their conversation, during which Mr. Wallace outlined the charge against Barash.

"Will I have to have a lawyer in a case like this?" Barash asked the detective.

Before he could reply, Eisenstadt spoke up.

"Sure you'll need a lawyer," he said, "and I'm the lawyer who will defend you."

As he spoke Eisenstadt took off his linen jacket, and, donning a neat dark fedora hat and well-pressed sack coat, accompanied the client, the detective and the complainant to court.

In 1932, Ben and Betty were living with Betty's parents. Because Betty's father was ill, Ben had taken over at the diner. He kept his office in the city but was behind the diner counter most of the time. He walked to work each morning in the dark. He opened the locks and turned on the stove. He brought in the milk and ice. He cleaned out the sugar dispensers that sat on each table. Congealed sugar crusted at the mouth of these bottles, and if a dispenser was not cleaned regularly, the sugar became impossible to pour.

A diner runs like a factory, an exercise in repetition, a struggle for efficiency, each day broken into a series of gestures, the gestures into flows, the flows into shifts, between which you can do the crossword puzzle, or read the newspaper, or stand outside and smoke. The morning shift was over by 8:00 a.m., by which time Ben had been joined by Betty or Betty's brother, Abe, who worked in the diner before and after class. In the dead hours between lunch and dinner, five or six men sometimes filled a table in back, filled it completely, leaning together and talking, their laughter rattling like machine-gun fire. These were members of the Jewish mob, named Murder Incorporated by the newspapers in deference to the gang's bloodthirsty skill and hundreds of shootings and garrotings done for the crime syndicate. This work, too, was broken into shifts, with the rush coming in the wee hours, when the streets of Brooklyn were as mysterious as the streets in a dream: torpedoes pursuing marks down alleys, into cellars and saloons; pistols coughing blue flames; sawed-off shotguns going BLAM, BLAM; clotheslines tightening until the face turns blue.

In the 1930s, the diner became a haunt for the boys of Murder Inc. In her later years, Betty talked about this a lot. It was a subject that she knew would interest me. For Jews of my generation—I don't know what you call us, but we are younger than real adults and older than everyone else—there is a perverse fascination with Jewish gangsters, the rogues' gallery that offers a liberating sense of diversity. It's amazing just how many Jews claim kinship with some ganef who rode shotgun on Arnold Rothstein's whiskey trucks, or worked the craps game on State Street, or stood lookout for Pretty Levine in Canarsie. Through such a gangster, a Jew can attach himself to a more exotic past, and shake off all the doctors and accountants in the family tree.

Betty said I should never write about the gangsters because they do not like their names in print, and it's not a letter to the editor they send. When I pointed out that these men had died long ago, she said, "They will enjoy killing you." She spoke of them with the reverence of Yeats, in "Easter, 1916," recording the names of the leaders of the Irish uprising:

MacDonagh and MacBride
And Connolly and Pearse
Now and in time to be,
Wherever green is worn,
Are changed, changed utterly:
A terrible beauty is born.

Here's Betty's poem, "Brownsville 1933":

Pittsburgh Phil and Kid Twist Reles
And Bugsy and Gangy and Tick Tock

They haunted Livonia and Pitkin and ate in delis
In Hebrew "Father" is translated as Abba
And Red Levine would never kill on Shabbas.

"Kid Twist later ratted and got thrown out of the window of the Half Moon Hotel in Coney Island," Betty told me. "They called him the canary who could sing but couldn't fly. Pittsburgh Phil Strauss was the most handsome man I have ever seen."

If Strauss spotted a cop in the street, he would call over Betty, who held out her apron as the boys dumped their guns in it. Then she would bury all that hardware under the onions behind the counter. Strauss, who did his killing with an ice pick, would toy with Uncle Abie, saying, "You're a big kid. Why are you doing lady's work?"

Betty was alone in the diner with Reles the morning in 1933 when she went into labor with her first child. She slumped across the counter. Reles ran over to help. This is the creation myth of Uncle Marvelous, midwifed by a lightning bolt. With great frowning concern, Reles led Betty out to his car, a notorious Brooklyn crash car, the long black sedan ghosting past the red brick of the storefronts and the stoops, all of this territory, from here to the Gowanus Canal, belonging to the Kid. "You got a problem, Betty, talk to me, 'cause all of it's mine."

Betty had been pregnant with twins. Marvin's brother died soon after the delivery. He was around just long enough to get a name: Ernest. Marvin is one of that legion of people who, for a time, rode shotgun with a phantom, the sibling who could not make it: dead in the womb, dead on delivery. Only the name remains, incorporated into the name of the living. If Marvin wants to make a point, he slaps his chest and says, "That's the truth from Marvin Ernest Eisenstadt!" For Ben, the lost twin was a tragedy. God shook him and he stayed shook. Marvin, the surviving son, the miracle, came to embody the hopes of two.

Gladys was born in 1935. Ellen in 1938. By the time Ellen was seven years old, the family dynamic was recognizable, the patterns and relationships that persist to this day. Because it's so hard to imagine a fully formed personality in a half-formed state, I picture the childhood versions of Marvin and Gladys and Ellen as shrunken-down versions of their adult selves, like children in Renaissance paintings, tiny bodies containing adult-size portions of envy and anger and fear.

For Marvin, life was mostly a matter of being in charge and out front, two years older and ages ahead.

For Gladys, life was the dread of the middle child, too late and too early, driven like many middle children by the question "Why me?" With its implication of "Why not her?" Which, on East Twenty-first Street in Brooklyn, was particularized as "Why not Ellen?"

For Ellen . . . well, Ellen is my mother, and she is a great mother, and I love her, and once, when I was sick at Camp Menominee in Eagle River, Wisconsin, and the sickness spread through the grounds, and first we were under quarantine and then we were to be sent home by bus, an eight-hour ride to Chicago, this mother of mine chartered a Cessna out of Palwaukee Airport in Wheeling, Illinois, and landed on a plowed field in Rhinelander, Wisconsin, and it was like a dream, being woken in the middle of the night, then driving out to the field, the roads glowing beneath the sort of grand, starry constellations that have ceased to exist, standing on the runway and watching as the distant red light tracked across the sky and the shape of the plane emerged from the darkness and the wheels bounced on the moist dirt and the plane slowed and turned and stopped and the little door opened and out stepped my mother, and she carried me back into the plane and we roared across the strip and then we were away, with the lights of the rinky-dink Wisconsin towns fading into the inky black, and her hand was so cool in my hand, and it would have been a dream, too, if I had not woken up the next morning in my bed at home.

So, no, I cannot be objective about my mother, but I don't think I need to be. I am the youngest in my own family, and I think, to a large extent, the youngest—because Ira was born so many years later, my mother is really the youngest in the first family of Betty and Ben—is almost always without blame, because the show was already going when we got there.

When I spoke to Gladys and Marvin, I expected them to pick apart the stories my mother had told me, or to call them lies, but this did not happen. In fact, Gladys and Marvin told the same stories, only in a different way, with a different emphasis. It was like seeing a familiar drama restaged as a musical or a farce. There were stories about the trips the Eisenstadt children took to Coney Island, each child given a quarter for food and rides. Gladys and Marvin spent their money right away. Ellen hung on to hers, pocketing and cherishing it because it was hers. That is, until her brother and sister went to work, as shameless as carnival barkers, guilting her up and separating her from that coin. "It was so cute," Gladys told me. "We got it away from her every time."

Gladys told me this story with laughter—adorable Ellen fun to play with and tease. Marvin told it the same way. These are small things, of course, tidbits, the misadventures experienced by all of us, part of learning the way of the world, but also not so small. The passing of the years can convince you that nothing that happened so long ago can be of much importance, but it's a trick. It's your adult self mocking your childhood self. Because these experiences set patterns you follow through life. I see the residue of Coney Island all over my mom, who always gives it away before it's taken away. If you ask my mother, "How's your dinner?" she slides over her whole goddamn plate and says, "Take it, please, take it and enjoy."

When Ellen was seven, the family moved to the house in Midwood, where my Aunt Gladys still lives. The neighborhood has evolved over the years and the house now sits amid colonies of Hasids and Haitians, West Indians beached, like my aunt, by the terrible history of sweets. But in the 1940s, the block was at the forefront of the American dream. Living in Midwood, Brooklyn, was like living in Scarsdale today: it meant you had made it.

The Eisenstadt house was narrow, with living, dining, and sitting rooms on the ground floor, and on the second floor, four bedrooms that would be lived in and abandoned. As the reviewers say, the house is another character in this story. It has witnessed all the action. Like the countries of Eastern Europe, it has seen its population go boom and bust. It has aged with its inhabitants. As you read this book, keep it forever in mind, superimposed over the action, the lights going on and off, the people coming and going, the summers and winters, the snows and heat waves and rain.

For Ben, the house was a tangible result of hard work. He had built the diner into a real business, saved money, bought a bigger diner, saved more money. It was a lesson in the old rules: He never spent on himself, never treated himself to a swanky suit or a nice car. He never took a loan, never carried a debt. He plowed every cent of profit back into the business. If there was a bad year, he could ride it out.

5.

On April 25, 1806, a British warship followed an American merchant vessel into New York Harbor, where, within sight of Pearl Street, the English signaled the Americans to anchor. (This was during the Napoleonic Wars; the British were seizing all goods bound for France.) When the Americans ignored the signal, the British shot their cannon across the American ship's bow. The first shot sailed over the ship into the water. The second took off the head of the helmsman. A crowd that witnessed the incident from the seawall below Wall Street stormed the docks, beat up British sailors, and raided British ships. The decapitated body of the helmsman was brought ashore, paraded in the streets, put on display at the Tontine Coffee House on Burling Slip, then carried to City Hall. The people demanded action. Thomas Jefferson, who was at the end of his second term as president, drafted the Embargo Act, which banned commercial trade with all belligerents.

Meant to keep the nation out of war, the Embargo Act brought misery to the harbor. By the winter of 1808, the sailors of New York were starving. Jefferson accordingly devised a federal program, putting the men to work building the Brooklyn Navy Yard, which would secure America's position as a sea power. The Yard was built on a crescent of East River shoreline purchased by the administration of John Adams. This land made its first appearance in city records in 1637, described as the property of Joris de Rapelje, a Walloon* who operated a ship factory. It came to be known as Walloon's Bay, or Waelnbogt Bay, later anglicized to Wallabout Bay. (During the Revolutionary War, the British filled the bay with decrepit prison ships in which thousands of American soldiers died.) Sailors were soon ferrying back and forth to Brooklyn, firming up the shoreline and leveling hills. When complete, the Navy Yard was a trim landscape of wooden houses set on a soft swell above the East River.[†]

In 1820, the first vessel was built from scratch in the Yard, a seventy-four-gun battleship assembled in the facility's Dry Dock Number Two, itself considered a mechanical wonder of the world. There is a Charlie Chaplin film in which you see a warship released from dry dock. It's all sepia tone—the hubbub of the harbor; the flags snapping and making visible the passage of the wind; the industrialists in high hats and the workmen in coveralls; the ship beautiful and heartbreakingly silent as it slides gracefully into the water, an occasion in which the heavy machinery of war appears weightless and transcendent.

The first modern submarine, designed by John Philip Holland, a schoolteacher from Paterson, New Jersey, was built in the Yard. The first steam warships were built there, including *The Maine*, the ship that exploded in Havana in 1898, sparking war with the Spanish. By the First World War, barracks had been built on Flushing Avenue. There were proving grounds where the marines drilled, houses for officers, and the site for Wallabout Market, with stalls for fruit sellers and wine merchants. The navy hospital was filled with cases of flu and scurvy. There was a loft at 8 Warrington Avenue where navy widows stitched bunting for the warships. On Cobb Dock, there was the meteor that Admiral Peary brought

---

*A race of Celts that migrated to North America from Belgium as traders and trappers.

[†]There are many sources on the history of the Navy Yard, but most interesting for me was *Illustrated Guide to the Brooklyn Navy Yard*, prepared by the Brooklyn Daily Eagle Information Bureau (Brooklyn: Eagle Book and Job Printing Department, 1900).

back from his fabled expedition to the Arctic. It weighed a hundred tons. Also on Cobb Dock was an iron coop that housed more than two hundred navy homing pigeons that carried messages to ships off the coast. Fleets of the birds could be seen each morning turning circles over the bay.

If you were in the navy, you probably spent time in the Yard, being processed and trained, living in the barracks, taking leave in the bars, or eating in the cafeteria across the street. Ben Eisenstadt purchased that cafeteria in 1940. The Navy Yard, after a lull following the First World War, was humming back to life. The taverns were smoky and crowded, the tenements were filled with laborers. On the night of December 7, 1941, as Ben locked up, thousands of young men stood in front of the gate of the Yard, waiting to enlist. The Japanese had attacked Pearl Harbor.

Just like that, Brooklyn had changed.

For kids, the Second World War was a time of tremendous excitement. The drama of the world finally matched the drama of the imagination. There were actual spies and enemy agents skulking on the waterfront. The monsters were real. Troopships burst into flames at the river docks and bodies washed ashore at night. The lights of the city were extinguished, not, as many people thought, to prevent aerial attack, but to foil German U-boats that might have targeted American ships silhouetted against the gaudy skyline of the city. The observation deck of the Wool-worth building was closed for fear it could offer enemy agents a clear view of the Navy Yard and the position of the ships at sea. The gold dome of the Federal Building, which on clear nights reflected the moon, was painted black. The torch in the hand of Lady Liberty was extinguished. Pedestrians were kept off the river bridges, from which a saboteur might drop a bomb onto a transport ship. German spies were caught before they could blow up Hells Gate Bridge and the Westchester Reservoir. An abandoned dinghy was found on Staten Island; in the ensuing manhunt, the spies were captured by some of the boys from Murder Incorporated. The chief enemy operative was tracked down and arrested in his apartment at 305 Riverside Drive. The war shattered the bubble that seemed to protect the city in even the worst years of the Depression. New York had been pulled into the tide of history. It was a hinge moment. To this day, if my father is confronted by someone he thinks is especially vicious, he says, "It's 1943 and this bastard is killing Jews."

By 1944, there were nine hundred thousand people in uniform in the city. It was in these years that Brooklyn achieved its peak state of Brooklyn-ness, becoming what it always wanted to become: a composite sketch of the nation, a police artist's rendering of the American face, with every state and town and backwater represented. This was the wartime Brooklyn of tattoo parlors and dance halls and beer gardens and drunken sailors.

If you have three drinks and turn around twice, you can almost get into the head of one of the doughboys, a farmhand who joined up while drunk, woke with an eagle tattoo and a receipt of induction, was shipped to Brooklyn, and got lost among the dagos and the yids. Check out the bars on Front Street! Check out the houses on Flatbush Avenue! And check out the bawdy houses on Vinegar Hill! And check out the sun on the harbor and the big smoky town and the diner serving mountains of eggs and rivers of booze! And check out the dude behind the counter! They say he's a lawyer! In this town, even the countermen are Jew lawyers!

6.

In 1944, Abraham Gellman, Betty's brother, enlisted in the army. He had previously volunteered and been rejected, because he had flat feet or something, but, two years into the war, the army would accept anyone. He joined, depending on whom you ask, because he was patriotic, because all his friends were in, because he was a good citizen, because only cripples and losers stayed out, because this really was "1943" and those bastards really were killing Jews.

Abie was a captain in the Army Medical Corps, a trauma surgeon. Marvin says he was big, over six feet tall, and handsome as hell, with all the Brooklyn girls swooning in his wake, but I bet he was small. I bet he was short and slight and not very good looking. Average. We Jews are a pretty small people, so, as the haters would have it, we operate by stealth and craft—it's no accident that Jewish basketball players invented the sneaky behind-the-back pass—and so put far too much value on size. In our stories, our relatives are always much bigger than we are, our stature being a fluke, because we were not breast fed, because we drank water full of paint, because we were one of a pair and the twin died. I could be wrong, of course. Abie could have been a colossus, storming through the borough like a Yiddish Paul Bunyan, a figure out of folktales: *One day, Uncle Abie dragged his lunch box to school and that is how we have the Gowanus Canal!*

Abie had fleshy lips and a high forehead. He was glamorous. He was the hope of the family. "He was my hero," Marvin told me. "We would walk in the street, and the men would salute him. He was a doctor. He was a big guy. He had a girlfriend. And he was religious. He kept kosher, and that was not easy to do in the barracks."

My mother remembers Abie as pure light, the sort of figure who, in the old paintings, is surrounded by sunbeams. She says he saved her life exactly twice: when she had whooping cough, and again when she had something more exotic. He came like a vision that second time, so hazy was she with fever. He took her temperature and spoke in a reassuring way and then stood in the door talking to Betty. He was twenty-six. He gave my mother a new medicine, which he had swiped from the hospital. Sulfa, the first of the wonder drugs. Possibly because of the fever, my mother was left with the sense that Abie was her real father, that he had left her in this house only while he was away, which is why she was treated, as she puts it, like an "also," that he was out there still, awaiting the right moment to return.

Betty's father, Isadore, always had a bad heart, but it had gotten so bad he could hardly walk a flight of stairs. The walls would reel. He would grab his chest and stumble. Sarah would say, "Don't be so dramatic!" Then one day the walls did not stop reeling, and the floor opened and in he went. Sarah was destroyed. She might have acted fed up, but Isadore was the last person who knew everything, who had lived through all of it. The red-haired man who had crossed the Russian frontier was laid out in a funeral home in Brooklyn. Abie, who was in training at Fort Dix, in New Jersey, got leave for the funeral. He turned up in khakis, tearful and tall. Everyone agreed he looked great. He spent the day with his mother. Betty could do nothing for Sarah, but Abie was a solace. When the light died from the windows, he walked through the apartment, saying goodbye.

I have tried to piece together details from the military life of Uncle Abie. He is a key figure in the history of the Eisenstadts. I have talked to relatives and read documents, but the information is sketchy. Key places and dates have been omitted from the military records because "loose lips sink ships." Yet, by examining old newspaper stories and government files, and by reading between the lines, I have been able to imagine the last days of Abraham Gellman:

After Fort Dix, he was sent to a military base in the South, where, though he was a doctor and an officer and would likely be assigned to a hospital, he had to drill and climb and shoot his gun—because the gun is your friend—and live in the barracks that were scattered like matchboxes across the buggy country. Because the war was winding down and he did not want to miss it, he volunteered for hazardous duty. He was sent to New Guinea. The transport ship sailed from an East River dock. From the rail, he could see Brooklyn, the streets, the factories, the smoke-spewing chimneys. The ship passed under a big river bridge, and for a moment, he was lost in shadow, girders high overhead, the green shore sliding through his fingers like silk. Then he was beyond the Narrows and into the open sea. The ship sailed for days through the swell, sometimes joined by other ships and sharking along in convoy, or sometimes alone.

He would lie in his bunk, smoking or writing his girl. A Jew on the sea, away from the towns, away from the other Jews, can let go and get free, and know but not care that he is going to die. Or he would stand on deck, staring at the sky, thinking about Isadore, dead now, dead and gone, dead, dead, dead, can't get any more dead, and does it matter, being dead for a week or for a thousand years, and when Isadore came out of Russia in the oxcart, he must have had dreams, because he was a human being, and had a stomach and a brain, and so must have wanted to see the world, and drink, and get drunk.

The ship sailed until it hung upside down on the far side of the ocean. In New Guinea, Abie lived in a hut backed by vines. He examined soldiers and talked them through fevers. He studied the effects of rare tropical diseases. His work was described as important. At night, he stared at the jungle. On the other side, a war was raging. On some islands, the Japanese fought until they ran out of bullets. Abie volunteered for duty as a combat surgeon. In the last months of the war, he came ashore with an infantry unit in the Philippines.

He splashed through the shallows and stormed the beach with the other soldiers, only he carried a medical kit in addition to a gun. The sand was scalloped near the shore. Palm trees strained in the breeze. He ran into the jungle. He fell in with his platoon. They humped into the wilderness. In towns, they fought from house to house. The biggest threat came from snipers. Five or six men might get clipped in an hour. He cut them open and plunged his hands in, searching for the bullet.

The rivers were smoky in the morning and dark ribbons at night. The days were malarial. The platoon was lost, no backup and no supplies. They lived off game and wild berries—eat the red ones; the blues take you on a trip that makes you see a terrible truth of time. The unit followed a road built by the Japanese. They were fighting in the cities, like the cities back home, the entire army converging on Luzon. From there, the soldiers would march on Manila. When the Americans took Manila, General MacArthur would give a speech.

The fighting was brutal. Corpses desecrated, gutted. Battles like Luzon convinced Truman to drop the bomb. The platoon was marching through a town. Left alone for a week, such towns are reclaimed by the jungle. Weeds curl around the traffic lights. A flash came from a building. A soldier fell. Then another. Then another. A sniper was marking the boys, the bullets cutting through leaves and into soft tissue, through soft tissue and onto the road. By the time the commander got the men back, ten soldiers had been hit. It was not the big war anymore. It was just a nasty thing happening on the road. Against orders, Abie broke cover and sat in the road with his bag. Those he could save, he dragged. In this manner, he saved eight men. Then, wham, a bullet caught him below the temple. The commander went through his pockets, saving letters, dog tags, and his cap. As it says in Deuteronomy: "So Moses the servant of the Lord died in the land of Moab, and the Lord buried him in a valley in the land, but no man knows of his sepulcher unto this day."

Abraham Gellman was killed on January 22, 1945. The telegram did not reach Sarah until March. Then the letters kept coming, some accompanied by effects, others by medals, the Silver Star and Purple Heart, with citations that made it clear that Abie had died a hero.

December 6, 1945

Mrs. Sarah Gellman
c/o Eisenstadt,
277 Montgomery Street
Brooklyn, N.Y.

My Dear Mrs. Gellman,

At the request of the President, I write to inform you that the Purple Heart has been awarded posthumously to your son, Captain Abraham Gellman, Medical Corps, who sacrificed his life in defense of his country.

Little that we can do or say will console you for the death of your loved one. We profoundly appreciate the greatness of your loss, for in a very real sense the loss suffered by any of us in the battle for our country, is a loss shared by all of us. When the medal, which you will receive shortly, reaches you, I want you to know that with it goes my sincerest sympathy, and the hope that time and the victory of our cause will finally lighten the burden of your grief.

Sincerely yours,

Robert Patterson
Secretary of War

It was not much help to Bubba that Abie died a hero. In the course of a season, she had lost her husband and her son. In the fall of 1946, after a long, gloomy night, she went to the roof of the family's apartment house,*

---

*The family was then living in an apartment on Montgomery Street; they would soon move to Flatbush.

where she tried to kill herself by jumping. Oh, the black comedy of it! This grief-stricken old yenta, her white hair in a neat bun, her eyes hidden behind Mother Goose spectacles, in a flowing dress and heavy stockings and sensible shoes, climbing the rickety stairs and throwing open the door and walking through the exhaust fans and vents, the borough spread below, the factories and the laundry lines, letting down her hair, which waves in the soft tidal wind, stepping onto the retaining wall and throwing open her arms and falling, her body turning over and over, the windows of the tenements drifting up like bubbles and the ground rising to meet her. But no, she did not jump. She did not kill herself. She got down off the wall. She listened to reason. She went back inside, where she became a tragic figure. "My grandmother was in terrible shock when Abie died," Marvin told me. "I think she tried to kill herself. They held her back."

And what about Betty?

There had been a family called the Gellmans. It consisted of Isadore, Sarah, Betty, and Abraham Gellman. Then Isadore and Abraham died, and it was only Sarah and Betty, and for Sarah, that was not enough. What about Betty's children? Still not enough. Sarah was willing to kill herself under the same roof as all those children (or on top of it), to cover them in the sort of shame not even a lifetime can wash away. In this chain of events (the death of Abie, the gloom of Bubba, the forsakenness of Betty) lies the birthplace of the family pathology. Betty can marry well, support her mother and father, fill the world with children, and it's still not enough.

"Bubba was bereft when Abie died. Her husband was never spoken of in great terms, but Abie was a deity."

This is my father talking. He brings to all questions of character the Arthur Miller–style analysis, the Brooklyn realism of the thirties and forties, which normally strikes me as old-fashioned and yet, because this really was Brooklyn in the thirties and forties, rings true: "Abie was a guy who—and there's no reason for me not to believe this—was religious, went to medical school; who, if there was a class on Saturday, would walk. He kept kosher, was kind, was wonderful, good with children and animals. And he became a doctor and went into the military and went to New Guinea and was killed. Betty was the oldest child, so when this boy was born, and the boy is a student and the boy is brilliant and the boy goes to medical school, she is pushed aside and the focus is on this kid Abie. It wasn't his fault they revered him. And he goes into the service. And Bubba's husband dies. And right after that, they get word Abie is dead. And Bubba is so distraught she wants to kill herself. Threatens to kill herself, maybe tries to kill herself but is prevented from doing so. Betty had three children, and still her mother is willing to throw away her life. So Betty got the impression she wasn't worth shit and her children weren't worth shit. And that had a big impact on her."

My mother loves the Norman Rockwell painting of the doughboy just home from the war, in uniform, in the street, looking at the tenement, and you just know it's an Irish neighborhood in Brooklyn, the meals on the stoves, the laundry hung out to dry, and the gold stars in the windows, one for every son lost in the fighting. I used to imagine this picture repainted by a Jew, the apartments filled with balabustas, the bathtubs filled with goldfish—why is the ugliest, most sullen fish in the sea called the jewfish?—the soldier with curly black hair and ears that pop like jug handles and a honker of a nose. For my mother, this painting brings back some of her earliest memories, when every gold star was Abie, and the boy in the street was Abie, too, not a returning hero but a ghost paying a last visit to the old block before stepping into the galaxy, which is like the ocean, cold at first, nice when you get used to it. If Abie had come back, he would have been just another uncle, with his own family and his own life, but as it happened, he never did come back, not even his body came back, so for my mother, Abie became just what she needed him to become—the vanished hero, the lost father.

A few years ago, Betty picked a fight with my mother. She wanted to know why I had never written about Abie.

Here is how Gladys later described the argument:*

*This comes from the deposition taken from Gladys on July 30, 2002, when my mother was considering contesting Betty's will.

My sister's son wrote a book, Tough Juice.* And we called him and we congratulated him and we did all the things that I thought we were supposed to do. And then he wrote another book called The Survivors† in which he talked about his father's family in relationship to—I didn't read the book, so I don't know—saving Israel. [And Ellen] got on the phone with my mother . . . and she started talking about my brother-in-law's family. And my mother got upset—she had a brother who was killed in World War Two. He was a doctor, he was 26 years old. He won the silver star. And she tried to tell my sister, "Well, your uncle was also a hero." And my sister did not acknowledge my mother's brother. When my mother got off the phone, she was really angry and said, "You know, she never pays attention." So I called my sister and I said, "You upset Mother because of what you said about the book." And my sister's response was, "Well, I can't be proud of my own son?" And I said, "That's not what I'm saying. I'm only saying Mother was offended that you didn't mention Abie."

*The book was called Tough Jews. Still, Tough Juice has a certain ring. It reminds me of that joke: What do you get when you squeeze a synagogue? Juice!

†The book was called The Avengers.

The challenge for Betty and Ben was this: SAVE BUBBA! If you can't rid her of sadness, maybe you can reengage her in life. Though Betty and Ben were not exactly young, they decided to have another child. Replacing a dead soldier by raising another is a classic move.

All the lost promise of Abie was stuffed into Ira. He was born in 1948. In old family pictures, he is often seated on Bubba's lap. Who could live up to that? Who wouldn't grow a tangly red beard and have about a gazillion cats? So it goes with all wars: the repercussions are endless.

7.

Then the war was won. The harbor was full of ships, there was music in the dives. The party went on for days; then the party was over. The borough stank like a hangover, like stale beer. The streets emptied out and the big hooks hung motionless over the Yard. The work orders dried up, the belts geared down. The sailors were demobbed, the shipbuilders went in search of work. The cafeteria was deserted. Ben stood behind the counter staring at the empty street. He was living off the money he had saved during the war, but he had a family and expenses, and money wants to be free — that's why it swims out of your pocket. He put his business up for sale. He got a good offer and a deposit, but the offer had been based on the wartime numbers. The buyer soon realized he had made a mistake. Over the objections of Betty, Ben tore up the contract and returned the deposit. He did not panic. He had been through a depression and a war.

No matter what you think of him, no matter if he was one of the few grandfathers who spanked, you must admit that Ben was a cool customer. He understood the big truth of this town: that New York is a market, a shopping mall from which there is no escape, with the very idea of escape, to Long Island or the Midwest, being the dream of green fields that keeps the drones pumping money into the machine; it's the greatest device ever invented to separate you from your money.* To live in the city with any dignity you therefore need something to sell, otherwise you are just another customer. In casting about for a product, Ben remembered his childhood and his job in his uncle's factory.

Ben shut down the diner, tore out the counters and booths. In 1945, he ordered a tea-bagging machine from a factory supply company in Quincy, Massachusetts. This is the ancient device I saw on my tour of the factory, springs and shutters and cranks that convert a raw material (tea) into a product (tea bag). He hung a new sign out front: THE CUMBERLAND PACKING COMPANY. The money for this venture came mostly from Sarah—the insurance payoff and the military pension that arrived after the death of Abie. Ben was now the owner of a small factory. He climbed all over his tea bagger, kicking and cursing and keeping it in gear. Sarah worked at his side, packing tea bags into small boxes, then packing the small boxes into big boxes. But who needed it? Ben was packing tea for a world filled with tea bags. The boxes piled up, the bills poured in, and the money swam away in great fishlike schools.

Ben had failed.

Betty and Ben went for lunch at Cookie's in Midwood. The meal at the end of the dream. Fog-shrouded streets, the distant whistle of a train. They talked about the lack of business, each tea bag a child and each child unwanted. The waitress crossed the room with a coffee pot. It was a crown on a velvet pillow. It was a coronation. Betty poured a cup, added cream, reached for the sugar—one of the heavy dispensers she knew from

*The suburban mall was an effort to replicate this trick in the provinces, bringing the density and pressure of New York to the sticks, which is why building a mall in New York, as was recently done at Columbus Circle, is redundant. Manhattan is already a mall, the dream shopping plaza of Peter Stuyvesant run amok, spread across the archipelago.

her days in the diner. She flipped and banged the bottle, but nothing came out. The mouth had crusted over, the sugar stopped like sand frozen in an hourglass, so the epiphany came as a stop in time: WHY NOT PACK SUGAR? I mean, look at this bottle, all clotted and clogged and disgusting. WHY NOT PACK SUGAR? Why not make the use of sugar clean and personal, one person, one pack, one time, and kiss the sugar bottle and the whole sticky mess goodbye? Ben got it right away. Because he and Betty communicated on a supersecret frequency, because the sugar bottle was messy and Americans wanted to avoid cleanup, because America was about being disposable, because America was about private property and here was a way to replace the dispenser, which was almost socialist, with individual, privately owned packets. WHY NOT PACK SUGAR?

MARVIN:

"My mother looks at the sugar dispenser—at that time it was either a dispenser or an open bowl with a spoon that people put in their coffee and then back in the bowl—and she thought it was unsanitary. And, eureka, like the Greek guy said, Why don't we put sugar in a tea bag for restaurants? It would be very sanitary."

ELLEN:

"It was summer. It was hot. My parents were sitting in Cookie's. My father was saying, 'I've got to do something. They are closing the Navy Yard.' Then he's pouring sugar into his coffee. At that time, you either had to use a lump of sugar, and if it was iced it would never dissolve. Or you put a spoon into your coffee and back into the bowl, which was unsanitary. And that's when my mother came up with the idea of loose sugar in a packet. It was desperation makes inspiration."

Ben worked on the tea bagger, trying to convince it to change its mission. In the end, he drove to the factory in Quincy, where, working with the engineers, he was able to reconfigure the machine into the world's first sugar packer. My grandfather was not the sort of man who invents the new thing. He was the sort of man who takes two things that already exist and combines them in a new and interesting way. In Fort Greene, the machine was soon spitting out the first sugar packets. Elegant and clean and personal. They looked almost exactly like the sugar packets of today—it's an invention that has not called for much improvement.*

When I asked Marvin if there had been anything like the sugar packet before, he said, "The closest thing was the pay envelope with a metal clip. They used it in offices. It was expensive to make."

Marvin said this, but Marvin was wrong. Before the sugar packet there had been, among other packages, the tea bag, the tin can, the cigarette, the cigar, all of it just an imitation of what has been going on since day two, when God separated the land from the water and covered the land with hills, and the hills with groves of fruit trees, each apple and orange and banana even more efficiently packed than the sugar coming off the belts in Brooklyn.

Modern packing appeared in 1815, in Delaware, with the invention of butcher paper, greasy brown wrap used to carry corned beef and smoked salmon; followed by the invention, in 1853, of the paper bag. Crucial early work was done by the chemist Gail Borden, who in the mid-1800s was badly shaken by newspaper accounts of the Donner Party, the starving snowbound emigrants who cannibalized their dead. To prevent such a tragedy from ever recurring, Borden promised to devise a way to store calories in small packages that would keep over great distances. He promised to "put a potato into a pill-box, a pumpkin into a tablespoon." Most successful were his canned foods and condensed milk. In the Civil War,

---

*In addition to family reminiscences, there are several good sources on the early history of Cumberland, including articles that have run in *The New York Times* and other newspapers (Ben's obituary, for example), the corporate history on Cumberland's own website, www.sweetnlow.com, passages in Hillel Schwartz's *Never Satisfied: A Cultural History of Diets, Fantasies and Fat* (New York: Free Press, 1986), and a chapter in a book by Rhonda Abrams called *Wear Clean Underwear: Business Wisdom from Mom* (New York: Villard, 1990).

the possession of these items (prototypes of the modern MRE, the military's "Meals Ready to Eat") was a great advantage for the Union.

Before modern packing, foodstuff had been laid out in markets and general stores in great piles. You walked along a counter, examining seeds, nuts, raisins, sugars, spices, and candies, plunging in your hands and filling your sack. This changed with widespread use of the microscope and the corresponding understanding of bacteria. A disease, it was now understood, could be carried through a store by a single industrious fly. A report issued by the Massachusetts Commission on the Cost of Living in 1911 perfectly captures the persnickety mood of the time:

> When one enters the door [of a general store outside of Boston] a bell rings, which calls the attendant from the barn, where he has been unharnessing or brushing the horses. Accordingly as one article or another is desired, he plunges his unwashed hands into the pork or pickle barrel, cuts cheese or butter, often drawing kerosene or molasses in the meantime, wiping the overflow on his coat sleeve or jumper. In the summer no attempt is made to keep out flies, and much of the merchandise is open to them for food. The maple syrup bottles stand nearby. And the keeper himself has been seen to take a swallow from them at different times, when his sweet tooth called.

In other words, Betty was right: it's not sanitary. In a flash, she had seen a way to reorganize sugar and bring some cleanliness to a germy world. To Waverley Root and Richard de Rochemont, historians of the American diet, such an invention is more than a clever innovation; it's a revolution in ideas. "Packaging is an almost mystical concept," they write in their book *Eating in America*, "which for the unimaginative may mean nothing more than enveloping food in some sort of covering; but for the philosophically inclined, what is essential about packaging is that it brings shape out of formlessness."

The Domino Sugar refinery was directly across the river from Lower Manhattan. In the imagination of my family, it's a mansion circled by bats. Through its parent company, American Sugar, it was linked to the founding families of New York—the Bayards, the Stewarts, the Roosevelts, the Havemeyers, the Van Cortlands—owners of the colonial refineries that once lined Duane Street and William Street and Pine Street. When the Confederate refineries were destroyed during the Civil War, New York was rendered the capital of sugar. By World War II, 40 percent of the world's supply was being processed in Brooklyn. For a time, these companies formed into a trust. Big Sugar. Even after the trust had been broken, the heads of the sugar companies still behaved like the members of a monopoly. They controlled supply and fixed prices and smothered competition.

When Ben met with the bosses of Domino, he was ignorant of all this history, a happy-go-lucky schmuck with designs in his pocket. He wanted Domino to hire him to pack their sugar. Because it's not the invention of a product that makes the fortune. It's the invention of a market. (For Henry Ford, the big invention was not the Model T but the market for the Model T.) If Domino contracted with Ben to pack their sugar, that was all the market he would ever need.

The executives asked questions and studied Ben's plans. They thanked him and shook his hand and said he would be hearing from them. He went back to Cumberland and waited. One week, two weeks. It took a month to get someone on the phone. He was finally told, "No thank you, Mr. Eisenstadt. Your machine is quite clever. In fact, we've already built one of our own."

Ben hung up, and the room sailed away and he was in the little wooden house with Dorothy, spinning through the twister, away and over the city, staring down at the streets and the factories and the warehouses, and the people looked like ants!

He had not even applied for a patent. He did not know about patents. He did not know about anything. He simply took his product to the men he thought could make the most use of it, and they could, which is why they stole it. This was the important early lesson in Ben's business life. It confirmed his worst fears. It made him resentful and suspicious.

Ben did not live long enough to see Domino Sugar shut its doors in

Brooklyn,* but it would have made him happy. He would have laughed. If this were a movie, you would have seen him laughing in shot after shot: walking to the bank, driving in his car, waking from a nap, soaping up his chest.

In the weeks following, Ben moped and bitched, then picked up the pieces and went back to work. He visited small refineries in Brooklyn and across the region, shops left out of the trust. He explained his machine and how he could pack their product. He signed contracts with a handful of lesser sugar companies and was soon turning out thousands of packets a day.

In the 1950s, Cumberland Packing was a prosperous little factory, part of the belt of industry that stretched along the Brooklyn waterfront. Ben employed a few dozen people. The company grossed perhaps a hundred thousand a year, most of it plowed right back into the factory: new machines, more workers. Ben brought home just enough money to buy a car, support a family, send his kids to summer camp. In addition to sugar, he was packing duck sauce, perfume, and tokens. My mother, who worked at the factory when she was in high school and college, says she could tell the nature of a run by the smell in the air. Cumberland had become a transit station, a place where the raw material of the borough was given shape and sent into the market.

*Domino continues to operate, of course, albeit with greatly reduced sugar sales. Renamed Domino Foods, it's headquartered in Yonkers, New York.

8.

My father lived twenty minutes by bus from my mother, but an epoch away. Flatbush was middle class and coming. Bensonhurst was red brick and open hydrants. If you lived in Flatbush, your grandparents or great-grandparents came from Shtetl-land (a theme park I hope to open in Wisconsin, which will include a ride called Cossack Attack!). If you lived in Bensonhurst, your *parents* came from Shtetl-land. Bensonhurst is on the edge of the borough, the sort of half-known terrain cartographers signify with sea monsters. Its western edge is the Belt Parkway. The Verrazano Narrows Bridge starts in Bensonhurst and goes away in the fog—a ladder with its top in the clouds. Kids from the neighborhood take pride in its hooligans and wiseguys. A few years ago, when Sammy Gravano, a Mafia capo who testified against John Gotti, told his story to Peter Maas (*Underboss: Sammy the Bull Gravano's Story of Life in the Mafia*) my father sent me a copy of the book annotated, as if it were a work by James Joyce, with such marginalia as: "We hung out on that corner, too." "This guy was related to Who-Ha by marriage."

My father's family lived in an apartment building on Eighty-fifth Street and Twenty-first Avenue. In those years, my father was the kid who always knew the way to get the thing, the kid with the intricate counter-intuitive plan. He was a smart-ass. He would make a career out of neighborhood wisdom, refashioning the talk and code of his street corner into sayings and aphorisms he would sell to the corporate leaders of America. My father has worked for IBM, Citicorp, General Motors, the FBI, and the CIA. He's an expert in the field of negotiation. His book *You Can Negotiate Anything** has sold more than two million copies. His other book, *Negotiate This*, was also a bestseller.

My father's father was named Morris Cohen. Morris Cohen was Herbie's Herbie. Sometimes, looking at my son, Aaron, I say, "I am your Herbie." Morris was part of that generation of Eastern European Jews who said, "Let's get out of this!" He walked away from Poland when he was fourteen. He worked on the docks in Antwerp. I think of him whenever I read those hateful lines in the great T. S. Eliot poem "Gerontion":

> My house is a decayed house,
> And the Jew squats on the window sill, the owner,
> Spawned in some estaminet of Antwerp,
> Blistered in Brussels, patched and peeled in London.

Morris earned passage to New York, lived on the Lower East Side, then in Williamsburg, Brooklyn. He worked with his hands. He brought his brothers across. He was one of that crew of brothers in the old photos, all with the same eyes. He had a sense of humor that could strike the weak-minded as mean. When, as a kid, I mistook his medication for children's aspirin and swallowed some nitroglycerin, I saw real fear in his eyes. What can you say about this man, dead such a long time, so important to my own father?

---

*This book sparked a family argument: in the acknowledgments, my father thanked Frank Sinatra, or as he called him, "Francis Albert Sinatra," but not Betty or Ben. "They were pissed," my mother told me. "[Betty] reads the acknowledgments and says to me, 'We did more for your husband than Frank Sinatra.' "

Grandma Esther outlived Morris by thirty years. Grandma Betty was careful about what she said and to whom. Esther said everything to everyone. She was the loudmouthed immigrant who suddenly becomes a member of your family. She took an afternoon to tell a story that could be told in five minutes, then wound it up by saying, "That's it in a nutshell." For me, an early memory is my father on the phone saying, *Ma, Ma, please, Ma, oh, Ma! Ma! Ma!* I once heard her ask a woman in her condo complex, "Why do you hate me, fatso?" I once heard her say to a Holocaust survivor, "You are one Hitler should not have let get away." When she took me and my sister to see *Yentl,* she asked for three tickets, one senior, two children. My sister was thirty, I was twenty-two. The three of us saw *Yentl* for four dollars. She could defrost a three-course meal in six minutes. She was, according to my father, the nation's foremost expert in cryogenics. She used the word *schvartze.* Cubans made her nervous. She believed there was a book in Jerusalem in which her name was inscribed in gold. She was old, but then she got really old. When I was driving her home, she demanded to see my license, studied it, then gave it back like a skeptical cop. She was in the early stages of dementia. She said the angel of death had lost her address. "He must have been distracted at a party and forgotten."

By the time my father was in high school, Morris had become the owner of a small factory. In revenue, it was probably similar to Cumberland. In outlook, it was on the opposite end of the spectrum. With Sweet'N Low, Ben would ride the health craze. His company belonged to the future. Morris manufactured leather bands for fedoras, bowlers, and panama hats. His company belonged to the past. The industry would be wiped out when John F. Kennedy began appearing bareheaded in public. When Kennedy was assassinated, E. B. White began his *New Yorker* obituary: "When we think of him, he is without a hat." Morris spent his life in a business that has vanished, throwing him into the deep past, as if he had been a blacksmith or a medieval barber. In these two grandfathers, you therefore see a great change in America: from the industrious hat-wearing crowds that once darkened Fifth Avenue to the calorie-obsessed grooving with Richard Simmons.

Morris's factory was on the corner of Eighth Street and Broadway, in a neighborhood of small shops and garment manufacturers. The streets were filled with pushcarts and coatracks. Pressing machines hammered in the attics. Spools drifted across the sky. The business was called N&M Cohen. N stood for Nathan, one of the brothers whom Morris brought over from Europe. N&M Cohen was reached by a rickety elevator. There were five or six sewing machines, a room where workers cut leather swatches into hat bindings. My father worked at the factory in the summer, taking the subway from Bensonhurst with Morris, swaying through the tunnels, sitting at the Automat. He carried rolls of fabric, ran order forms across the district, worked on the sewing machines. As he got older, the quality of his work fell off. His mind wandered. Every day was like the first day of spring, and he could feel the wind on his neck. Morris said, "Please, Herbert, just stack the boxes, then you can go." He was a freshman at NYU, commuting from home. At night, when he sat down to do his homework, the curb below his window filled with members of his club, the Warriors, now old and fat, but then a bunch of guys in matching haircuts and coats. They stood in the street like a chorus line, chattering and tossing basketballs. Herbie was distracted by them. Herbie was distracted by everything.

He dropped out of college and joined the army. He trained at Fort Dix, in New Jersey, then Camp Chaffee, in Arkansas. He marched, got yelled at, climbed poles, scaled walls, and fired guns. He was shipped to Germany as part of the American army of occupation. He was moved east by train, the cars snaking through the black country, the heads and the hats of the enlisted men all swaying together. When the train reached a city (Wiesbaden, Stuttgart) a sergeant called out names. The men pulled down their packs and gathered their gear. Herbie was still on the train

after all the other names had been called. He was stationed on the East German border, in Bad Kissingen, a resort town that had become a flash point in the cold war. It was ideal tank country.

He trained as a clerk typist, but his classification had been changed to gunner. He drove a weasel, an armored car with a cannon on back. His unit was made up of kids from the Piedmonts, the Appalachians, and the

Ozarks. There were incidents on the frontier. Some crazy grunt determined to kill a commie would shoot up a guard tower. He was transferred to a post in town. I've seen pictures. It's like a town in a fairy tale, a carpet of red roofs, the green hills of a valley. He worked in an office, wrote legal documents, and coached basketball. On leave, he traveled to Italy and Morocco.

Then he was sent home.

He stood on the deck of the ship watching Manhattan rise out of the sea. He took the subway to Brooklyn. He walked through Bensonhurst in the rain. Well, I really have no idea what kind of day it was, but it should have been raining, because that's how he felt inside. He returned to NYU. He was among a select group of students: veterans attending school on the GI Bill of Rights. They were in their twenties, had facial hair, wore capes, used French words, ordered dark beer, and knew ten different names for schnitzel.

When my father wasn't in class, he sat in the NYU cafeteria. He read and reread the plays of Eugene O'Neill. One day, he saw a girl eating alone. She had brown hair. She was eighteen. He asked if she had seen his friend Marty Goldman. She said no. She said her name was Ellen Eisenstadt. She went home and told her father, "I have met the man I am going to marry."

Pointing at his eyes, heart, then crotch, Ben said, "Do you love him here, here, or here."

"I love him all three of those places, Pop."

For a man, such a story is dispiriting. It means Herbie did not have much say in the matter. He did not have much chance. He thought he was in control, but in fact he had been spotted like a big rhino feeding in the tall grass, or sunning on the savannah, spotted and tagged and brought down with the tranq gun, then choppered away, carried by thick ropes over the dense jungle floor.

"I liked Ben," Herbie told me. "I admired the man. He was smart and shrewd. He knew world affairs. He knew lots of things. He was more conservative than your mother and me. He called us commies. But I liked him. In those years, he seemed good. So what happened? Well, a lot of things. Or nothing. I don't really know."

But there was an event—an event so important that it's never talked about.

Soon after Herbie and Ellen were engaged, Morris sat down with Ben for the sort of man-to-man that establishes a future. Morris Cohen had two children—a daughter, Renee, and Herbie. He had retired with Esther to Miami Beach. He had sold his business and put his savings in T-bills and utilities. He proposed to invest this money in Cumberland, which was small but growing and in need of capital. In return, Ben would take Herbie into the business—a traditional arrangement that would help Ben and help Herbie and also provide for Ellen. Morris did not think he was asking Ben for a favor. He thought he was offering a gift. More than money, he was offering the services of Herbie. (Like a lot of fathers, Morris saw his son as himself perfected, with the flaws and impurities boiled away.) Ben said he would think about it. When Morris followed up, Ben said he was still thinking about it. After a time, because he was prideful and confused, Morris stopped asking.

In this way, Ben said no.

Why did Ben say no?

Because he wanted his business for himself; because he did not want a partner; because he did not need the money; because it would confuse the hierarchy; because who is this pushy immigrant with his pushy son?; because Ben already had a son and his name was Marvin.

I am not sure why Ben said no, and I am not sure what Herbie would have done had Ben said yes. Herbie says he never would have taken a job at the factory. He wanted to make his own way and not be part of someone else's scheme. As Saul Bellow said, "You define yourself, or you are defined." But in such protests I hear the sting of injury. Was there a moment in the early 1960s, after Morris had talked to Ben, that, in Herbie's mind, he had already taken a job at the factory?

———

When I was in the house after Ben's funeral, I came across a photo of my father in an old photo album. His face was sharp and willful, and I could see him as he must have first appeared to Ben, an intruder, the end of the domestic dream, the force beyond control, as if Ellen, out of her yearning, had called down a vampire. For a man like Ben, who prized the idea of family in the abstract, this business of sons-in-law was tricky. Stupid fathers lock up their daughters and forbid them to have such relationships. Ben had a smarter play: he would rush the marriage, he would call Ellen's bluff, he would say, "You love him here, here, and here? Then take him there, there, and there."

"They thought if it happened fast, it would fail," my mother told me. "And I would come back and say they were right and everything would be like it was before."

Shortly after Ellen and Herbert started dating, Ben, from behind his newspaper, which is how he confronted the world, said, "I don't believe in casual dating. If you love this boy, you will get engaged."

And so they were engaged.

Then, from behind his newspaper, Ben said, "I don't believe in long engagements. If you love this boy, you will set a date."

And so a date was set.

Then Ben said, "If you plan to marry this boy, I want to talk to his parents."

So Ben, Betty, and Ellen drove to Bensonhurst and ambushed those poor immigrants, Morris and Esther, just back from Florida, unpacking and shouting from room to room.

Ellen: "My father burst in. And he said, 'The kids are getting married. I will pay for this and that. You will pay for that and this. Done!' Herbie's parents didn't know what was going on. Esther kept saying, 'Who's getting married?'"

Gladys: "I knew your dad from school. Your dad was not ready to get married. So Ellen, Grandma, and Grandpa went over to your dad's house. Ellen was eighteen. They rang the bell. Herbert was not even there. They barged in. Esther said, 'Who are you?'"

"Ellen said, 'I am going to marry Herbert.'"

Morris said, "Who is marrying who?"

Ben said, "If it's what the kids want, it's what the kids want."

Esther said, "*A glick ahf dir! Far-tshadikt! Er zol vaksen vi a tsibeleh, mit dem kop in drerd!*"*

Ben said, "Let's work out the details and we're done."

And so the rhino was sighted, shot full of tranq, and choppered to the zoo.

From behind his paper Ben said, "I don't believe in getting engaged and setting a date and meeting the parents and not getting on with it. If you love this boy, choose a hall."

And so Ben and Ellen were in the Cadillac speeding over the black-top. When Ellen was a girl, she used to go for walks with Ben after dinner. One night, when they got back to the house, Betty was waiting on the porch. She marched Ben inside and scolded him behind the kitchen door. She said it was wrong for a man to spend so much time alone with a young girl, even if she was his daughter. Maybe Ben rushed the wedding because he felt betrayed. If he had to give Ellen away, he wanted to do it fast. They went into a half a dozen halls, fantasy palaces, where, for one night, even a Brooklyn girl could play princess. They talked to the managers and looked at the menus and studied the seating charts. Each room was imprinted with its history of weddings and bar mitzvahs, the afterimage of events so powerful they left a stain in the fabric.

*"Good luck to you! My head is confused. He should grow like an onion, with his head in the ground!"

9.

In 1957, Gladys took some money and left home. Her brother Marvin was living in Greenwich Village and her sister, Ellen, was engaged to be married. Perhaps Gladys felt that life was going on without her. She rented a room off Washington Square. She was twenty years old. During the day, she went to class. At night, she called Betty and said she was not coming home. In those weeks, questions were being asked in Flatbush: Just what is Gladys doing? Just who is Gladys living with? This was the romantic moment in the life of my aunt. It did not last very long. Her life is a novel in which everything exciting happens in the first twenty pages, followed by decades of bedridden remembering. For nieces and nephews, it's a passage that reads like a hidden text that might explain everything. As in, "Tell me, Uncle Willie, what happened to Biff when he went to see you on the road?"

Betty sent emissaries to talk with Gladys. Marvin went, and so did my father. "Gladys had a little place. I can even show you where it was, not an apartment, a dumpy hotel," my father told me. "Off Eighth Street. I

went with Howie Weiss, a friend of mine. Howie spoke to her. I spoke to her. I said, 'Please! Your parents are upset! Come home!'"

In the end, Ben dragged Gladys back to Flatbush. She was angry. You had to check her the way you check the weather. If it was a good day, she was full of charm. If it was a bad day, she was electrical and dangerous. "Summer was coming, and Ben was thinking about Gladys," my father told me, "and he suddenly realized that, over the previous year and a half, she had earned like three and a half credits in school. Everything else was incomplete. So Ben decides Gladys either has to really go to school or get a job. This went on and on. He finally gave her an ultimatum. He said, 'Come Monday, you are getting a job.'"

On Monday morning, Gladys was not at breakfast, nor was she in the hall or the bathroom. She was in bed, her body covered in sores.

Years later, when asked why she did not finish college, Gladys said, "It's hard to answer. It's a myriad of things, and I really can't put a finger on it, really. I wasn't feeling very well."

Gladys had in fact suffered an outbreak of psoriasis, a skin disease she developed in early adolescence. Psoriasis afflicts 2 percent of the world's population. In a healthy person, dead skin sheds every six or seven days. In a psoriatic, dead skin doesn't slough off for months. Bacteria builds up, turning the skin red and scaly. The disease mimics the healing process, a burst of new skin growth that protects cuts and burns; in a sense, psoriasis is the body healing but never healed.

In some instances (this is true of my aunt) the condition is accompanied by arthritis, which can deform hands and fingers. But even in the worst cases, the disease is simply not disabling. It is suffered instead as a chronic annoyance, with good days and bad days. In his book *Essential Pathology*, Emanuel Rubin writes, "By far the most disturbing aspect of psoriasis is its appearance. Sufferers' lives can be completely taken over by maneuvers designed to avoid exposing the affected skin to the public eye."

Specialists have spent careers trying to determine the causes of an outbreak. Most agree it's in some part psychological. In *The Encyclopedia of Family Health*, Marshall Cavendish writes, "Psoriasis may be triggered by a stressful event, an examination or bereavement, and studies indicate psoriasis may be an outward expression of subconscious problems."

Following the outbreak, Ben basically gave up on Gladys, no longer demanding she get a job or even leave the house. Ben and Betty did not take her to a doctor, but instead let her stay in bed, where, in a sense, she remains to this day.

Speaking to my mother and father, I get the impression that Betty was embarrassed by the disease, and wanted to keep her afflicted daughter hidden.

"Betty acted like Gladys had the plague," my mother told me. "She would rather people think my sister was dead than that she didn't look right."

"My parents never took Gladys to the hospital," said Marvin. "[Gladys] was sensitive about people seeing her. And so, unfortunately, because my parents could afford to take care of her, she never ventured out of the house."

A typical treatment for psoriasis would consist of cortisone shots, a low-fat diet, and sunshine. In cases where the disease is accompanied by arthritis, you need exercise. Gladys lay in a dark, cold room and hardly moved. Following that first big outbreak, she was in bed for almost two years. Through a friend in medical school, my father was able to get her cortisone.

When Gladys was finally taken to a doctor, she was told that her illness, especially her arthritis, had been exacerbated by the long stay in bed. "Her muscles had atrophied," said my father.

In the end, the doctors decided to operate, fusing parts of her body so she could have some use of them. "In those days, with arthritis, if it was bad, they fused your joints," Marvin explained.

"I had a knee cap removed, I had a leg fused, I had a wrist fusion and I had a bone taken out of my hip to put in my wrist," Gladys later said. "I had my fingers on [my left] hand fused."

"She was very, very sensitive about being seen," Marvin told me. "In the beginning, she tried to do things. She went to doctors, got treatments, even worked at Cumberland. But the condition kept getting worse, especially the arthritis. She became a cripple. And she's a very, very bright girl and, as I said, and again, this part is between us, she always loved my mother, and my mother, for whatever reason, did not like her."

After surgery, Gladys settled into bed, where, other than a rare trip to another bed in another house, she stayed for decades. She made camp on the first floor, next to Betty and Ben, from where she could control access to the love of her parents. Because love is finite. Because love is scarcer than water. Even though she has confined herself to one room, mostly to one part of one room, she is still able to wield tremendous power, her tiny voice made large by the telephone. Gladys is the product of technology. Her tongue is thousands of miles of fiber-optic cable. Her ears are satellite dishes. Her eyes are TV cameras. Sometimes I think there can be no one else in the world like my aunt Gladys and she must be a topic of gossip on the block, but other times I think Brooklyn must be filled with many such ladies.

10.

My parents were married on June 14, 1958, at the Park Manor in Flatbush. There was shag carpet and a coat check and more than a hundred guests in frilly gowns and white dinner jackets. There was a choice of meat or fish. There were refiners and manufacturers, the business associates of Ben. There were Moishes and Schmeulies, each of whom identified himself by a street in a liquidated Polish town. There was a band that the old people agreed was too loud. I imagine this event as it would have been chronicled in the wedding section of *The New York Times*.

Herbert Cohen, Ellen Eisenstadt

Herbert Cohen and Ellen Eisenstadt are to be married today on the Eastern Parkway in Brooklyn. The bride, 19, is, according to her sister, Gladys, too young to get married. The bride will raise three children in Illinois. Behind the wheel, she will suffer from a strange illness known as "night blindness." She will grow unaccountably weepy whenever a Helen Reddy song comes on the radio.

Ellen Eisenstadt is the youngest daughter of Benjamin and Betty (formerly Bessie, formerly Pessie) Eisenstadt of Flatbush. Benjamin Eisenstadt is a lawyer and he used to run a diner. He loves the cartoon character Popeye, with whom he identifies. In 1945, he invented the sugar packet. In 1946, the idea was stolen by the suits over at Domino.

The mother of the bride, Betty Eisenstadt, did not learn to speak English until she was eight years old. She was the only Jew at the Girls High School. She attended New York University, where she studied English with Thomas Wolfe, whom she was later to describe, though not in these words, as an anti-Semitic prick.

Betty Eisenstadt is a proponent of a cutting-edge parenting technique known as "Love Is Finite." Marvin, the brother of the bride, can walk on his hands.

Through her father, the bride is related to a Jew with flaming-red hair who crossed the Russian frontier in a hay cart. Her grandmother, Sarah, known as Bubba, came to this country so *you* could have a better life. Thirteen years ago, after Bubba's son, Abraham Gellman, a genuine war hero, was shot to death in the Pacific, Bubba tried to jump off a roof.

The bridegroom, 25, is a night student at NYU Law School. His sister, Renee, though only four years older, was eight years ahead in school. He will later have a house in suburban Chicago, three children, and a dog. He will be hard on his first and second born, and lenient with the third. How he will love that dog! He will work for Allstate Insurance, rising to the executive suite, where he will be the only Hebrew. Each morning, he will walk into the office and say, "Company Jew, passing through."

The groom is the son of Morris and Esther Cohen of Bensonhurst, apartment-house people. Morris spends half the year in the true promised land of the Jews (North Miami Beach). Until he retired, Morris owned The N&M company, which manufactured hat bindings. The mother of the groom, Esther Cohen, did so much good work for the state of Israel that her name, or so she believes, is inscribed in an actual golden book in Jerusalem. Through his mother, the groom is related to nobody, generations of them, in fact, cobblers and usurers and furriers and farmers who left no trace. Through his father, he is a direct descendant of Aaron, the brother of Moses, who brought the Law down from Sinai.

When I went to see Gladys, she talked about how curious she found it that Ellen did not ask her to be her maid of honor. "I did not make much of it at the time," she told me. "But when I think back on it—it was not me but your mother's friend Susan who was the maid of honor—I find it funny."

This complaint intrigued me because when my mother talks about the wedding, she lingers on the same detail: the fact that Gladys had not been in the ceremony. But according to Ellen, Gladys was supposed to be the maid of honor. She had been asked, had accepted, had the dress made, and went through the rehearsal. Then, at the last moment, with the people gathered and the music playing, she refused to participate. "She had a fit," my mother told me. "She refused to walk down the aisle, so I had to ask my friend Susan, who was a bridesmaid, to step in as the maid of honor."

The key details agree: Susan was in, Gladys was out. But who made the decision? If I could answer this question, maybe I could get a handle on the bigger mysteries. I asked my mother to send me her wedding album, hoping the pictures might offer a clue.

It's bound in fake white leather. In gold stencil it says, HERB AND ELLEN. It's water damaged. It's come through the flood with the rest of us. It's a bible. I devour it.

Exhibit A: This picture shows Herbert and Ellen among their attendants. Herbert is in a white dinner jacket. Ellen is in a gooey gown. Next to Ellen, holding a big bouquet of flowers, is my mother's friend Susan. So yes, Susan was in the ceremony. Off to one side is Marvin in a dinner jacket. Why? Because Marvin was Herbie's best man! Would Marvin have been Herbie's best man if Gladys had been excluded? Would Ben

and Betty have stood for it? But wait, here is Gladys, on the other side of Susan, in a gown that matches the wedding dress. From this dress and from her place in the picture, next to the best man, it is clear Gladys was

the maid of honor. But she looks angry. Her foot is turned away, as if, the moment the shutter snaps, she will dissolve into hysterics.

Exhibit B: a family photo of the Eisenstadts. Everyone is here. Ben, and Betty, and Marvin, and Ellen, and Bubba, and Ira. Betty and Bubba wear dresses that are similar to Gladys's. But wait! Where is Gladys? She is not here! Is it possible that Betty would pose for such a photo without Gladys? Unless Gladys had freaked!

Here's what I suggest: Gladys had been the maid of honor. She had the flowers and the dress. Then, after the photo of the attendants but before the family portrait, she blew her stack. (The wedding photographer always misses the really big moment.) Because her little sister was getting married, because she would be left alone in the house, because a storm was blowing across her frontal lobe. She absented herself from the wedding and now believes she was excluded. Well, I guess she was excluded, only not by Ellen. She excluded herself. Gladys took herself out of the wedding just as Gladys took herself out of life.

More pictures: Marvin walking down the aisle, handsome as a screen star, with a blond crew cut. My parents on an interior balcony, waving, as in the last scene in *North by Northwest*, in which Cary Grant pulls Eva Marie Saint up onto the bed in the sleeping car. Bubba, the folds in her neck like tea leaves in which you can read the future. There is a picture of chubby, prepubescent Ira laughing with David Blumenthal, the first-born grandson of Morris and Esther Cohen, a jug-eared little kid who years later will be Ben's cardiologist. But my favorite picture shows my mother and father walking down the aisle, the glass broken, the deed done. A picture of me and my wife in my own wedding album echoes this shot so precisely it makes me feel as if I am not living my life but instead existing as a part of a big organism that never dies.

Several years ago, a home movie of the wedding surfaced. It was shot on film and later transferred to VHS. There is a seasicky image of an old Jew in a prayer shawl, eyes hollow and dark, as if he knows this is a film being shown decades later and that he is dead. In one frame, you see my mother and her father standing together behind the tables. My mother is stunning in a way that makes me blush. She drops her eyes. Ben turns her face toward his and kisses her on the mouth. Orange blotches appear on the film and the movie jumps, and it's the end of the night and everyone has gone.

11.

Marvin began working full time at Cumberland Packing in 1956. He had graduated from the University of Vermont, where he studied chemistry. There was some thought of his attending medical school, carrying on the legacy of Uncle Abraham. The dilemma is presented thus: Marvelous comes out of college full of piss and vinegar, rice and beans, salt and pepper, and can do whatever he wants, so stands there like Lady Justice, weighing the two ways of doing good—go to medical school and save sick kids and stuff, or go to the factory.

In the end, he decided to ride to the rescue of Ben.

"Grandpa didn't want Marvin to go into the business," Gladys told me. "When Marvin got out of the army, Grandpa said, 'Look, I don't know what this business is going to turn out to be and I might run into a lot of trauma.' But for whatever reason, Marvin said, 'I want to be there for you, Pop. I want to be with you.'"

A great family is built by the will of a patriarch. The rest of the story is just the dissolution of this will, a dwindling of the energy that built the castle, founded the bank, invented the sugar packet. It's why family firms tend to last no more than three generations. First comes the pioneer, the old man with knowledge of the world. Then comes the son who frets and fears and lays in stores of antibiotics but always for the wrong disease. Then comes the grandson, who either wants to have fun or—and this is more dangerous—wants to outperform Pop. For the third generation, it seems the money will always be there because it always has been. The challenge for a family firm is to devise a way to beat human nature.

How does a rich man raise a son who is not a rich man's son?

You might study the old private firms of Europe, because some went public, some went defunct, but some stayed in the family for generations. Take the Warburgs, for example, a Jewish banking family that prospered from the 1700s to the mid-1900s—a reign that ended only with the rise of Hitler.* The patriarch of the Warburgs, Simon von Cassel, emigrated from Hesse to Warburg, a Prussian town near the Rhine, in 1559.† This man appears out of nowhere, like a stranger at the edge of a wood. His progeny would be scattered among the banking capitals of the Continent. By looking at the workings of this firm, which seemed to exist in a perpetual first generation, one can devise a few general rules for the preservation of a family firm.

1. Do Not Observe Primogeniture:
    Birth order has no significance, as it has no bearing on savvy, intelligence, or leadership. In fact, the first born is like the first batch of pancakes, which often needs to be chucked, not because there was anything wrong with the batter but because the grill was not hot enough. In the end, the best leader might turn out to be the youngest. In other words, don't bestow leadership; have it be fought for and won.

*See Ron Chernow, *The Warburgs: The Twentieth-Century Odyssey of a Remarkable Jewish Family* (New York: Random House, 1993).

†The family took its famous name in 1668, when Simon's great-grandson Juspa-Joseph left Warburg for Altona, a town on the Elbe River, where he came to be known as Joseph von Warburg, later shortened to Joseph Warburg.

2. There Is Nothing Immediate About Immediate Family:
   Do not restrict your search for a successor to the nuclear family. Sometimes the far-flung branches create the dynamos (a cousin raised on a farm in Bavaria, a middle child raised in an English Tudor in Illinois), because the power belongs to the man from the provinces, an outsider who understands the world because he sees it from beyond the glass. The Warburgs searched wide for talent, in one case recruiting the middle son of a disgraced sister who had vanished years before. The children of such outcasts most resemble the patriarch, exhibiting the desperation and drive of the first generation. In spite of any former grievances, the Warburgs promoted such recruits to positions even above their own sons. Because in the end, the firm is the family.

3. Make the Kid Work for It:
   Even when a future leader is spotted, he should not be given a position of power immediately. After a Warburg finished school, he was sent to a distant city, where his name carried little meaning, and put to work. In this way, the family short-circuited the system and cheated time, creating a pool of first generationers. Unlike my uncle Marvin or cousin Jeff, who have had little experience in the world outside of Cumberland Packing, and so have no real confidence (Marvin is a man telling a joke he himself does not get), the Warburgs would be brought back to Hamburg only after decades with another firm in another town, bringing the knowledge of another office, and, more important, the confidence of one who has made his own way.

Shortly after Marvin started at the factory, Ben gave his son half ownership of the company. Ben did this in recognition of the problems just mentioned. By turning Marvin into a partner, he hoped to instill in him the responsibility and terror of ownership. This is the story as the family tells it, anyway: because if you dig through the documents, it gets more complicated. The assets of the business, which is entirely family owned, are in fact divided into two kinds of stock: fifteen shares of class-A voting stock which actually controls the company; several hundred shares of class-B nonvoting stock, or common stock, ownership of which entitles you to dividends but to no real role in the decision making.* The holder of such stock has about as much say in Cumberland as the holder of Israel bonds has in the foreign policy of Jerusalem. Thus dividing the stock allowed Ben maximum control. He could give without giving, like the dollar on the string, or the trap door in the contract. He handed out nonvoting shares to Marvin, and later to Ira and Jeff, but kept control of the class-A stock: five shares were given to his oldest son, but the rest he divided between himself and Betty, a distribution that mimics the dynamic of the family. Map the stock and you map the love.

Marvin learned the business from the ground up. In the early days, he hung out with the assembly-line workers and mechanics, mostly immigrants from South America and the Caribbean. Many of these men are still at the factory. Whenever a reporter visits, Marvin walks through the plant grabbing workers seemingly at random and asking, "How long have you worked at Cumberland?" Ten years, eighteen years, forty years. He spent his youth with these men, in the break rooms and mixing chambers, laughing and telling stories. He speaks of these as his years at sea, as if he had been Henry V wandering in disguise among his soldiers, or Peter the Great hiking through Europe dressed as a pauper. He says, "Everything I learned, I learned in the school of hard knocks." But everyone knew who Marvin was: not just the son of the owner but an owner himself. Such a regular guy turns up in the lunchroom the way a screw turns up in the joint. Everything gets quiet and the phony grins appear. Or maybe these men saw Marvin as a great development, a weak son who could be colonized and exploited like a third world country.

For Marvin, the years drifted by as a succession of faces, the immigrant factory hands, like the sombrero wearers in a Diego Rivera mural, crashed on the loading bay between shifts, Sweet'N Low packets stacked behind them, the pink packets under the hard blue sky, tenements and smoke stacks, the dirty river, the men laughing and singing their sad songs and passing the reefer and the jug as the gringo son of the boss sits

---

*A 1995 audit estimated the class-A voting stock at $27,620 a share. The total value of the class-B nonvoting stock was estimated at $40 million.

among them, laughing, too, because he is dumb and doesn't know he is the butt of the joke. *Mañana man, mañana.* Tomorrow we work, but today, *mañana, man!*

These men, who have worked at the factory for decades, are silent witnesses to the rise and fall of Cumberland Packing.

Witnesses?

Yes, literally.

Marvin arrived at the factory each morning before sunup. He walked the floors and examined the presses and belts. *Goddamn, he was a handsome man!* Thin hipped, blue eyed. Into gadgets. A genius with his hands. An aristocrat of machines. He took them apart and put them together. He crawled under the belts and climbed into the rafters. He was covered in grease, his face turning above the factory. You can amass a pile of patents awarded to Marvin, each elegant drawing accompanied by a byzantine description of a new formula, a new sugar substitute, a new device. When I think of my uncle in those years, I think of a creative world-tamer, so, sadly, I have come to see his story as one of wasted potential. He was out front for years, soaking up the sun in the family portrait, a golden boy of the postwar boom. Yet this figure of energy and promise spent himself and withered. The flaw in his character ripened. It was part of his talent, the glitch that made the early success possible. It was the focus that gave him the insight into equipment but crippled him when it came to people.

In 1956, Ben and Marvin began the research that would culminate, later that year, in the invention of Sweet'N Low. There are legends about this discovery, as well there should be. It's the place where the stream goes under the rocks and emerges as a swift and dangerous river, where the needling problems of a middle-class Brooklyn family become the soap-opera stuff of the superrich.

According to legend, the invention was an expression of character. That is, the nature of Sweet'N Low can tell you about the nature of Ben, is an extension of Ben, or is Ben himself in another form. Sweet'N Low as a sacrament. Sweet'N Low as the holy wafer. Take it onto your tongue and let it dissolve. The rush of sweetness is followed by a bitter aftertaste. That aftertaste is the soul of Ben.

My mother says the spark came when Ben was on a diet. Ben was always on a diet because he was never happy with who he was—a psychosis that runs through the family. We gain and lose like boxers freaking out before a weigh-in. When my father is on a diet, he goes through the house tossing out candy and dumping Windex on the coffee cake. He can drop sixty pounds just like that. On the refrigerator, he keeps a picture of himself at his fattest to remind himself that lurking in each of us "is a small-town southern sheriff." He travels with packets of Sweet'N Low rubber-banded like flash cards, precious as poppers. "Because of this diet, Grandpa Ben was not eating anything with sugar," said my mother. "In those days, the only substitute was Sucaryl, a combination of saccharin and another artificial sweetener called cyclamate.* It came in little pills that you carried in a vial. You put one into a cup of coffee. Or there was a liquid that came in an eye dropper. If you were having ice tea, you might add two drops. But the liquid was too sweet. And the pills never dissolved. My father loved grapefruit. He would crush the pills and spread it on the grapefruit, but that never really worked. It bothered him. It was a problem he wanted to solve."

For Ben, grapefruit is like the apple of Newton, that part of the material world that cracks him on the skull and jars loose the obstruction.

"I have no idea how he came up with it," Gladys told me. "Yes, he was on a diet, but I don't know. People were dieting and using saccharin so, okay, I guess he decided, 'Let's invent a sugar substitute.'"

Is this what happened?

Well, Ben was on a diet and he did sprinkle mashed up-saccharin and cyclamate pills on his grapefruit, but he did not take the next logical step on his own. The idea for an artificial sweetener in powder form was in fact brought to him by the executives at a long-defunct pharmaceutical company. These men asked Ben if he could devise a sugar substitute that could

---

*For more on cyclamate, which was introduced by Abbott Laboratories in 1950, see the article called "Abbott Labs Introduces Artificial Sweetener Cyclamate," included in the book *Great Events: 1900–2001* (Salem Press, Inc., 2002).

be packed by Cumberland in the same way the company was packing sugar. Fake sugar, real packets. To these men, fake sugar was imagined less as a food than as a medicine. It would be sold to hospitals and drugstores. It would be used mostly by diabetics. With this simple idea, the pharmaceutical executives were offering a solution to a problem new in history, the American problem of plenty. Not the scarcity of food, but too much. Too many burgers, too many shakes, too many candy bars, too many calories.

"The drug company came to us," said Marvin. "They wanted us to make a sugar substitute. At that time, there was just Sucaryl, put out by Abbott Laboratories."

Even if they did not know it, Ben and Marvin were entering into a plot to overthrow sugar, which had been the king of the Western diet for five hundred years.

12.

Sugar cane was domesticated in New Guinea in 8000 B.C., a taste for sweets being written into our genetic code. Coffee, tea, beer, corned beef, olives, pickles, borscht—these are tastes you have to acquire. Sweets you like the moment the fruit touches your tongue. It's the first thing you crave. In the caveman days, so goes the thinking, a sweet taste indicated that a food was safe to eat. Bitterness meant death. Sweetness meant life. So wild cane was pulled down and picked and bundled and carried on foot and by boat, until, by 6000 B.C., it had reached the Philippines and Indonesia, a stash of cane growing in the sun outside an island shanty. The morning of Man. It was not yet called sugar. It was called manna, like the manna from heaven that fed the Jews on their way out of Egypt.

Sugar appeared in the oldest books. Dioscorides, an ancient historian, wrote of "a kind of concentrated honey called Saccharon found in the reeds in India and in Arabia Felix, alike in consistence to salt. It is good for the belly and the stomach, being dissolved in water and so drunk, helping the pained bladder." In 327 B.C., while searching for the source of the Euphrates, Nearchus, a general in the army of Alexander the Great, came across "a reed in India that brings forth honey without the help of bees." By 200 B.C., refined sugar, as opposed to the wild growing stalk, had turned up. It was a key ingredient in an ancient Indian cookbook, which included recipes for rice pudding (milk and refined sugar), porridge (barley meal and refined sugar), and some sort of fruity summer drink (distilled spirits and refined sugar).

Refining had been the protected knowledge of the ancients, which, like the secrets of masonry and pyramid building, was passed from father to son. A Sanskrit document from 100 B.C. described a primitive version of the process in a sort of pharmacist's handbook. *The Buddhagosa,* an ancient Hindu text, mentioned a mystical process in which crystals were extracted from cane. In A.D. 627, when the Byzantine emperor Heraclius seized the palace of Persian emperor Chosroes II, Christian soldiers stumbled on a warehouse of what was probably refined sugar, sacks of white crystals described to the invaders as "an Indian delicacy."

By A.D. 700, the refining process was basically the same as it is today: Scores of men—migrants, refugees, or slaves—walking through the green swaying aisles of cane, singing and swinging the scythe, the blade reflecting the sun like a heliograph, dripping with cane juice or dripping with blood. Because of the violent, fatiguing nature of the work, harvesters often lose fingers or limbs. They live in huts or shanties or tent camps. Twice a year, they burn the fields, which leaves the cane scorched and ashy and ready for harvesting. The sweet smoke is dense in the low equatorial sky, great flocks of birds turning over the fields into the shape of the cross, or the star and crescent, or the scythe, the instrument of the fields, the symbol of the slave rebellion.

The harvested cane is carried into a mixing house, where it is peeled and piled. The men then go to work, beating and stomping it into a pulp. What remains when the debris is cleared is cane juice, which is poured into tremendous vats and cooked over tremendous fires. As the juice bubbles, crystals appear. As the juice cools, it turns brown and gooey. It is poured into huge funnels shaped like orange safety cones. It shimmies and drips, a river of syrup pooling beneath, the by-product of the trade, molasses, sold as a cheap foodstuff or fermented into rum. What's left in the cone dries into crystals. This is refined sugar. The longer the process is allowed to continue, the more molasses drains and the whiter the sugar: brown sugar, and Cumberland's Sugar in the Raw, is sugar that has gone only partway through the process and is still stained with molasses.

Once it's refined, you can see just what a miracle sugar is: it's easy to transport, it keeps, it's nice at parties, and it's delicious. Because it has been reduced to such purity (the essence hidden in every fruit), refined sugar carries a terrific cargo of calories in a very small package.

By the 1300s, the world had entered the age of sugar. The Muslims, who learned its secrets in the course of their invasions of Asia, carried it overland to the Middle East, Asia Minor, and North Africa. "Sugar followed the Koran," as the old saying goes. The caliphs had declared a ban on alcohol and caffeine—no coffee in the desert, no wine by the well, nothing to electrify the senses—so sugar became the treat at the end of the trail. The Arabs were pioneers in the concoction of sugar drinks, predecessors to our own oceans of Coca-Cola. Because it was so expensive, an ostentatious display of sugar was a show of power. *The Zahir* tells of an eleventh-century caliph who celebrated a feast day by having a court artist sculpt 157 marzipan figures and seven tent-size marzipan palaces. (A medieval candy made from ground almonds and sugar, marzipan is even more supple than terra-cotta.) In 1412, another caliph had a mosque carved out of marzipan. Worshippers prayed in the mosque, then it was eaten by the poor.

Muslims built the first sugar plantations on the Atlantic coast of North Africa. To flourish, sugar cane needs a thousand millimeters of rain a year and a twelve-month growing season. That means, the torrid zone. That means, "What are we? A mile from the sun?" Because it was such hard work, the fields were planted and harvested by pagans captured on the European frontier. Because these men were mostly Slavic, cane workers came to be knows as slavs, later corrupted to *slaves*. From the beginning, Europeans therefore knew sugar as a crop best harvested by slaves. So begins perhaps the darkest chapter in our history.

Sugar came west in the course of the Crusades, the first of which was launched by an edict of Pope Urban II in 1095. For the Crusaders, sugar was encountered as the wealth and variety of the Orient. In a book about the First Crusade (1096–1099) based on the reminiscences of returning soldiers, Albert van Aachen, a medieval historian, writes: "In the fields of Tripoli is found in abundance a honey reed which they call *Zuchra*. The people are accustomed to suck enthusiastically on this reed, delighting themselves with beneficial juices, and seem unable to sate themselves with this pleasure in spite of their sweetness. It was on this taste that people sustained themselves during the sieges of El-barieh, Marrah, and Arkah, when tormented by fearsome hunger."

The Crusaders seized plantations in Africa, or took cuttings and planted their own fields outside Jerusalem, or beyond the walls of Acre, a fortress underlaid by chambers and an escape route to the sea. When the returning soldiers planted cane in Flanders or in Westminster, the stalks withered. Britain and France do not have the climate for sugar. In the end, this *not having* would be a kind of blessing, as it would drive the British and French to build navies and dominate the world. History is made by those who love sweets but who do not have the fields in which sugarcane grows.

Before sugar, the European diet, even for the nobility, had been perhaps the blandest in history. The most common food (the first fast food) was gruel. A typical meal was many courses of gruel, a drumstick, you're done. On occasion, a dish was sweetened by sorghum or honey. Dessert did not appear until the sixteenth century. By 1580, the French nobles were eating a third course. Dessert came to the commoners only in the 1800s, first to England, where it was almost always pudding.

In the Middle Ages, sugar was so rare that the Europeans considered it a spice, classed with pepper, nutmeg, mace, ginger, cardamom, coriander, saffron, a treasure from the East, measured not in cups but in thimbles, sprinkled on like salt, just enough to get the bland thing down. It first appeared in official British records in the twelfth century, and in 1226, three pounds of Alexandrian sugar were ordered for the table of King Henry III. It was used as much for texture as for taste. A relic of sugar as a spice is seen in the crystals scattered on the Christmas cookie. Sugar was also treated as a medicine, prescribed, like all wonder drugs, for everything. For sleepiness and sleeplessness, for weight loss and weight gain, for constipation and the runs. For fever, dry cough, chapped lips, stomach disease, body aches. Church officials said, as sugar was a drug, it was not bound by the dietary rules. "Though they are nutritious," wrote Thomas Aquinas, "sugared spices are not eaten with the end in mind of nourishment but rather for ease in digestion; accordingly, they do not break the fast any more than taking of any other medicine."

In 1581, the Flemish cartographer Abraham Ortelius wrote, "What used to be kept by apothecaries for sick people is now commonly devoured out of gluttony." By then, sugar use had become so common among British nobles that the negative effects had begun to surface. A sixteenth-century German traveler wrote of his visit with Queen Elizabeth: "Her eyes are small yet black and pleasant; her nose is a little hooked, her lips narrow and her teeth are black (a defect the English seem subject to from their too great use of sugar)."

The more sugar the aristocrats ate, the more they wanted to eat. As the demand grew, so did the search for new sources of cane, like the search, in our own time, for new sources of oil. The Age of Exploration, which in school we were taught was a search for knowledge, because man is curious and needs a frontier, was actually a quest for a way around the Muslims, who clogged the trade routes and blocked the way to the sugar of the East. It was at this moment, when the West turned away from the East, and its leaders said, in essence, *Forget it, we'll grow our own*, that the Muslim imperium took its first sad steps downhill.

In the fifteenth century, the Christian nations set out in search of tropical islands where they could build their own plantations, plant their own fields, and work to death their own slaves. On his second crossing, Christopher Columbus carried sugarcane and slaves, the entire story of the New World stored in a single ship. Within a decade, cane fields had been carved out of the brush all across the Caribbean. Every few years, a new island was colonized and planted in the same way every few years a new theme hotel opens on the strip in Vegas. Jamaica, Cuba, Barbados.

The defining product of the New World (sugar) was an import. The defining people of the New World (black slaves) were also an import. They lived on islands of sugar, in shanties buried in a sea of stalks, amid rows as ordered as circuitry inside a transistor radio. Lifetimes in the fields, cutting and stomping and boiling and shipping the cane to the refineries of Antwerp, London, Paris. Banner year followed banner year. The price of sugar fell. It entered the diet of the merchants. When the shop owners got the taste, they flipped. It's economics. It's a circle. The price falls, the demand grows; the demand grows, more islands are planted; more islands are planted, more people are enslaved; more people are enslaved, the price falls.* The sugar trade was one of the biggest economic booms in history, one that started in the age of Shakespeare and did not break until after the cancellation of *The Love Boat*.

The men drawn to the boom were often the worst people in Europe, the dregs of the dregs. It's always thus with bubbles that form on the far side of creation. Who would volunteer for work in the titanium mines on Mars? Those who turned up in the overgrown capitals of the Antilles were runaways and criminals and pirates and slave traders and corrupt governors and defrocked clergy and disgraced veterans—ne'er-do-wells getting blasted in the dives, sailing out before first light, laying up for the Spanish galleon, killing the crew, and making off with the gold the Conquistadors had carried out of the jungle, stealing stolen goods, the treasure of the Incas. The drink of the islands was rum, which tastes like the ash and pine forests of the New World.

The story of sugar is the story of the Americas. Everyone is in it: the plotting officials of the East India Company; the political hacks going straight from the House of Lords to the board of directors; the British Navy backing up every threat; the fading aristocrats set for a last hurrah in some glorious statehouse overlooking the harbor; the hustlers and pirates working the gaps; then, at the bottom, the fuel that powered the whole

---

*This was called the triangular trade: cargo ships filled with trinkets sailed to Africa, where the trinkets were traded for shackled chain gangs of slaves, who were loaded into the now-empty holds of the cargo ships and carried across the sea to the Caribbean islands, where the people were traded for sugar, which was loaded into the holds and carried back to the point of departure, completing the triangle. The second leg was the Middle Passage, in the course of which millions of Africans died and were dumped into the ocean.

machine: the slaves, the men and women who did the actual work that made the wheels spin.

By the nineteenth century, slavery had become a moral issue. There were demands for abolition. The East India Company produced sugar bowls that carried the legend NOT MADE BY SLAVES. The British turned against slavery only when steam power and other advances made the harvesting and refining of sugarcane far less labor intensive. That is, slavery became reprehensible only when slaves were no longer needed. As a result, the European nations loosened their grip on the colonies, and so began the age of rebellion. In island after island, the slaves threw off their shackles. In Barbados. In Puerto Rico. In Jamaica. Cuba was the last, with slavery outlawed in 1880. The legacy is a sea of lost colonies, now known mostly as places to vacation, some sunny and fun, some dark and edgy. Like St. Lucia, with its volcanic peaks rising steeply from the ocean, where you are gently advised not to leave the compound, because inside the compound is vacation, but outside is history. On a trip to town you are chased by ghouls, by a man waving a scythe, because you are in the ruined house of sugar. The slave trade snatched these people, their ancestors, I mean, shackled and carried and dumped them on these islands and did not free them so much as abandon them. The best case is a place like Barbados, a Hamptons for pink people from Nottingham and Essex, where the descendants of slaves work at restaurants and hotels and serve and clean up after the descendants of masters, the entire system built on the ghosts of the Caribs.

The first slave rebellion, the insurrection that, with its tremendous violence, made the others possible, happened on the island of Haiti. That island is a mess, the sin of the trade made manifest. There have been twenty coups in Haiti. When you see it in the news, you are amazed by its beauty: how can anyone be unhappy in such a place? The roads climb terraced hills, each switchback opening on a vista of sea and sky, colonial towns pooling like fog in the valleys. The slaves came to greatly outnumber the masters in Haiti, and the plantations expanded until they were unknowable. Hundreds of slaves escaped to the overgrown north side of the island, where they built camps from which they hounded the plantation owners. These men were called Maroons. The most storied of them was François Macandal, who led mobs through the fields, killing every white person he came across. Before it, the mob carried a pike on which a white baby had been impaled. This was the birth of the great white fear. When white people get scared, black people die. The Maroons thought Macandal was a *boko,* a sorcerer called by the winds. In 1758, when he was burned by plantation owners, the stake snapped and for a moment he seemed to dance in the flames.

The big revolt came after the Revolution in France, an unintended consequence of all the fraternity talk in Paris. The slaves got wind of this talk and believed it, as did the in-between classes of mulattoes and octoroons and blacks who had been freed, or had bought their freedom. The government in Paris legislated rights for these people, but the laws were ignored in the colony. When the whites lost the allegiance of the mulattoes and the octoroons, they lost control of the island. The revolt took shape only when it was joined by François Dominique Toussaint, the greatest revolutionary in the history of the Caribbean. Toussaint was fifty when he joined the rebellion. A slave. Too old to work in the cane, he had been employed as a carriage driver. He secured safe passage off the island for his former master and his master's family. There are only a few pictures of Toussaint. In them, he is dressed like a French aristocrat, in the hat and plumage of the soon-to-be-vanquished class. Toussaint dressed like the leaders of the colony the way, in our own time, the driver of the limousine dresses like the CEO. Toussaint was the most dangerous sort of man: the slave who has learned to read his master's books. He studied the classics in the estate house library. It was said that he learned to defeat the French by reading *Julius Caesar.* He became known as Toussaint L'Ouverture, (Toussaint "The Opening"), the first of those Castros and Guevaras who so thrilled the intellectual class of the West. To feel free, people must believe that somewhere a slave is in revolt. Toussaint turned the mob into an army, won seven battles in seven days, and drove the masters from the island.

Napoleon sent a battalion to reclaim Haiti. Fifty thousand French soldiers died in the effort, most of them from malaria. Toussaint was captured and shipped to France. He was locked in a prison high in the Alps, a strange, cold place, as far as you can get from Port-au-Prince. He sickened and died. The merchants of France feared Toussaint and what he implied about the coming order in the same way that the royals of Europe feared Napoleon. When Napoleon was captured, he, too, was sent into exile in an alien climate, as if in sentencing Toussaint, Napoleon had been choosing his own fate.

Of course, you cannot kill Toussaint. Because Toussaint is a symbol. He is freedom in a jail far from home. He is the slave who has dared raise his fist to power. In the world of sugar, there is the plantation owner and there is Toussaint.

Pablo Neruda wrote a hymn to the revolutionary (here translated by James Wright).*

> Out of its own tangled sweetness
> Haiti raises mournful petals,
> and elaborate gardens, magnificent
> structures, and rocks the sea
> as a dark grandfather rocks
> his ancient dignity of skin and space.
>
> Toussaint L'Ouverture knits together
> the vegetable kingdom,
> the majesty chained,
> the monotonous voice of the drums
> and attacks, cuts off retreats, rises,
> orders, expels, defies

---

*Wordsworth wrote the first poem about the rebel, "To Toussaint L'Ouverture," penned while the former slave was imprisoned in the Alps: "O miserable chieftain! where and when / Wilt thou find patience? Yet die not; do thou / Wear rather in thy bonds a cheerful brow: / Though fallen thyself, never to rise again, / Live, and take comfort. Thou hast left behind / Powers that will work for thee; air, earth, and skies; / There's not a breathing of the common wind / That will forget thee; thou hast great allies; / Thy friends are exultations, agonies, / And love, and man's unconquerable mind."

like a natural monarch,
until he falls in the shadowy net
and they carry him over the seas,
dragged along and trampled down
like the return of his race,
thrown into the secret death
of the ship holds and the cellars.
But on the island the boulders burn,
the hidden branches speak,
hopes are passed on,
the walls of the fortress rise.
Liberty is your own forest,
dark brother, don't lose
the memory of your sufferings,
may the ancestral heroes
have your magic sea foam in their keeping.

Even in the bloodiest years of revolt, sugar consumption continued to climb. In 1839, the Western refineries produced 245,000 tons of sugar. In 1860, they produced 1.37 million tons of sugar. In 1890, they produced 6 million tons of sugar. Most dazzling are the figures that track individual consumption. In 1700, an average Englishman consumed four pounds of sugar annually. In 1800, an average Englishman consumed twenty pounds annually. In 1900, an average American consumed forty pounds of sugar per year. In 1960, an average American consumed sixty pounds per year. Over time, we have become fat, supersizing junkies. By 1970, sugar accounted for 10 percent of all the calories consumed in the world. That same year, Americans, on average, ingested 265 combined pounds of fat and sugar. Your common citizen, even now, in the age of Atkins, consumes 3,200 calories a day. When questioned at the end of the day, most people can account for only 1,600 of these calories. Chips, cones, creams, fries—we have no memory of our crimes. We are whales swimming open-mouthed through the food court. We are what we eat, and we don't know what that is.

As the use of sugar increased, teeth rotted, kids turned hyper, and people died. Diabetes, which had been unknown before 1600, became an epidemic. By the middle 1900s, a new sort of fat man had appeared, waves and oceans and great heaving ripples of fat. In its world-conquering ways, sugar had created the conditions for its own demise—the need for alternatives.*

*On the history of sugar see *Sweetness and Power: The Place of Sugar in Modern History*, by Sidney W. Mintz (New York: Viking, 1985); *Tastes of Paradise: A Social History of Spices, Stimulants, and Intoxicants*, by Wolfgang Schivelbusch (New York: Pantheon, 1992); *Bittersweet: The Story of Sugar*, by Peter Macinnis (Crows Nest, Australia: Allen & Unwin, 2002); *Eating in America*, by Waverly Root and Richard de Rochemont (New York: Morrow, 1976); *Refined Tastes: Sugar, Confectionery, and Consumers in Nineteenth-Century America*, by Wendy A. Woloson (Baltimore: Johns Hopkins University Press, 2002), and, as already mentioned, *Never Satisfied: A Cultural History of Diets, Fantasies, and Fat* by Hillel Schwartz.

13.

One evening in 1879, Constantine Fahlberg shoved a piece of bread so far into his mouth that his fingers touched his tongue. *Ka-pow!* "Before going home, I had washed my hands thoroughly," he later wrote. "I was very surprised at dinner when my hands tasted sweet."

Earlier that day, while testing a derivative of coal tar, an experiment suggested by Ira Remsen, a professor and the manager of the lab at Johns Hopkins University in Baltimore, Fahlberg had become distracted and his beaker overflowed. When he raced back to the lab and licked the stain, his mouth filled with flavor. One year later, in the *American Chemical Journal*, Remsen and Fahlberg wrote that this substance "possesses a very marked sweet taste, being much sweeter than cane sugar. The taste is perfectly pure. The minutest quantity of the substance, a bit of its powder scarcely visible, if placed upon the tip of the tongue, causes a sensation of pleasant sweetness throughout the entire cavity of the mouth."

Constantine Fahlberg was born in Tambov, Russia, in 1850. He attended gymnasium in Estonia, studied chemistry in Leipzig, and trained in sugar analysis, the crucial skill of the day, in Berlin. He was part of the modern priesthood that understood how the magic worked. He moved to New York City in 1874. He came to be known as the nation's foremost expert on sugar. He was called to court again and again. He made a grand entrance. In 1877, when the H. W. Perot Import Firms, the largest sugar supplier in Baltimore, had a large shipment of imported sugar impounded as impure, the company hired Fahlberg to run tests and appear as an expert witness. With this in mind, Perot asked Ira Remsen, a chemist and the president of Johns Hopkins, to let Fahlberg use Remsen's lab at the school.*

Ira Remsen was born in New York on February 10, 1846, the son of Rosanna Secor and James Vanderbilt Remsen.[†] He founded the nation's first journal of chemical research, and is considered the father of American chemistry. He began tinkering with sulfobenzoic acids as a student in Germany, work that would be the basis for the invention of saccharin. In 1878, he became the second president of Johns Hopkins University. In temperament, he was the opposite of Fahlberg. He considered himself too pure for the market. He once said, "I will not sully my hands with industry."

Fahlberg soon finished his work for H. W. Perot. Because there was a delay in court, he began tinkering with experiments Remsen had been talking about for years. Fahlberg was like a jazz musician picking up a line that Remsen had established, tossed around, and toyed with but had never carried to a conclusion. This work had to do with the derivatives of coal tar and some of the obscure properties of sulfuric acids, how such acids break down, and how the resulting compounds behave. The result was a chemical so sweet it could be used in quantities small enough to amount to no calories. Fahlberg had invented it by accident, while he was supposed to be working on something else, with another scientist's research, in a lab not his own.

---

*Helpful for this section was the article "Making Governmental Policy Under Conditions of Scientific Uncertainty: A Century of Controversy about Saccharin in Congress and the Laboratory," by Paul M. Priebe and George B. Kaufman, *Minerva* 18, no. 4 (Winter 1980): 556–74.

[†]See the biographical sketch of Remsen on the website of the Sheridan Libraries at Johns Hopkins, where most of Remsen's papers are archived.

The origins of saccharin have become a matter of intense debate. According to a monograph written by Kathryn Jacob, "This discovery is shrouded in controversy. It's become something of a Johns Hopkins folk myth."* In most versions of this myth, Fahlberg is the Judas from Tambov, packing his notes and catching the midnight train to Washington, D.C., where he hurries to the patent office and claims Ira Remsen's work as his own. In fact, Fahlberg did share the credit with Remsen, at least in the beginning. The findings were initially published under a joint by-line.

Then the H. W. Perot case ended, and the pages flew off the calendar.

While contracted to work for Harrison Brothers, a Philadelphia chemical plant, Fahlberg continued his research into coal tar, perfecting the formula. In 1882, he traveled to Leipzig, where a rich uncle gave him money to search for a way to mass-produce the chemical. He began testing it on people. Saccharin was among the first of the artificial foods, a product not of the fields or of the trees but of the lab. It was the beginning of a revolution as great as any political revolution: the overthrowing of the old diet. He fed volunteers saccharin, then, over several hours, tested their pee, determining how much of the saccharin turned up. Almost all of it did. Saccharin goes right through you. As far as Fahlberg was concerned, it was therefore no more dangerous than a bad thought. He applied for and received a patent in Germany, which was honored in the United States. In other words, Fahlberg got his patent in the way least likely to attract attention or protest from Remsen. He then returned to America and opened the world's first saccharin factory. It was on 117th Street and the East River, just a few miles up the tidal wash from the great sugar refineries of Brooklyn.

For Remsen, most galling was the name under which the chemical was patented. It had always been called by its scientific name: benzoic sulfide. In the legal documents, in the newspapers, and above the door of the factory it was now called, "Fahlberg's saccharin." The word *saccharin* is a play on the Latin term for sugar: *saccharum*. The *Fahlberg* in "Fahlberg's saccharin" is pure marketing and pure genius. It demonstrates the power

*Cited in "The Discovery of Saccharin: A Centennial Retrospect," by George B. Kaufman and Paul M. Priebe, published in *Ambix*, the Society for the History of Alchemy and Chemistry 25, no. 3 (November 1978): 191–207.

of branding, how getting your name on the new thing early is the key to everything. Even when Remsen complained, he had to use the name of his nemesis: "The expression 'Fahlberg's saccharin' is absolutely unauthorized," he wrote in 1877. "I hope it will not appear again. The only possible justification is the fact that Fahlberg had the compound patented without discussing the matter with me. This fact requires no comment."

Fahlberg came to be seen as a usurper, the brutal face of capitalism. It did not matter to Remsen or to his supporters that Fahlberg did actually invent the compound—built on the work of Remsen, yes, but the entire world is built on the work of some fool too dumb to put his name on it. Or that Fahlberg did not in fact patent saccharin but only his method for producing it—a deed not to the butter but to the butter churn. Or that once the process had been patented, he was free to call it whatever he wanted. "Fahlberg is a scoundrel," wrote Remsen. "It nauseates me to hear my name mentioned in the same breath with his."

By 1890, saccharin had found a growing market, being prescribed by doctors for nausea, headaches, and corpulence. It was used in canned foods as a preservative. It was added to coffee and tea by diabetics. For the first time in history, a food was valued not for being nutritional but for having no nutritional value whatsoever. Because no one knew what the compound would do to a body, its success would eventually give rise to a whole bureaucracy of regulators and fake-food cops charged with protecting the American people from their own habits. (The Pure Food and Drug Act, passed in 1906, was the earliest attempt really to get a handle on the fast-changing food supply.) In 1907, Harvey Washington Wiley, America's chief chemist, proposed the first saccharin ban, making his case directly to President Teddy Roosevelt.*

Whenever you look into the story of the American diet, and the story of our fat people, you come across this encounter: Roosevelt sitting on the

---

*On the ups and downs of saccharin, see "Sweets for the Sweet: Saccharin, Knowledge, and the Contemporary Regulatory Nexus," by Alan I. Marcus, *Journal of Policy History* 9 no. 1 (Winter 1997):33–47.

edge of his desk in the Oval Office, legs crossed at the ankle, hair brushed to the side, buckteeth shining like piano keys, woolen vest stretched across his frankly corpulent midsection, chatting up the captains of industry who have gathered for the meeting. The president sees himself as a man of science, and until this moment, he has been largely receptive to the ideas of his chief chemist. But now Wiley is making his case, raising a vial of saccharin, like a vial of crack cocaine or anthrax, and saying that thousands of pounds of this poison are sold every year as a preservative or sweetener. *Nothing good to eat can derive from coal tar. It should be banned.*

A factory boss protests: "Mr. President, my firm saved four thousand dollars last year by using saccharin instead of sugar."

"Yes, Mr. President," says Dr. Wiley, "and everyone who eats those products is deceived, believing he is eating sugar, and moreover his health is threatened by this drug."

"Anyone who says saccharin is injurious to health is an idiot," snaps Roosevelt. "Dr. Rixey gives it to me every day." (It was prescribed for corpulence.)

In 1913, the first saccharin ban was signed by President William Howard Taft, who, not coincidentally, was our last fat president.* That we have not had a truly fat commander in chief in the last hundred years suggests that this was a moment of change in body type, or in how we value body type, the beginning of the end of the glorious fat man—a change that would be a key to the success of Sweet'N Low. Whereas girth had long signified prosperity and ease, it had come to mean laziness and sloppiness, the fat man as laggard. Roosevelt had refused to ban saccharin because Roosevelt was the first modern president: he wanted to look like a machine.

The ban lasted less than a year. Within months of its passage, Archduke Franz Ferdinand got his head blown off in Sarajevo and the armies filled the parade grounds and we were into the era of big wars. Destroyers

---

*Clinton could get chubby, but Taft was monstrously fat, a frequenter of "big and tall" men's shops, famous as the president who got stuck in a bathtub, which is easy to picture, but hard to picture clearly.

sat off the coast, U-boats patrolled the depths, tankers were hit below the waterline, and the oceans filled with molasses. Sugar was priced right off the market, so saccharin was brought back as a cheap alternative, another drug spread by conflict. Like tobacco in the Thirty Years War, like cocaine in the Civil War, like morphine in the Crimean War, like LSD in the Cold War.

After the First World War, when the seas opened, saccharin use dipped, but after the Second World War, in which it became part of the arsenal of democracy—loaded onto transport trucks alongside the powdered eggs and condensed milk, a preservative that made possible the trick of modern warfare—the use of saccharin held steady, then began to climb. Because you got hooked in the war but stayed hooked in the peace, because women who had taken jobs during the war kept on working afterward, making fewer meals at home and coming to rely on prepared and canned foods. In 1950, Abbott Labs began producing Sucaryl, its saccharin-cyclamate formula sold in liquid and pill form, for diabetics and the corpulent, and also for people who just wanted to look skinny.

14.

In 1957, Ben hired a chemist to help him devise a saccharin mixture that would approximate the look and feel of sugar.* Much is made of Marvin's chemistry degree, but in truth, Dr. Kracauer was the professional on the project. Paul Kracauer is like Pete Best, the first drummer of the Beatles, mostly expunged from lore, but the name endures on the patents. When my mother mentions his name, it's with drama, like the name of a villain in a silent movie: "Dr. Kracauer." I picture it written in wavy freak-show letters: DOCTOR KRACAUER RETURNS! I guess this is because of the name itself, which has an Eastern European concentration camp ring, but also because of my sense that here is the evil genius behind it all.

In devising the formula, Ben was especially wary of saccharin's bitter aftertaste. "In many cases this bitter aftertaste actually makes the person

*On one of the patents, this quality is described as "mouth-feel."

nauseous," Ben wrote in his patent application.* The saccharin would therefore have to be cut with a neutral substance the way cocaine is cut with baking powder. Several years before, the scientists at Abbott Labs had come up with a formula considered the industry gold standard. The 10 : 1 mix: ten parts cyclamate, which is not as sweet as saccharin, but has no aftertaste, and one part saccharin. A perfect complement. When the cyclamate is combined with saccharin in an amount that equals the sweetness of one teaspoon of sugar, it yields a pill the size of a mini M&M. The aftertaste is there, but muted. If Ben wanted to fill an entire packet with the formula, he would need another ingredient to bulk up the mix and approximate the texture of sugar.

Dr. Kracauer came up with several variations, which he mixed into drinks, dispensers and teaspoons spread across the kitchen table in Flatbush. Ben drank cup after cup of coffee, each sweetened with a different mixture.

Dr. Kracauer watched with eagle eyes, then said, "This or that?"

"Ben was tearing his hair out," my father told me. "He would stare at these coffee cups, three or four or five, then he would make me taste each and tell him which was best as he conferred with Dr. Kracauer."

Marvin found the missing ingredient in a cookbook. According to an old recipe, lactose bulked up food and leached out taste. With the addition of lactose, Ben was able to perfect the formula that became Sweet'N Low. Fahlberg's saccharin had been an artificial sweetener. This was fake sugar, a counterfeit, part of the postwar process whereby the world of our grandfathers would be replaced by a facsimile. But when Ben and Marvin returned to the pharmaceutical company, the executives hardly seemed to remember them, were not sure what Ben was talking about, and did not want to taste that cup of coffee, because they were no longer interested. "We had done all this work and they just didn't care," Marvin

*In an attempt to taste the product in various forms, I made several dishes from *The Sweet'N Low Cook Book* (New York: Smithmark Publishers). Recipes include Bran Apple Cookies, Lemon Chiffon Pie, and Crab and Cheese Casserole. (The Sweet'N Low Lemon Chiffon Pie resembles actual Lemon Chiffon Pie in the same the way that stage scenery from the musical *Guys & Dolls* resembles actual New York City.)

told me. "And we thought we had really accomplished something. Put it in a cup of coffee and it tastes like sugar. But they changed their mind. Maybe they thought the market was too small."

The big moment from which all the other moments flowed was therefore brought about not by an act of genius or will, but out of a first-generation determination not to let good work go to waste. "Well, my dad was angry, and so was I," said Marvin. "We had worked very hard and very long on this and hated to watch it go down the drain. So we decided, you know, let's just make it and pack it and distribute it ourselves."

By showing the government that this new saccharin formula, with lactose as its secret ingredient, was the closest fake thing to real sugar, Ben and Marvin won a "use patent." For eighteen years, only Cumberland would be allowed to manufacture the formula. "Now of course those eighteen years have gone by," Marvin told me. "But once you develop that magical brand name, nothing can touch you. If someone put out the exact same product without our name, we would outsell them eight to one."

From there, it was just a matter of marketing:

What will the product be called?

What will the packet look like?

What color will it be?

Where will it be sold?

To whom will it be sold?

When I asked Marvin who was responsible for what, he told me that he made most of the big decisions, but Ben had been "an inspiration." "I always tried to be better than him," said Marvin. "But I could never fill his shoes. He was, after all, the one who innovated this from a cafeteria."

"The product was developed by Ben and Dr. Kracauer," said my father. "I watched it happen. Marvin kept the machines running. He was good at fixing things. He was like a mechanic. His job was to keep those things going."

When pressed for specifics, Marvin said, "Well, the name Sweet'N Low was [Ben's] invention. It was a phrase from his favorite Tennyson poem."

Marvin mentions this often: the name of the product comes from Ben's favorite Tennyson poem, but it's not exactly true. As Huck Finn would say, it's a stretcher, a way to class up the joint. The name Sweet'N Low does not come from Ben's favorite Tennyson poem, but from a song written with the words of the poem—the sheet music credits Alfred Lord Tennyson and J. Barnby—that had been a hit in the early 1900s, when Ben was a kid.* Up until a few years ago, if you called Cumberland and said, "This is Rich Cohen, I am trying to reach my uncle Marvin," and were told to wait as your cousins (I imagine) raced around, saying, "Well, what should we do? Should we talk to him?" the hold music was "Sweet and Low," a melancholy dirge on a loop, what the military band plays as the boys march to hell: *sweet and low, sweet and low, wind of the western sea.*

Here's the sheet music:

I looked up the poem that supplied the lyrics. (In fact, the phrase "sweet and low" was used often by Tennyson.) It's called "The Princess":

> Sweet and low, sweet and low,
> Wind of the western sea,
> Low, low, breathe and blow,
> Wind of the western sea!
> Over the rolling waters go,

*This version of the song had been arranged by John Hyatt Brewer and was performed by a male vocal quartet. The original composer of the music, Sir Joseph Barnby, died in 1896.

Come from the dying moon, and blow,
Blow him again to me;
While my little one, while my pretty one, sleeps.
Sleep and rest, sleep and rest,
Father will come to thee soon;
Rest, rest, on mother's breast
Father will come to thee soon,
Father will come to his babe in the nest.
Silver sails all out of the west,
Under the silver moon:
Sleep, my little one, sleep, my pretty one, sleep.

Marvin says he came up with the packet color, that he entertained and rejected blue because blue does not occur in nature. But this sounds to me like Marvin reading a criticism of Equal, which would not appear for twenty years, back into the historical record. I say this because (1) blueberries; and (2) sky. Gladys told me that it was Ben who chose pink because Ben thought pink would stand out among the white sugar packets on the diner tables. The packet and the logo were designed by Aunt Barbara, an amateur artist who, on vacations, used to paint funny faces on tennis balls. Her work on the packet was just beautiful: the name of the product as notes on a musical staff. It has become a classic, as much a symbol of plastic America as the soup cans of Andy Warhol.*

Ben launched the product in 1957, at first positioning it as a medicine, an aid to diabetics. He sold it to restaurants and hospitals, simply adding Sweet'N Low to the river of product already flowing out of the factory. Those first shipments were devoured. Packets were swiped from restaurants and stolen from hospitals. People called Cumberland. They wanted to buy boxes wholesale. Ben and Marvin had tapped into the zeitgeist; they had boarded a bullet train called Fat but Still Hungry. Like you go to the airport and step on a moving walkway and it turns out that walkway

---

*In 1974, when Cumberland applied for a renewal on its packet design, Sweet'N Low was listed as the one millionth trademark granted in the United States. This news was reported in *The New York Times*.

is moving a thousand miles an hour. "Then it really happened," Marvin told me. "We got a call from the head buyer of the A&P, the supermarket chain with hundreds of stores across the nation. Manufacturers would kill to get their product in there. They told us they wanted to start stocking Sweet'N Low. That's when we knew this was really going to be something big."

Ben bought billboards on buses. The first ads showed a woman holding a glass of ice tea over the words: "I call my sugar Sweet'N Low." Others seemed more or less improvised, like signs painted directly onto the bricks of the city. *Do any survive?* I imagine a wall in Brooklyn, the neighborhood gone punk, the paint faded. You can see red brick peeking through, as if the picture and the story itself were being reclaimed by the borough. It's done up like pop art, in reds and yellows. It shows Marvin raising a pink packet. It shows Gladys in her bed. It shows Ellen walking down the aisle. It shows Herbie on a train in the West German night. It shows Betty staring into a jewelry box. It shows Bubba preparing to jump. It shows the Belt Parkway and Avenue M and Flatbush Avenue. It shows the town houses and stoops, the bridges painted in exaggerated detail. It shows the factory ringed by workmen, the air hazed with saccharin dust, the product pouring off the belts. In the middle of it all, the subway cars and trucks spinning around him into a halo, is Ben, Vishnu-like, with hundreds of arms and thousands of fingers, pointing everywhere at once:

"Look upon my works!"

15.

In 1967, my parents moved to Illinois, where my father, a corporate executive for Allstate Insurance Company, had been transferred. For my
family, it was like a second crossing. To the Herbies and Ellens of Brooklyn, America was the thirteen colonies plus Miami Beach. The rest of the
country was just the words in the Irving Berlin song: mountains, prairies,
oceans, foam. And yokels. And cross burners. When my parents speak of
their first years in Illinois, it's in the way that, at school, the teachers spoke
of the journeys of Marquette and Joliet, the French explorers who
mapped the lakes and rivers of the Upper Midwest: *Your father came into
this country dressed in buckskin. He carried only a Bible. This was a wild
country then. There were no Jews in the territory, nor any from Brooklyn.
You could not find* The New York Times, *or good Peking duck. The bagels
were like donuts, and the spaghetti was like papier-mâché. The neighbors
were happy when we moved in. They said, "Thank God, we thought they
would sell to Catholics."*

Libertyville was surrounded by farms. My father chose it because it
was near the tollway. There was a barbershop, a Ford dealer, a Dairy

Queen. Chicago has since flowed over its rim, turning such towns into suburbs, but Libertyville was then still an outpost of nowhere America. In 1968, Ben and Betty visited for my bris. My brother was five, my sister was eight. They were students at Hawthorne school, where the bad kids got paddled. Because I had been sickly—handsome but small—the bris was put off until I was five weeks old. I can remember large parts of that ceremony, or think I can, though everyone calls that nuts. I remember the layout of the house perfectly, a wood-and-brick colonial amid a sea of oak trees. That house was summer, the smell of laundry, the street dead-ending at the Des Plaines River, which was warm and drowsy, and marked the termination point of the known world. Because I was born in Illinois, I came to know my grandparents at a distance. I hardly saw them. For me, the world began with Ellen and Herbie. I came to think of myself as a first-generation American, the only Cohen untouched by Brooklyn.

When I was five, we moved to Glencoe, a town on the lake north of Chicago. I have talked and written so much about this town that it's become a dream, its streets overhung by trees, its pathways leading to the lake. It gets tangled in my mind until every street leads to every other street, and every road ends at the beach, and the house parties rage, and the parents have gone on vacation, and the cops don't care, and the teachers are busy grading makeup exams, and all the seasons and moods collapse into a series of images: a sailboat at the pier in August, a lifeguard

asleep in the changing house, the shadow of a passing plane. It's sad because I know the town is not worth all this romantic attention. But for me it's the town against which all others are measured. I wish it had been Cannery Row in Monterey, which is a poem and a quality of light, or Miguel Street in Port of Spain, but it wasn't. It was Vernon Road in Glencoe.

My father told me we were the only Jews in Glencoe, which was not true. About 30 percent of the people in town were Jewish, which is one of the reasons we moved there. In Libertyville, there really were no Jews, which meant a forty-minute drive to the preschool at the synagogue. I was returning from such a trip with the nanny, Bea, when our station wagon was rear-ended. Bea threw me against the seat as she went into the steering wheel. When I looked at her, she said, "Everything will be fine." As she said this, all her teeth fell out. I was unconscious when the paramedics arrived, my eyelashes scattered across my shirtfront. From shock. For my mother, this was the end of Libertyville. She found a house in Glencoe, closing the deal while my father was out of town. In choosing Glencoe, because of the good schools, she was part of a demographic shift that continues. The Jews are coming! A friend told me Glencoe is now so Jewish that it's referred to as Glen-Cohen. I hated this at first. I did not like it that the many small ideas of my town were being replaced by one big idea, but the more I think about it, the more I like it. In Glen-Cohen, you have the suggestion of a hybrid, a new kind of Jew raised on the icy shores of a great lake. In Poland we were Kohens, in Brooklyn we were Cohens, in the Middle West we are Glen-Cohens.

My father was not lying when he said there were no Jews in Glencoe. As far as he was concerned, there weren't. Not what he recognized as Jews, anyway. To him a Jew is from Brooklyn. A Jew knows Yiddish. A Jew is wound like a spring. These easy-mannered Glen-Cohens, how would you even know they were Jewish? This is how my father happens to see the world, and it left me with a sense that there was something bogus about where I was growing up. The bagels were a joke, and so were the people. The only real place was back East. Brooklyn was where you came from, Manhattan was where you went. My world was out of bounds. It was always preseason. Every player was a scrub. My father encouraged me to ditch the Cubs, my favorite baseball team, for his much more successful Dodgers, formerly of Brooklyn. He said a Cubs fan learns to accept defeat as the natural condition of life. On holidays, we would fly to New York to get a taste of "real food" and see "real theater."

When I was in sixth grade, I wrote a story for English class about a child born and raised in middle America who, when he starts speaking, dumbfounds his parents and doctors by speaking with a heavy New York accent. In this story, I now hear a cry for help; proof of the condition bred by my father's intense, backward-looking love for the home country. The members of my family were expatriates, New Yorkers trapped in Illinois, landlocked and dreaming of the Narrows, with the longing of exiles.

When my brother was applying to college, my father said he could go anywhere but NYU, so that's where he went. Steven sent back pictures of Greenwich Village. He took the train to Flatbush to see Betty and Ben and Gladys. At Christmas, my mother asked him to bring home an order of chow mein from her favorite restaurant in Chinatown. He stowed it in the overhead bin. It stank up the plane. When he got it home, the carton was sweaty. We stood around the kitchen table as my mother opened it and stared inside and held it to her nose. She dipped in a fork and slurped up a noodle. She passed the box around like a joint. We each took

a bite. It was not much better than the chow mein at Chin's Chop Suey in Glencoe, but it was from New York, and that's what mattered.

By moving to Illinois, my parents had set their children on a trajectory away from the Eisenstadts. It's like the famous study by Darwin in which members of the same species, separated by a mountain range or a body of water, or in our case a short plane flight, evolve into two separate species. We saw our cousins only on vacation, or on visits to New York, or during visits New York made to us. Looking through the photo album of my bar mitzvah, from 1981, I can tell the families had already grown apart. I shared the bema (the altar from which the rabbi speaks to the congregation) with an ungainly boy whose voice was changing. As a result, I was a contrast gainer. The reception was at the Continental Plaza in Chicago. The band played "Under My Thumb" and "Three Times a Lady" and "Celebration." The cake was shaped like a Torah. A friend of my mother's pressed a Tom Collins into my hand and said, "Today you are a man!" The Eisenstadts turn up in the album like birds blown off course, big and sunny and blond, alighting on table twelve. If they are not the object of a photo, they lurk in the backround like water towers. Uncle Marvin in a Duke Ellington captain's cap. Cousins Jill and Debra with wavy Farah Fawcett hair. Little Steven, who at nine is already as tall as I am. How do you forgive someone for that? Cousin Jeffrey, his eyes glazed and shirt unbuttoned halfway down his chest. On behalf of his entire family, Uncle Marvin gave me a two-hundred-dollar check written on a Cumberland account.

The New York Yankees, in town to play the White Sox, were staying at the same hotel. In the elevator, my father ran into some of the old-time players who traveled with the team. He invited them to stop by the reception. I like to show new friends the photo album and watch as they page through the aunts and uncles and then stop dead at the picture of me and the natty little man with the steel-gray hair and the big glasses.

"Hey, isn't that . . ."

"Yes, friend, that's me and the Scooter, Yankee great Phil Rizutto!"

Or the picture of me and the huge man in a blue blazer, my small hand swallowed by his giant palm.

"Hey, isn't that . . ."

"Yes, friend, that's me and Cardinal slugger Bill White!"

It's a New York team of course, not the White Sox or the Cubs, because New York is where the real world begins.

16.

By 1975, Cumberland was manufacturing forty million packets of Sweet'N Low a day and grossing more than twenty million dollars a year. Ben and Marvin, intending to produce a tidbit for diabetics, had plugged into the general ennui, the estrangement people had come to feel from even their own bodies. The company was offering a cure for the illness of the age, an answer to the cry from the wilderness: *Help, I'm fat!*

Weight watching is a neurotic activity that was known as far back as the third century B.C., when Philon the Byzantine sold a prototype of the modern diet pill. Called "the hunger- and thirst-checking pill," it consisted of sesame seeds, oil, honey, almonds, and sea onion. But intense weight watching is characteristic of the age of excess, so it did not appear until the eighteenth century. In Victorian England, dieting became a fad among the bourgeoisie. The tubby burghers haunted specialty shops, where they obsessively weighed themselves on fish scales. The modern diet appeared in America in the nineteenth century. The first of the gurus was Sylvester Graham, a Presbyterian minister who turned his attention from the spirit to the flesh. He was a famous early vegetarian. To facilitate his high-fiber diet, he invented the graham cracker. For Graham, eating correctly was more than just a matter of good health; it was a quest for salvation. As part of his program, he recommended "hard mattresses, open bedroom windows, chastity, cold showers, loose clothing, pure water and vigorous exercise."*

Sylvester Graham was the seventeenth child of Reverend John Graham, who died when Sylvester was two years old. His mother was declared deranged and locked away in an asylum. Graham was raised by relatives. As an adolescent, he worked in a mill in West Suffield, Connecticut, traveled with a horse dealer, and studied theology. In 1826, he was ordained in the Presbyterian Church. He wore a frock coat and a shirt fastened at the chin. He looked like the sort of minister who is hiding a terrible secret, eating and purging on the side. He lectured on the evils of tea, coffee, and tobacco. The hollows of his eyes were ghostly. For the rise in sugar consumption, he feared a terrible reckoning. He was haunted by the accretion of waste. The word *gluttony* hung over him like a cloud. He was repulsed by the excess of modern life. He said, "Gluttony and not starvation is the greatest of all causes of evil." It seems fitting that our modern sense of food was invented by a minister badly hung up on the ugliness of the body. His disciples, who called themselves Grahamites, preached the message with zeal. They vowed to reform "a nation of gluttons."† The Grahamites offered a comprehensive plan: what and when and how much to consume. Followers dined by weight, setting their dish on a scale before each meal and limiting themselves to a certain amount of pounds per day.

This was a strange new idea—having to be taught how to eat. Modern diet books began appearing in the 1890s. The most popular of these were written by Sarah Tyson Rorer, the leader of the "Reducing Movement." Rorer ran a culinary school in Philadelphia and also wrote for the *Ladies' Home Journal*. Her bestseller *The Philadelphia Cook Book*, is the work of

*This is taken from the Graham family papers, archived at the University of Illinois.

†Much information in this section comes from *Never Satisfied: A Cultural History of Diets, Fantasies and Fat*, by Hillel Schwartz. My favorite section is called "The Social Decline of Fat People."

a fanatic. She writes, "An excess of flesh is to be looked upon as one of the most objectionable forms of disease, and must be treated as such." The first modern health club opened in Chicago in 1914. It was called the "reducing salon," and its literature boasts of Gardner Reducing Machines with adjustable rollers. By the early 1900s, weight-loss powders and elixirs had flooded the market. If you walked into a general store in 1892, you would have found Russell's Anti-Corpulent Preparation Cream, Jean Down's Get Slim Powder, Every Woman's Flesh Reducer, and Howell's Reducing Paste. George Burwell's Obesity Belt consisted of 150 electrically charged discs placed in denim. Shock your way to salvation. Or the reducing chair, a positive spin on the electric chair—muscles zapped, pounds terminated.

It was the start of the age in which we still live, the moment that body type was first revalued, the end of the glorious fat man. The prosperous fat man became the jolly fat man, and the jolly fat man became the lonely fat man, and the lonely fat man became the dangerous fat man. In 1914, the dietician Vance Thompson wrote, "The Fat Man may clown and slap himself and wag a droll forefinger, but he is not merry at all; and if one should sink a shaft down to his heart—or rather, drive a tunnel through to it—one would discover that it is a sad heart, black with melancholy."

A new body type emerged with the new literature and the new architecture of the new country. It was akin to the sinewy prose of Lincoln and Twain, to the clean lines of the skyscraper and the power of the horseless carriage. The American century would be about speed, grace, efficiency. "Flyers, and dancers and efficiency experts were preparing the way for a society intolerant of fat," Hillel Schwartz writes. "The best body would now be an aerodynamic body, curved but slender, controlled but light."

The key measure of this new age was the calorie, accepted as unit of measure in 1906 as part of the greater effort to put everything on the clock, to render the whole of creation quantifiable. According to the *World Book Encyclopedia*, a calorie is "the amount of energy that is needed to raise the temperature of one gram of water by one degree Celsius." In other words, a calorie is the amount of energy you need to complete a given task. Whatever you do not burn through work or exercise is stored as fat. Because different foods burn at different heats, different foods have different caloric values: sugar is rocket fuel, saccharin is water. (Measurements are made with an instrument called a "calorimeter.") The calorie, like the dollar, is a key measure in our economy, a unit upon which much hustling and suffering is based. With its invention, dieticians came to see the body as a factory where the goal was to spend every dollar you earned. If you spent more than you earned, you wasted away and died. If you earned more than you spent, you accumulated a surplus and grew fat and melancholy.

Weight watching came into its own after World War II. America was a different country after the war, the plastic country created by advertising, where you invent the product, then invent the market, invent the medicine, then invent the disease. Invent Ritalin, then invent attention deficit disorder. Invent antacid, then invent acid reflux disease. The entire system is based on this practice: convince people they're sick, then sell them the cure. For the diet economy, the illness is obesity, which, no matter how many diet products are sold, only worsens and spreads, because the definition keeps changing and the people in the ads keep getting skinnier. In 1933, 10 percent of Americans considered themselves obese; by 1973, that number had climbed to 35 percent; today, it's close to 50 percent: an epidemic not only of fat people, but of people who think they are fat.*

Hyman Kirsch, a Russian immigrant who owned a soft drink factory in Williamsburg, Brooklyn, began producing Kirsch's No-Cal Ginger Ale in 1952, followed by Kirsch's No-Cal Orange and Kirsch's No-Cal Lime, diet drinks sweetened with cyclamate and marketed to diabetics. The cans were sold in pharmacies and grocery stores. It was soon clear that the drinks were being purchased not only by diabetics but also by those who wanted to stay slim. People like my father tried the cola, saw it had no calories, went back for more, then bought whole cases of it. All across the

*According to the most recent report issued by the National Center for Health Statistics (2004), 64 percent of Americans over age twenty are overweight, while 30 percent suffer from obesity, which the *Encyclopedia Britannica* defines as, "a body weight 20 percent or more over the optimum."

country the weight conscious were soon sending away to Brooklyn for No-Cal. This was the first suggestion of the size of the market. "A guy named Kirsch and his father, Hyman, were the innovators," Marvin told me. "It was a little thing but it kept on going, and suddenly you were like, *ahhh*, this can really be something. Pepsi and Coke loved the idea. It was after Kirsch's that they came out with their own diet sodas. Because of Kirsch's, people became diet conscious, aware of sugar-free products. Kirsch's started the diet revolution in the United States."

Pick one of the new diet companies of that era and watch it grow— this will give you a sense of the explosiveness of the boom. Weight Watchers is a good example because it has many of the elements of an American religion: you confess, you come to terms with who you are, you swear off your old sinful life, you are born again. The company was founded in 1961 by Jean Nidetch, a formerly fat woman who had lost weight with the help of an obesity clinic run by New York City. She cobbled together some of the principles she learned at the clinic and started a program of her own. In 1964, Weight Watchers generated $160,000 in sales. In 1970, its sales were $8 million; in 1979, $39 million. Today it generates sales of over $1 billion a year.

Cumberland surfed the same wave.

By 1996, the company was producing fifty million packets of Sweet'N Low a day. "I don't think Ben thought that the business would even support the family," Gladys told me. "But it just grew and grew. It's the amazing thing about a business. It takes off. It doesn't stop. You don't know why. It's like a living thing. It mutates. It becomes something you never planned on."

How did my mother realize that her family was rich?

Maybe it was in the voice of Ben, a new confidence, or his occasional promise to send money,* or maybe it was Betty, the jewelry she kept accumulating.

*He never did, always backing away from his promise, saying it was a bad time because he was "not liquid."

Maybe it was the town house Ira bought on the Upper West Side, or his bushy red beard and purse and cryptic Zen koans—"What's the last thing you want to hear your crazy uncle say?"—the sort of life available only to the super-rich.

Maybe it was the house Marvin bought in the Rockaways. *Lives in Queens, commutes to Brooklyn.* My aunt later cited this house as proof of modesty. "Our home, for thirty-six years, has been in the Rockaways (Queens) and we have been living in the same house for twenty-seven years. All our children were educated in the public school system."* But this house is a mansion in Neponsit, which had once been an oceanfront enclave for robber barons. It's about as far as you can get by subway, the last stop on the A train, which cuts across the steely waters of Jamaica Bay before dead-ending a few hundred yards from the Atlantic. When the train doors open, you hear seagulls.

When I was a kid, Marvin's house seemed to me like an extension of Marvin. It was Marvelous, it was dreamy, it could do handsprings and somersaults. It was the house that saccharin built. Each room was approached down a long hallway, and each window was filled with light. There was a gate in the backyard that opened directly onto the sand. Since I grew up in the middle of the country, a landlocked product of the grasslands—and Chicago towers above it, and the corn grows all around it—a thousand miles from the ocean, for me the sound and the smell of the Atlantic are a dream. I once sat behind Marvin's house eating steamers, and they were salty and fresh and tasted like a delicacy from another life.

In my mind, the house in the Rockaways has become tangled up with the biggest house in my hometown. Wherever you go in the Midwest, there is a biggest house in town. It's the house you point out to newcomers. In Glencoe, it had ten bedrooms and sat on a bluff high over the ravine. I knew the kid who lived there. His father had a handlebar mustache and stood in the driveway without a shirt. Much later, when this man was sent to prison for attempted murder, the house was put up for auction. All the busybodies in town walked through the rooms gossiping.

*This comes again from my aunt Barbara's letter to the judge sentencing Marvin, pleading for leniency.

To me, Marvin's house is that house. It's also the house behind the gate where the billionaire W. Clement Stone lived on Sheridan Road in Winnetka, Illinois. It's the commandant's house above the Brooklyn Navy Yard, and the house in the creepy Edwin Arlington Robinson poem we had to memorize in junior high.

RICHARD CORY

Whenever Richard Cory went down town,
We people on the pavement looked at him:
He was a gentleman from sole to crown,
Clean favored, and imperially slim.

And he was always quietly arrayed,
And he was always human when he talked;
But still he fluttered pulses when he said,
"Good-morning," and he glittered when he walked.

And he was rich—yes, richer than a king—
And admirably schooled in every grace;
In fine we thought that he was everything
To make us wish that we were in his place.

So on we worked, and waited for the light,
And went without the meat, and cursed the bread;
And Richard Cory, one calm summer night,
Went home and put a bullet through his head.

How did my mother realize her family was rich?

Maybe it was the articles in *The Wall Street Journal* and *The New York Times* about Cumberland, its patents, its products, its practices, its philosophy, the pictures of Ben in a bad suit, Marvin boyish into his middle years, hands in his pocket, jingling and full of American energy.

Maybe it was the omnipresence of the product itself, nowhere but in Brooklyn at first, then in every restaurant on the North Shore of Chicago.

Each packet of Sweet'N Low is a poker chip, each packet is a doubloon. Walk around the casino and start counting, and pretty soon you realize the kind of money we're talking about. My mother might want to forget Ben, but every time she sat down for a meal, there he was, or this totem of the old man. On a trip to Israel, in a café overlooking the Dead Sea— really, one of the most terrible landscapes on the planet—we came across a stack of the pink packets. As if Ben were in every country, in every language. My mother said, "Sweet'N Low! In Hebrew! I'll have to tell Pop."

I think I saw the exact moment when my mother realized that every member of her family was rich. Marvin was giving us a tour of his house. Down halls, through bedrooms, onto the lawn, into the sea salt and slanting light, and back into the living room, where a piano was being played. The big moment came when my mother realized the piano was playing itself. It was the first time I had seen a player piano outside the Haunted House in Disney World. Marvin said this was no ordinary player piano. It did not play a mechanical rendition of a song. It played the song exactly as it had been played by the man or woman who made the piano roll. It had nuance, style. If Beethoven had been hooked to the recording mech-anism, the resulting roll, fed into the piano, would have been the song ex-actly as played by the maestro himself. The pedals even went up and down! Marvin's piano was playing "Rhapsody in Blue," and it was as if the ghost of George Gershwin had taken a seat at the bench—his handsome face, his hawk nose, a cigarette dangling.

What do you want to hear, Marv? "They All Laughed" Hah! Hah! I bet they did!

To the Brooklyn Jews of that era, Gershwin stood for everything so-phisticated, dreamy, and unattainable. His music was the music of the metropolis, of vodka martinis and the '21' Club. It struck hidden depths in my mother. The ache of it turned up on her face the way a complicated emotion turns up on the face of a starlet in a silent movie. She was living in Glencoe, Illinois! The land of Lincoln! Where the S is silent! And here was Marvin with the ghost of Gershwin in a kingdom by the sea.

In our family, the phrase "Gershwin's piano rolls" has itself become evocative. It conjures Madison Avenue and the Pierre Hotel and every-thing you want but cannot quite reach. When a compact disc of the piano rolls was released a few years ago, I ran out and bought it. I listened to it again and again. I studied the picture on the jacket. I read the liner notes. George Gershwin died of a brain tumor when he was thirty-nine years old, leaving behind his brother and lyricist, Ira. After George's death, Ira wrote the lyrics for "Our Love Is Here to Stay," the melody his brother had been working on when he died. My apartment is not far from the apartment where Gershwin wrote the song. It's on one of those nar-row West Side streets that runs down to Riverside Park. In the autumn, the sky above such streets is so melancholy and insubstantial you can al-most brush it aside and stare into space. In the words of that song ("In time the Rockies may crumble, / Gibraltar may tumble, / They're only made of clay, but / Our love is here to stay") I hear a tribute to the great-est kind of love. Not romantic love, or parental love. Brotherly love. My mother used to tell me to take care of my brother and sister because "no one else will ever be as close to you in this world."

My parents recently bought a house in South Florida, in a gated community surrounded by other gated communities, in the town where

Mohammad Atta had his last whiskey sour. They made this purchase quickly and weirdly, buying not just the house but everything in it. Furniture, books, linen, paintings, car, golf clubs, and even golf shoes, as if my father were an agent for the CIA who needed a new cover fast.

As my father showed me the souvenirs on the mantel, he said proudly, "I always wanted tchotchkes."

I said, "But these are not your tchotchkes."

He said, "Tchotchkes are tchotchkes."

Their favorite possession is the piano, which, soon after they moved in, they sent to a shop, where it was broken down and converted into a player piano. One day, when my mother called to "see how I was doing," I could hear this tremendous racket. It was as if she were calling from an orchestra pit.

I said, "What's all the noise?"

She said, cool and matter-of-fact, "Oh, the player piano is here. It's playing Gershwin's piano rolls."

17.

In the late 1800s, food was being reinvented in precisely the same way as the city. The move was toward punch and compression, the direction was up. The first skyscraper, built in Chicago in 1885, was twelve stories. The Petronas Towers, built in Kuala Lumpur in 1998, are eighty-eight stories. Saccharin, discovered in 1879, is three hundred times sweeter than sugar. Aspartame, discovered in 1965, is two hundred times sweeter. Sucralose, discovered in 1976, is six hundred times sweeter. Neotame, the newest artificial sweetener, approved by the FDA in 2002, is seven thousand to thirteen thousand times sweeter than sugar.* By the end of the nineteenth century, the grocery stores and apothecaries had become terrible fun houses: you never knew what you were going to get, what was going to help you, and what was going to kill you. According to a government pamphlet, "Conditions in the U.S. Food and Drug industry a century ago can hardly be imagined. Use of chemical preservatives and toxic colors

---

*Neotame is made by the NutraSweet Company, which also makes aspartame. See Stephanie M. Horvath's "NutraSweet Gets FDA Approval for Artificial Sweetener Neotame," *The Wall Street Journal*, July 8, 2002.

was virtually uncontrolled." In 1862, a single chemist in the Department of Agriculture was given the job of policing a cataract of artificial foods and preservatives. But the real cleanup began in 1883, when Harvey Washington Wiley was named to run the division that would eventually become the FDA. Wiley is the man who made the grocery store a decent place to raise a family.

Wiley was born in Kent, Indiana. He studied at Hanover College in Indiana and at Harvard, and he was the state chemist of Indiana. He taught the first chemistry course at Purdue. He was notified of his federal appointment by wire. He appeared on the streets of the capital like Jimmy Stewart in *Mr. Smith Goes to Washington*, the spirit of the West come to save the East from its addiction to goofballs. In photographs, he looks like a frontier sheriff—a big beard, a big important belly, a big round hat, and big pointy boots. He was determined to take on the chemical companies, the most powerful interests of the day. The FDA now has its own building, ten thousand employees and a budget of more than two billion dollars a year, but back then it was just Wiley and his assistant in the basement of the Department of Agriculture.*

Wiley came to an existing organization yet is considered the FDA's founder. He took a half-realized body and gave it a mission. He measured, sampled, made cuttings, boiled, mixed, stirred, smelled, tasted, and squeezed. He wrote a book called *Songs of Agricultural Chemists*. He was obsessed with the preservatives hidden in products all over the grocery store—the obvious short-term effects, the mysterious long-term effects. He faced down congressional committees staffed by politicians in the pocket of big business. Because of him, the first food and drug laws were passed. He trained the chemists that would dominate the industry. He found them in schools and factories, called them to throw down their nets and become fishers of souls. They searched for outbreak,

*For information on the history of the FDA, see the Food and Drug Administration's website. Also *Protecting America's Health: The FDA, Business, and One Hundred Years of Regulation*, by Philip J. Hilts (New York: Alfred A. Knopf, 2003); and *Regulatory Law and Policy: Cases and Materials*, 2nd ed., by Sidney A. Shapiro and Joseph P. Tomain (Charlottesville, Va.: Lexis Law Publishing, 1998).

fraud, adulteration. They had been assembled in the manner of a crack squad in an old movie: this one because he can throw the knife; that one because he can hit a moving target; this one because he can reach into your chest, pull out your heart, and show it to you. In pictures, these chemists look like a gang of gunslingers, bad men recruited to clean up a bad town.

Just how do you determine the safety of a preservative or sweetener? Knowing the chemical properties and nutritional values will not necessarily tell you what such a food will do in the bloodstream. Wiley came up with a two-step solution that was simple, effective, and unimaginable today.

> *Step one*: feed dishes made with the preservative or sweetener to
> volunteers.
> *Step two*: see if any die.

The Poison Squad was the name given to the group of young men to whom, once a week, Wiley fed chemicals and preservatives and artificial sweeteners. It's like the invention of a fabulist, something out of García Márquez. Within a few months of the first meal, the members of the Poison Squad had become pop stars, admired by every man, loved by every woman. They ate, survived, and ate again. They were test pilots, solo aviators risking their bodies for the greater good.

In 1903, Lew Dockstader's Minstrels had a hit called "Song of the Poison Squad":

> O, they may get over it
> but they'll never look the same,
> that kind of bill of fare
> would drive most men insane,
> next week he'll give them mothballs,
> à la Newburgh or else plain;
> O, they may get over it
> but they'll never look the same.

Wiley built a dining room for the Poison Squad, which he called the "Hygienic Table." It was like a coach in a luxury train, the Alps drifting across the windows. The chef was an FDA chemist named William Carter.* He cooked steak, sausage, chicken, pies, and pastries with borax, salicylic acid, sulfurous benzoic acid, and formaldehyde.

It was Wiley's way of publicizing the risks of the new foods, of sounding the alarm, of making every consumer see himself or herself as an unknowing member of the Poison Squad. Wiley had cleverly associated preservatives with poison, an association that lingers in the public mind. Saccharin might be condemned, it might be cleared, but the health-conscious continue to avoid it. That's the legacy of the Poison Squad.

The bosses of the chemical companies came to resent the FDA. They accused its agents of taking bribes, and Wiley himself of being a socialist. There were hearings. Wiley was exonerated. But wrecked. The trial had become the punishment. In 1912, he resigned under a cloud. He went to work for *Good Housekeeping* magazine, where he developed the Good Housekeeping Seal of Approval. In 1951, to mark the fiftieth anniversary of the Pure Food and Drug Act, a postage stamp was issued with Wiley's likeness.

In the end, Wiley's philosophy triumphed. By the middle twentieth century, preservatives and artificial foods had been organized into two basic categories: good and bad. There was by then a mechanism for determining safety, tests by the FDA, more tests by the companies themselves.† (With preservatives, as in France, it's guilty until proven innocent.) If questions are raised by these tests, there are still more tests, meetings, discussions, and more tests. If a preservative passes these tests, it is put on the FDA's list of approved preservatives, compiled under the

*Carter was the first black scientist to work at the FDA, and he continued there for years, moving from the kitchen to the lab, where he stayed until the mid-1940s.

†The Pure Food and Drug Act requires chemical companies to test the safety of their own products. If the government had to investigate every new additive and preservative, the cost would run into the billions.

acronym GRAS: Generally Regarded as Safe. If it fails, it's withheld from stores. If it's already in stores, it's pulled from the shelves.

At the time of Ben's use of it in Sweet'N Low, cyclamate had long been of concern to the FDA. It was discovered in 1937. While experimenting with antifever drugs, a University of Illinois chemistry student named Michael Sveda set down his cigarette on a lab bench. When he picked it up and took a drag, it tasted as if it had been dipped in syrup. In the course of tinkering, Sveda had freed a hydrogen molecule from a bond, resulting in a compound thirty times sweeter than sugar. Though still not as sweet as saccharin, the compound was sweet enough to be used in quantities amounting to zero calories. Unlike saccharin, it had no aftertaste.*

Sveda licensed his discovery to Abbott Laboratories, which, within a few years, was turning out great mountains of the stuff. By 1953, scientists at Abbott had devised the cyclamate/saccharin mixture that was soon being used in Kirsch's No-Cal Cola, Diet Rite, Tab, and Sweet'N Low. In 1959, after an extensive study, the FDA added cyclamate to its approved list of preservatives. Because it was assumed that the use of cyclamate would be limited almost exclusively to diabetics, the approval was explained as a lesser of evils: better a diabetic use cyclamate than live in a world with no alternative to sugar and so be tempted into a wilderness of jelly donuts.†

In the 1960s, the FDA reconsidered: cyclamate was not being used exclusively or even mostly by diabetics, but, like saccharin, had crossed into the mainstream, where it was being ingested by millions of perfectly

---

*Sources on cyclamate include the article "Picking Up the Tab," by James Fallows, published in *The Washington Monthly* in 1992, and "The Science and Politics of Cyclamate," by William R. Havender, *Public Interest* 71(1983):17–32.

†For information on Abbott Labs, one of the most influential companies of the modern era, look at *The Long White Line: The Story of Abbott Laboratories* by Herman Kogan (New York: Random House, 1963).

healthy calorie counters. To the chemists at the FDA, the trend seemed reminiscent of a long history of unnecessary disasters:

In 1937, a scientist working for a Tennessee drug company had mixed sulfamide in water, creating a sore throat "elixir." As it was impossible to get the sulfamide to dissolve, the chemist added a "mixing agent," diethyl glycol, also known as antifreeze. A hundred and seven people died before the alarm was sounded, most of them children. Executives at the drug company at first refused to reveal their "secret" formula. The inventor later killed himself.

In 1959, three weeks before Thanksgiving, the entire American cranberry crop was recalled and tested for aminotriazole, a cancerous weed killer.

In 1976, a Russian study suggested that red dye no. 2, used to color jelly beans and licorice, but also maraschino cherries and apples—to color them in like pictures in a comic book—caused cancer in rats. Skeptics said the report was disinformation, the Soviets trying to take the color right out of our candy. Because they're commies, they think that red belongs to them!

Worst was the tragedy of thalidomide, an orange pill prescribed to women in the first trimester of pregnancy for insomnia and morning sickness. It was never approved for use in the United States because the head of the FDA, Frances Kelsey* (her name deserves to be remembered) said that, as it was for pregnant women, it had not been tested nearly enough. *Guilty until proven innocent.* In the early 1960s, thalidomide was prescribed widely in Europe, Mexico and Canada. Because it was taken for morning sickness, which typically occurs in the first months of pregnancy, the birth defects, when they began to be noticed, were to the parts of the body that develop early: fingers, arms and legs. According to the FDA, "Even a single dose of thalidomide during early pregnancy may cause major defects." Ten thousand babies were born severely affected. They came to be known as thalidomide babies, as if the sedative had joined with the genetic code to create a new species. Babies were born with flippers in-

*On October 7, 2000, Dr. Frances O. Kelsey (Ph.D., M.D.) was inducted into the National Women's Hall of Fame in Seneca Falls, New York.

stead of arms, or with long forearms and no hands, or with no arms and no ears. Or their eyes didn't work, or their nervous systems, or their hearts. As you get close to the borders of Canada or Mexico, where the pill was prescribed widely, you see them, middle-aged now, paying for a few bad months in the 1960s. It was a sad triumph for the FDA, vindication of the "slow-as-molasses" style that had made it a target of the drug companies.*

When I was nine, we went on a trip to New Mexico. At a mall in Albuquerque, New Mexico, I was approached by a kid with dark skin and dark eyes. He asked me something. At that age, kids feel an intense solidarity and fall together like charged molecules. But when I turned to answer, I noticed that this kid did not have arms. He had flippers. I did not know about thalidomide or thalidomide babies. I only knew that I felt sick. I ran. When my mother caught me, I was going up the escalator. She said, "You can run away from him, but *he* can't run away from him."

In the late 1960s, a series of experiments suggested that large intakes of cyclamate coincide with an uptick in cancer. The incidences were rare, the tests inconclusive, but the mere mention of the word *cancer* tripped the Delaney Clause, a rider to the Food, Drug and Cosmetic Act that says that any food additive or preservative shown to cause cancer in any living thing must be banned. No questions. Zero tolerance. Ban it! *What if it cures AIDS but in rare cases causes mild skin cancer?* Don't care! Ban it! *What if it saves the lives of epileptics but causes cancer in hamsters?* Not interested! Ban it! The Delaney Clause was like the mandatory minimum that sends the pot smoker to prison for life.

In late 1969, the FDA announced its decision to remove cyclamate from its list of approved preservatives and ban its use in foods and nonprescription drugs. When the word *cancer* hit the newspapers, people panicked. Diet products were pulled from the shelves, a river of cola went hissing down the gutters. (It makes me think of the chapter in A *Tale of Two Cities* called "The Wine Shop," in which a mob kicks open a cask

*Off the market since the 1960s, thalidomide was recently approved for the treatment of leprosy and certain kinds of cancer. Users must enter their names into a registry and, if sexually active, use two kinds of birth control and be tested regularly for pregnancy.

and merlot runs in the streets, and in it you see the blood of the coming revolution.) With one stroke, entire product lines had been wiped out. Tab: gone. Diet Rite: gone. Diet Crush: gone. The tabletop sweeteners that competed with Sweet'N Low (Wee Cal, Sweet Mate): gone. Factories closed, and hustling, Ben-like entrepreneurs accepted corporate positions. The term "job security" came to have a nice ring. Everyone was wounded, everyone bled. Everyone except Ben and Marvin. For Ben and Marvin, the cyclamate ban came as a blessing. "From every disaster we made a victory," Marvin told me. "Because we took advantage of it."

Because they were prepared.

Because they knew the ban was coming.

But how?

Cumberland Packing bought its cyclamate from Abbott Labs, a chemical plant headquartered in Abbott Park, Illinois, just a few miles from Libertyville, where my parents were living. My mother knew many of the company wives. From playground scuttlebutt (in such towns, the wives are like the astronaut wives in *The Right Stuff*) my mother learned that cyclamate would soon be banned and that Abbott would not fight the ban. If a company the size of Abbott chose to fight, the works could be gummed up for years, long enough for the Diet Rites and Tabs to adjust and be ready.

"Abbott was supposed to fight the ban," my mother told me. "But I found out they wouldn't. I called my father and told him. Because of that, when the ban did come, he had a head start on the entire industry. I never did get credit. It was like he did not remember I had told him. What did I want? Not much. A phone call. 'Thank you. You helped us.'"

But according to Marvin, he was ready for the ban simply because he "had a gut feeling." It was because of this feeling and because of his cautious, plan-for-every-contingency style that, he says, "belt and suspenders Marvin developed a product without cyclamate [before the ban]."

In fact, Ben and Marvin already had notes for an alternative formula, which they had drawn up years before while searching for a perfectly kosher Sweet'N Low. (Because the original formula contained lactose, a dairy product, it could not be used by religious Jews during or just after meals—in a cup of coffee, say—that included meat.) Marvin dug out these plans, got together with his "key personnel," and went to work. Once they had stripped away the cyclamate, the saccharin aftertaste reemerged like a repressed memory. Marvin tried everything, in the end finding the answer (once again) in a cookbook: cream of tartar, an ingredient that adds bulk without adding calories; and dextrose, an ingredient that leaches out aftertaste. "I was at Cumberland mixing and mixing, tasting and tasting, but what I didn't realize is that, when you do that, after a while, you don't taste anything," Marvin told me. "I began to panic: This doesn't taste sweet! It doesn't have any taste at all! But some other people tasted it and said, 'It tastes okay.' We weren't very scientific. We didn't take focus groups. But a week later, I sat in a restaurant that already had the new product and watched people that used Sweet'N Low to see if they made funny faces. They didn't. It was smooth. Some people said it didn't taste as good. Some people said it tasted better. A taste is funny. It's mental."

Immediately after the ban was announced, but before it was enacted, Ben called his distributors and buyers and told them to junk the old product and he would send them boxes of Sweet'N Low made without cyclamate. "We got rid of all that stuff and we didn't have to," Marvin said. "This was before the ban went into effect. Then we put out the new stuff. We borrowed over a million dollars to cover all the costs. There were headlines in the papers saying that Cumberland Packing, the makers of Sweet'N Low, had reformulated their product. They showed us in Chicago dumping old Sweet'N Low with cyclamate into a landfill."

A few years later, on November 30, 1975, Marvin was quoted in *The New York Times* as saying, "We retooled the machines, designed new packages and dumped about $2 million worth of inventory into about a dozen landfills around the country."

If the cyclamate ban had not been enacted, Cumberland would have been out millions of dollars for research and junked product. But when the ban was enacted and all of Sweet'N Low's competitors were pulled from the shelves, Ben and Marvin were perfectly positioned, with boxes of their new cyclamate-free sweetener already in stores. *The belt snapped, the suspenders held!* In those weeks, when the vacuum left by Wee Cal and Diet Rite and Tab opened up, the pink packets swirled in. Cumberland Packing went from being a midsize company in a competitive field to being the only company in a major industry. Within a few months, sales had tripled. Sweet'N Low became number one.

"That's how we became a brand name," Marvin told me. "Because our competitors, Pillsbury and the others, couldn't make that decision: to dump the old product *before* the ban. It was a gutsy decision, the kind only a private company can make. Because if it was a mistake, what would happen? My wife would yell at me. But if you work at a big corporation and make that mistake, you get fired. So those guys hung on and hung on to their old formulations and got crushed. We had a head start."*

I've always had a heroic picture of my grandfather in those years, the founder, the inventor, the man who made it all happen, but in Marvin's telling, Ben is almost entirely absent.

I told my uncle I was confused, and asked, "Just what did Grandpa do?"

Marvin thought for a moment, and looked at his hands, and looked at my hands, and said, "He gave me my head. When I wanted to make a new formulation, Dad said, 'Go ahead.' When I wanted to put it on the market before the ban, he said, 'Go ahead' to that, too. Ben's role, first of all, was to go along with everything I did. He could have said no, let's not take the chance, let's not dump all this stuff. But he got behind it one hundred percent, even though he said there was no reason to make a new formulation. He went along and was proud of his son, and I was proud of him for being proud of me."

*According to articles that ran in *The New York Times* on October 20 and October 21, 1969, General Foods, Pillsbury, Pepsi-Cola, Coca-Cola, and Royal Crown were all ready with non-cyclamate products within a few weeks of the ban—but those few weeks made all the difference.

18.

In these years, you could see what made Cumberland Packing a legend in Fort Greene. It is what the instructors at business school call "the founder's effect," the love and care only the creator can provide. More than any of his successors, the founder has the right to risk and fail. As long as the founder is in control, God is in the garden. When God goes, no one will ever again speak with the same authority. Ben hired and fired, saved, upgraded, invested. He was unquestionable, beyond corruption. In a recent survey, 82 percent of American CEOs admitted to cheating at golf.* Ben never even played golf, or tennis, or bought a nice car, or a new house, or a nice suit, or went on vacation. He was austere. He was driven to grow, expand, win. It was not enough to come in first. He wanted to lap the field. Even after Cumberland had become the industry leader, Ben kept on investing and inventing: Nu-Salt, Butter Buds, Sugar in the Raw.

*See Daniel Kadlec, "Worldcom: The Fall of a Telecom Titan," *Time*, July 8, 2002, page 20.

When Ben turned control over to his son, Cumberland owned its building and all its machines. Its debt was spectacularly light. For this reason, when New York City rents soared, forcing most of the old manufacturing firms to flee to the suburbs or across the country or the world, Cumberland stayed on, the last of the clipper ships. The factory supplied Fort Greene with taxes and jobs, and the borough supplied the factory with a sophisticated big-city workforce. People spent their entire lives in front of the packing machines. When the factory got into trouble, politicians protected it not just because Marvin gave money to their campaigns, which he did, but also because the business of Cumberland had become the business of Brooklyn.

Marvin has since let the factory dilapidate. I love that word because it suggests the beauty of decay. It makes me think of a chemical sunset over New Jersey. It looks great going away. It dies pretty. The factory has rusted, the walls sag, the paint is peeling, and paint chips are falling to the floor.* I am not saying Cumberland is about to go under, or that Marvin has run the place into the ground. It isn't, and he hasn't. The factory makes more money now than it ever has, but only because other, more ambitious men at other companies have grown the market. Cumberland, which used to lead, has fallen into a distant third in market share—a smaller piece of a much bigger pie. The industry continues to change, but the men at Cumberland no longer have the stomach or desire to change with it.

Of course, it was not just Ben who built Cumberland. It was Ben plus Marvin, the camaraderie, the rivalry. They spun around each other like stars whipsawing through the void: the patriarch who spoke with authority, the hustling son trying to outperform Pop. Because of this dynamic, the factory had a freewheeling ability to adapt. Take for example the oil embargo of 1973, when the OPEC nations shut down the gasoline flow in response to America's support of Israel during the Yom Kippur War. Trans-

*I refer to a specific inspection report filed on March 23, 2001, by the New York State Department of Agriculture and Markets, Division of Food Safety and Inspection Services. The report, which I received as a result of a FOIA request, cited the factory for "peeling and hanging paint," "floor has peeling/missing surface," "walls are in disrepair," "warehouse floor exhibited litter and debrie [sic] accumulation," "product residue noted on walls and floor at 127 building, packing area."

ported almost entirely by truck, Sweet'N Low was acutely dependent on a regular supply of cheap gas. A spike in prices would raise costs. If the pumps went dry, the packets would pile up and the belts would rumble to a stop. One day, after a few of the Cumberland drivers had been turned away from some nearby pumps, Ben and Marvin went back and simply bought the entire station. "That was me," Marvin said. "In 1973, we had trucks to go around the city. And there was a Gulf station four blocks down. The owner knew us and would give us a preference. But this particular day—I think it was a Wednesday—there was a long line of cars and the father wasn't around and the son chased us away. He said he was too busy for us. I tried to explain. He said, 'Don't bother me.' Now, I'm the kind of guy that wears a belt *and* suspenders. So the next day, I went over and bought that gas station. For years we made money on the gas."

It's the great strength of the family-owned business. No meetings, no accountants, no bureaucracy. Just a problem and a solution. In the 1970s, as gas prices fluctuated, Sweet'N Low remained cheap and plentiful. But this same incident also shows what was wrong with the company, and the son of its founder—the weakness or flaw that would lead Marvin into scandal. "A funny thing happened with the gas station," he went on. "After we bought it, we went over with the keys, but there were these two German shepherds chained up in front. I could not get past them. They were vicious. It took me a week before I could get into the station. One of the dogs got loose, and I was scared to death it would kill somebody. But we finally got it worked out. I found someone who gave the dogs to a farm."

Gave the dogs to a farm?

It's the cover on the fish tank all over again. What do you call that? Willful blindness? Naïveté? Letting others do your dirty work?

Is ignorance innocence?

When I was ten, my dog turned a strange color and barked as if she did not know me, and her eyes were yellow. She was seventeen. My father took her away in the car, and when he came back he was alone. He said the dog was now living on a beautiful farm in the country. My brother said, "You mean a farm in the clouds." I did not know what my brother was talking about because I was a child, but I am not a child anymore.

19.

The FDA turned its attention to saccharin, which had long been an obsession of the fake-food cops, in the 1970s. With the banning of cyclamate, these officials had shown that it was possible to take on the pharmaceutical industry, even with big money at stake. (A saccharin ban would mean the loss of $1.9 billion a year to the diet and pharmaceutical companies.) By 1972, several saccharin studies were under way. The most damning of these was done in Canada, where one hundred rats were fed monster doses of the artificial sweetener. It was shot directly into their bodies—the equivalent of eight hundred cans of Diet Coke a day. Fourteen of these rats eventually developed bladder tumors. Twelve of them were male. A megadose of saccharin, it was concluded, results in bladder tumors in male rats.*

*An article that ran in *Science* on March 3, 1978, entitled "The Relative Risks of Saccharin and Calorie Ingestion," is helpful in following the methods and meanings of these tests. Among other things, it explains the results in a way that is easy to understand. It says that drinking a diet soft drink takes nine seconds off your life. It also says that consuming ten extra kilocalories takes nine seconds off your life. If, after reading this book, you decide not to drink a Diet Coke, add nine seconds. If you replace that

If it causes cancer in male rats, will it do the same in men?

As a parent, Marvin had lived through the thalidomide tragedy. His oldest son was born in 1960, his oldest daughter in 1963. In those years, the newspapers were filled with terrible photographs. Ask anyone who had a kid around that time about thalidomide and watch their face. No matter what my uncle said about the methods of big government, at some level he must have realized that the FDA may have saved his own family. What did he think when the key ingredients of Sweet'N Low failed these tests? He talked about the wrongheadedness of the government decision, the injustice of it, but I never once heard him ask, "What if I kill my customers?" "What if I reap a harvest of ruined genes?" Was there ever a moment when, crossing the factory floor amid the great plumes of chemical dust, Marvin asked himself, "My God, what if it really does cause cancer?"

The Canadians removed saccharin from the market in early 1977, and the American authorities followed close behind. Once a link to cancer had been established, the Delaney Clause kicked in and Sherwin Gardner, the commissioner of the FDA, really had no choice. In March 1977, saccharin was banned in the United States. For the first time since Constantine Fahlberg's beaker overflowed, consumers would be left with no alternative to sugar.

On March 10, 1977, *The New York Times* ran the story on the front page: "FDA Banning Saccharin Use on Cancer Links." In that moment, it was Cumberland's turn to teeter on the edge of the abyss. In the ensuing weeks, Marvin argued, pontificated, wisecracked, shouted his head off, and complained. He went on TV and radio. He talked to anyone who would listen. He became the champion of the diet economy. In a *Times* story headlined "Industry Responds to Ban of Saccharin," Marvin said that to equal the amount of saccharin given those rats, "an individual would have to drink diet soft drinks at the impossible rate of more than 1,000 bottles a day." In another story, he said, "Your organs would have to be bathed in the stuff." Reading these articles today, you can still feel the

---

Diet Coke with a Coke, ingesting ten extra kilocalories, subtract the nine seconds you just got back. You are damned if you drink, damned if you drink something else. Living nine seconds is subtracting nine seconds, using is using up.

panicky energy of my handsome uncle. The Calorie Control Council, a lobbying group then headed by Marvin, took out a full-page ad in the national newspapers that showed my uncle buried neck-deep in pink packets. According to the copy, this was the amount of Sweet'N Low a person would have to eat every day to approach the intake of the study rats.

MARVIN:

"In Canada, they fed rats the equivalent of eight hundred cans of diet soda a day for three generations. If you want to equate that with Sweet'N Low, it's 10,000 packets a day, day in, day out. The mother, the babies, the embryo, bathed in saccharin. If they had given them that much sugar, salt, pepper, or water they would've died, but that would be OK. Because the Delaney Amendment said any food additive that causes cancer in man or animal must be banned. The FDA was very determined because of thalidomide, which they banned but the Europeans did not and all these babies were born with no arms and no legs. So the FDA was cautious. Maybe rightly. I'm not saying they were wrong. But they were going to ban saccharin. I was on Channel 2 with Frank Field. His son is the weather man Storm Field. I was nervous because I had never been on TV before. I was in the studio and I remember Betty Furness, who used to sell refrigerators, was sitting next to me. I was prepared to show just how ridiculous the experiments were: in three generations, fourteen male rats developed bladder cancer. And on that kind of basis they might ban a product that's been used for over a hundred years and during both world wars when there were shortages. In fact, diabetics had a lower rate of bladder cancer than the rest of the population. So we were armed with all this terrific scientific information. Then, just as I'm about to go on, Frank Field comes in with a teletype. It says: The government has just banned saccharin. I was promised by our councilman they would not ban saccharin without giving us a hearing. The blood rushed out of my head. I thought I was going to faint. Betty Furness put her arm around me and said, 'Don't worry, Mr. Eisenstadt, everything will be okay.' The next thing I know, I'm on TV with those hot lights on me and Frank Field says, 'What's it like being put out of business?' I got angry. And because I got angry my blood pressure went up. And because my blood pressure went up, my sensibilities came back. I went into the details of this experiment. I told the truth about sugar: how it causes everything from rabies to pimples to diabetes to teeth falling out. I said, 'If you ban saccharin, the only thing left is sugar. You have no other choice. Take the diabetic kid who goes into a candy store and orders a diet soda. If there's no diet soda, what's he going to order? Sugar soda. This kid is going to hurt himself because you're not giving the public a choice. Just because of this stupid experiment on rats.'"

The letters poured in to Congress: doctors worried about diabetics; dentists worried about tooth decay. For the first time in our history, the ugly word *gingivitis* was whispered in the corridors of power. More than the gap-toothed or the insulin-starved, it was the calorie counters who made the difference. When weighing the possibility of a future tumor against the here and now of a skinny life, the consumers chose the here and now. In the week after the ban, Congress received more than a hundred thousand letters, more than received in any comparable period during the Vietnam War.

When the politicians finally weighed in, the bureaucrats were relieved: the FDA had strayed beyond its depth, wandered smack into the zeitgeist. They did not understand the crazed nature of their own time. On March 18, 1977, a week after the ban was announced, Ted Kennedy, the chairman of the Senate Subcommittee on Health and Scientific Research, moved for a delay. That June, Senator Kennedy pushed through a moratorium: the ban would remain on the books but would not be enforced. The effects of saccharin would be studied further. In the meantime, all saccharin products would carry a warning. The entire matter would come back before Congress in two years, at which time either the ban would be enforced, or saccharin would be cleared, or the moratorium would be extended. In November 1977, Jimmy Carter signed the Saccharin Study and Labeling Act into law.

The Sweet'N Low packet would now carry the label: USE OF THIS PRODUCT MAY BE HAZARDOUS TO YOUR HEALTH. THIS PRODUCT CONTAINS SACCHARIN, WHICH HAS BEEN DETERMINED TO CAUSE CANCER IN LABORATORY ANIMALS.

"Ted Kennedy proposed that," Marvin told me. "And it was unfair. Because it said the product causes cancer in animals. But it was only rats."

Soon after the ban was announced, Marvin told *The New York Times* that he was laying off seven hundred workers, which was his way of warning the politicians and union leaders: "These rats and their cancer is your tragedy, too!" But no one was laid off at Cumberland. In fact, the factory actually had to add an additional shift to cover demand. Sales were skyrocketing. The junkies were hoarding. By 1979, forty-four million Americans were using saccharin daily—six million more than had used it before the ban. For Marvin, the question had gone from "How does it feel to be put out of business?" to "How did you do it?"

And yet, looking back over the history of the company, you have to conclude that these events (ban, moratorium) were a disaster. If the ban had been lifted, the factory would have gone back to business as usual. If the ban had been imposed, Marvin and Ben would have been forced to reinvent Sweet'N Low as they had done before the ban of cyclamate. Instead, saccharin was thrown into limbo, alive with an asterisk, its future in doubt. A chasm opened, a need for an alternative to the existing alternatives; an ideal opportunity for Cumberland, leagues ahead of its competitors, to use its brand name and its resources to invent the future. But in a way common to executives of the second generation, Marvin got fixated on the past, on preserving. It was in these years, with my uncle hung up on the moratorium, on managing it, extending it, and extending it again, that the big pharmaceutical companies developed the artificial sweeteners that have come to dominate the industry (aspartame, sucralose).* All the while, the factory where Bubba once hand-packed sugar was living from hearing to hearing, moratorium to moratorium. Its executives entered the dirty game of politics. The ban had triggered a series of events that led almost inevitably to the scandal that would break over the factory and darken Ben's final days.

*Buried in a *New York Times* article published the week the ban was announced is a sentence that suggests the true import of the moment. "GD Searle makes aspartame, an artificial sweetener at present kept off the market because of a dispute between the company and regulators. The plan to ban saccharin has triggered new interest in aspartame."

PART TWO

CUMBERLAND PACKING IN FORT GREENE IS AMONG THE LAST
OF THE OLD-TIME FACTORIES THAT USED TO LINE THE BROOKLYN
WATERFRONT. IT'S WHERE BEN REALIZED HIS DREAM,
AND WHERE THAT DREAM WENT OFF THE RAILS.

20.

One morning, I rented a car, picked up my friend Burke, who has a towering head of Dylanesque hair, crossed Central Park at Eighty-sixth Street, and turned north onto Park Avenue, which climbs before its long descent into Manhattan Valley. As the road falls away, the subway tracks appear, dug out like a worm, turned into an elevated, rolling across the valley floor. You don't think of Manhattan as having a valley floor, but here it is, barnacled by concrete, the Park Avenue palaces giving way to the projects, the sort of urban view you see at the beginning of poor-and-black-is-funny television shows like *Good Times*. Burke shivered and said, "It got so seventies out!" Graffiti weather.

We took 125th Street to the East River Drive, then went north. I like driving away from the city, especially on a crisp summer morning, when the clouds are stacked like circling airplanes, when the bridges and the smokestacks are spotted by shadows. And look! The shadows, the trees, the cars, the people in the cars, the thoughts in the people—all of it moves! I feel like I'm getting away with something, like I have called in sick to school, but I am not sick at all! I like leaving when it rains, too, when the wipers snap and the cars come at you and at you in the rain, or at first light, when the sky over the airport is raw and industrial red.

We took the Triborough Bridge to the Grand Central Parkway, which swings back like a comma, giving you a great goodbye look at the city. Whenever I see Manhattan going away, I say, *Thank God I got out of that alive!*

Whenever I return, I say, *Thank God they let me back in.*

We went east on the Long Island Expressway. It's strange for a Midwesterner, going east to get away. Once you reach New York, you should be out of east. Manhattan should have its back to the wall of the country, but here we were, rolling past Olympia Boulevard and Elysian Fields. The border between Queens and Long Island is so indistinct you don't even notice it. You just look up at the signs and know that you have moved from your grandparents' world of apartment houses and subway stops to the perfect suburbia of the next generation, the Hicksvilles and Roslyns where the Jews of Brooklyn rebuilt Flatbush among the old Dutch farms. If F. Scott Fitzgerald could only see his new world, carved into subdivisions! *Forget the Buchanans, it belongs to the Blumenthals!* To the natives, it's one word: *Guyland.* How I hate that! Freshman year in college, I lived with a kid from Merrick, Long Island. One night, as I dozed off, I mumbled, "Long Island sucks," and the kid was on me, shouting, "You wish, you wish you was from Guyland! We got everything on Guyland! We got the museum! We got the sports team!" Pointing at his bicep, he said, "Do you want to tangle with this gun!" The story of the Jews runs right through Guyland. (I wish it didn't, because Guyland is a dead end.) But it does. It's where the Jews of America fell into the quotidian. Like the character in a Walker Percy novel who gets so lost he thinks he's home.

We've got everything on Guyland.

We exited beyond Great Neck, about forty-five minutes from the city. As Robert Frost puts it, "Neither Out Far Nor In Deep." We took a service road past auto shops and weedy fields with cars up on blocks and Guylanders in muscle shirts saying, *Now really wind her out.* We crossed an intersection, went over a hill, and were in Old Westbury, the distilled essence of Guyland. In the 1920s, the robber barons cut this town out of the potato fields. They built a polo club, a country club, a golf course, and huge mansions, many of which have been torn down to make way for even huger mansions. In 1928, when planners routed the Northern State Parkway through Old Westbury, the residents—this shows the kind of power we're talking about—forced New York State to push the highway five miles off course, which is why, as you head to the Hamptons, you dogleg left for no apparent reason.* The town is known for its high concentration of reputed gangsters. It's like one of those suburban towns where the members of a pro football team live among the lily-white locals. It's like that, only instead of athletes, it's reputed mobsters. Not the runners or torpedoes, but the Mafia lawyers and bosses who live on suburban estates like country squires. The streets stink of new money. When John Gotti, Jr., was indicted for racketeering, Victoria Gotti, his sister, offered her Old Westbury estate as collateral for a ten-million-dollar bail bond.†

We drove along tree-lined streets, the kind where, if you are a stranger, you feel the eyes on you, the busybody eyes peering out from behind living room curtains, the security-system eyes tracking each passing car, the vigilante eyes of the Neighborhood Watch. We turned into St. Andrews Court, a loop of concrete lined with houses behind security gates and tall hedges. (From above, this loop must form a dollar sign.) It's a cookie-cutter subdivision in which every cookie is a McMansion. Even when a family is on vacation, such houses swarm with activity: the pool man adjusting the hot tub, the yardman checking the underground sprinklers, the engineer monitoring the security system, the tree surgeon pruning the Japanese maple, the Mexican gardeners in their manure-smelling truck rattling down the hushed street. If you sit on a ridge above such a development at dusk as the lights come on, the houses look like an armada of battleships waiting off the coast for zero hour.

We parked in front of 18 St. Andrews Court. Burke raced up the driveway and snapped off some pictures. When he got back in the car, his

---

*This detour was nicknamed Objector's Bend. A source on all things concerning New York City highways is the website www.nycroads.com.

†This was reported in the Associated Press, among other places. This house is now the setting of A&E's reality television show *Growing Up Gotti*.

hair was wild and he was out of breath. He shouted, "Next house!" Ten St. Andrews Court was just a few doors away. As Burke crawled through the hedges and then captured the house from every angle, I said to myself, "Beautiful! Just freakin' beautiful!" These houses, which belonged to two former top executives of Cumberland Packing, were largely built with money stolen from the company. They were the scandal made physical. Though this was my first visit, I felt I already knew everything about the houses: their floor plans, their pool designs, their security systems, their finished basements. I knew this from reading hundreds of pages of documents, the court testimony of contractors, electricians, and plumbers.

The house at 10 St. Andrews Court belonged to Oswaldo "Gil" Mederos, who had been hired by Ben in 1954. Gil Mederos was really a glorified handyman, a self-trained mechanic who never graduated from high school. He worked with Marvin in the old days, when my uncle was still in coveralls. By the 1980s, Marvin had promoted him to the position of chief financial officer. According to his title, Mederos was responsible for the factory's cash flow, purchasing, and selling. This house had been his dream. He oversaw its construction down to the smallest detail: the three-story foyer that makes a man feel like a god; the seventeen-thousand-dollar front door imported from northern Italy; the curvy backyard pool fed by a waterfall; the hot tub; the gazebo; the forest trail illuminated by ground lights.

The house at 18 St. Andrews Court belonged to Joseph Asaro, who, according to the *The Washington Post*, had been identified as an associate of the Bonanno crime family.* Joe Asaro was Cumberland's vice president for governmental affairs. It was his job to manage the saccharin ban and the moratorium. He teamed with Marvin, or seduced, or fooled, or intimidated him into criminality. This was all part of a criminal conspiracy entered into by some of the company's chief officers in the 1980s and

---

*According to the article, which appeared in *The Washington Post* on September 2, 1994, Asaro had been "identified as an associate of the Bonanno crime family in a prosecution memo . . ." But in a story published in the *New York Post* on April 13, 1995, the U.S. Attorney's office seemed to back off that characterization. "News reports have linked Asaro to the Bonanno crime family," it read, "but federal prosecutors and his lawyer denied it."

1990s. These men pillaged the factory, writing fake invoices, soliciting bribes and kickbacks, cheating the IRS, making illegal campaign contributions, and defrauding Cumberland out of millions of dollars.

By the time Joe Asaro's picture made it into the newspapers, he was in his fifties, a tycoon from Old Westbury. His eyes are dark in these pictures, his features close set and intense. He did not learn English until his teens, so even when he got up in the world, he spoke in the sort of palooka voice that rings with the gruff edge of the street. "My supervisor teached me the trade," he later said while testifying against his former colleagues at Cumberland. He was a fixer, the sort of man who knows how the world really works. Ben might say, "Call Joe Asaro, he'll take care of it." Marvin might shout into a phone, "Do you want me to talk to Joe Asaro?" Asaro's Rolodex was filled with important names, his office as photo-filled as a delicatessen on Sixth Avenue: Asaro and Ronald Reagan, Asaro and Daniel Patrick Moynihan, Asaro and Bob Dole, Asaro and George Bush, Asaro and Alfonse D'Amato. According to *The New York Times*, "Within [Cumberland], workers traded stories of Mr. Asaro's boasts that he could dine with the Pope."

What I know about Asaro I know from newspaper stories, legal documents, and court testimony. (I have never met him.) He immigrated to the United States from Sicily in 1960. He came with his brothers, Frank and Salvatore Asaro, part of the flood of immigrants that was remaking the New York waterfront. He knocked around, did odd jobs. He worked at a clothing factory. He worked in construction. By the early 1970s, he was running a small construction company on Long Island. It was in this capacity that he came to Cumberland. Marvin told me that it was Ben who first hired Asaro. Or else he just appeared, like a dervish, out of a cloud of debris. "Back in the mid-seventies, I was in the contracting business," Asaro said in court. "I was doing work for Cumberland, renovation, alterations to the factory and offices. That's how I started."

"Joseph Asaro came to our plant," Marvin testified. "We had to build some warehouses. He was brought in by an architect as a contractor and he built—his crew built two warehouses."

I like that dash—it shows Marvin correcting himself. Because Asaro never built anything. He ran a crew, and the crew built a warehouse and Asaro took a cut. Even then, he was on the grift. He had been hired to build a warehouse, and he billed for that work, but he also billed for other work that was never done, or not done for Cumberland. Here is a courtroom exchange between Asaro and Irving Anolik, the defense lawyer who represented Gil Mederos.

ANOLIK: Before you became an employee, had you submitted any
    sort of invoices to Cumberland that were false?
ASARO: A few of them, yes.
ANOLIK: What sort of invoices did you submit that were false?
ASARO: There was work done at Robert Fernandez's* house. He
    asked me to do that. I did that.

In 1982, Joe Asaro, a Sicilian immigrant who had done a small construction job for the factory, in the course of which he filed fake invoices, was hired as a vice president of Cumberland Packing—a mind-boggling jump. Marvin says the decision was made by Ben for reasons that remain mysterious. Ben did not come up with the formula, did not foresee the cyclamate ban, did not buy the gas station, but he did hire Joe Asaro.

Irving Anolik's cross-examination of Asaro was filled with innuendo. Imagine a prosecutor probing Carlo Gambino on his actual knowledge of the olive oil business:

*Robert Fernandez was a vice president of Cumberland Packing. When he retired, in 1991, he was honored by Edolphus Towns, a congressman from the Tenth Congressional District, County of Kings, New York, who, standing on the floor of the House of Representatives, read the following statement into the record: "Mr. Speaker, I rise to salute the accomplishments of Mr. Robert Fernandez. Mr. Fernandez was born in Camaguey, Cuba. As a child he was an adventurer. He had a burning desire to come to America. At the age of sixteen his ambition was realized and he arrived in the United States. He joined the merchant marine and traveled extensively. Mr. Fernandez began his professional career by working for the Cumberland Packing Company. He rose through the organization to become a foreman and subsequently became vice president. He worked for that company for thirty years."

ANOLIK: What experience did you have in construction?

ASARO: Back in Italy, that's what I was doing for a living.

ANOLIK: What sort of training did you have?

ASARO: My supervisor taught me how to read blueprints.

ANOLIK: Would it be fair to say you have no special licenses or degrees in the construction business?

ASARO: I don't have a degree or special license, no.

Once Asaro was set up at Cumberland, in an office not far from the offices of Ben and Marvin, it was unclear just what he was supposed to do. "It was a myriad of positions," Marvin testified. "He started as renovations. He would get the materials, get the right contractors, do that himself."

"Being that I knew a lot of the construction, [Marvin] told me to handle all the construction, renovations, whatever," said Asaro.

When I talked to Marvin about the scandal, I got a different picture of Joe Asaro, his usefulness, and his role at the factory. "I had a guy named Gil Mederos who was my comptroller and a guy named Joe Asaro who was politically connected," Marvin told me.* "Originally he started—my father hired Joe Asaro. And he began to—he built our warehouse . . . and we hired him as a political consultant. And he knew everybody. He would go to Washington; he knew all these people. And the guy was almost illiterate. I mean really Mafia type. And once he really helped me in the sense that I had a cleaning service here through the union and we finally didn't need them and they threatened to blow up my car or to put my house on fire. And I told Joe Asaro about this and he went over there and he told them that, you know—I guess he was connected somehow. And they left me alone. I was left alone."

By 1987, Joe Asaro was a top-ranking officer at Cumberland, in charge of all construction and purchasing. If a foreman needed to replace a piece

*Marvin told me this during a phone call a few days after my visit to the factory in the summer of 2003.

of equipment, he went to see Asaro, who combed through the purchasing forms, queried, and probed. If everything looked okay, he signed off. The papers were then sent to the comptroller and chief financial officer, Gil Mederos, who had previously worked as a mechanic and on mixtures and recipes, but was now in charge of corporate cash flow. (Once a year, Mederos tuned Marvin's car; he also was the one who covered and cleaned out the aquarium during the tropical fish kill.) If Mederos approved an order, he signed the forms, not in his own hand but with a rubber stamp of his nickname. In court this was called "the Gil stamp." Irving Anolik, Mederos's lawyer, told the jury that there might in fact have been more than one Gil stamp. He said the cost of having such a stamp duplicated at a stationery store was about five dollars. The last office down the hall belonged to the president of the company, Marvin Eisenstadt, who was in charge of Gil Mederos, who was in charge of Joe Asaro, who was in charge of everything else.

Shortly after he started working for the company, Asaro noticed invoices for mysterious construction jobs that were being ordered without his permission. He tracked these to Mario Mederos, Gil's brother. Mario did not work in the main factory building but across the street, in the Navy Yard. Like his brother, Mario had been hired by Ben in the 1950s. Over the years, he had worked in almost every job at Cumberland. "He started as a floor man," Marvin said in court. "He would seal boxes, things of that na-

ture. He worked on the machinery. We had a machine that involved people, and he would run those. As we progressed, as we grew, we had a separate facility around the corner, and he really set that up."

Mario and Gil Mederos had been building the business when Marvin was still in college. When Marvin graduated, they helped train him and taught him the ins and outs. What happened to these brothers in their later years, when Ben was gone, when the grown-ups were dead, is a tragedy. Either they saw Marvin as nothing, and so took terrible advantage of him, or Marvin saw them as peasants, and did what plantation owners have always done to peasants.

When Asaro noticed Mario's unaccounted-for construction orders, he spoke to Marvin. He said something like "If Mario can go around buying all this on his own, then what's my job?"

Marvin called Mario in for a meeting. *See me*, like a message scribbled by a teacher on a shoddy term paper. It's a short walk from the Yard, down warehouse lanes lined with spools of cable and wire, railroad tracks, nails, tools—a million opportunities for tetanus—across the road, and in the side door to the Cumberland executive suite, which looks like it hasn't been remodeled since the 1970s. I can feel the unease this encounter must have caused my uncle, a man who assiduously avoids confrontation. *Just don't tell your aunt you talked to me! Just keep me out of it!* It's why he turned to Asaro in the first place: he wanted someone to take care of his problem with the cleaning service, place a call, live through the nasty moments, make it go away. *After that, I was left alone.* My uncle's fear rises from the pages of the court transcript; it smells like bad wiring. If Marvin called Mario for a meeting, it can only mean that Marvin was less afraid of Mario than he was of Asaro. Mario, who had worked at the factory since the Eisenhower administration, was marooned across the street in the Navy Yard, whereas Asaro, who a few years before had been outside building a warehouse with his crew, had an office in the executive suite, his door embossed with the outlandish title VICE PRESIDENT OF GOVERNMENTAL AFFAIRS.

Marvin said, "Look, Mario. This is the way I want it to be. Go through Joe for any contracting. Whatever space you need, you will tell Joe, and Joe will take it from that point."

A few weeks later, Mario sat down with Asaro. He told Asaro he had come up with a way to greatly increase their income. When all the particulars are boiled away, Mario's plan sounds like simple theft. He and Asaro would set up shell companies, fake businesses that would interpose themselves in the Cumberland flow chart as phony middle men: buying cheap raw materials, then, at a tremendous markup, selling them to the factory; or charging the factory for work that was never done, for deliveries that were never made, for products that never existed. The checks paid by Cumberland would then be deposited into the accounts of the shell companies, and in this way would be available to the conspirators. The shell companies could also pay contractors to do personal work for Asaro and Mederos, on their own property or on outside projects, and bill it all to Cumberland.

In short, these men would use the factory as their personal piggy bank: for walking-around money, to pay for vacations, to build their houses and fund their schemes. It reads like a precursor to the corporate scandals that would break across the country a few years later, Enron and Arthur Andersen and Tyco International, where CEO L. Dennis Kozlowski treated the company accounts as his private stash. The government later argued that Mederos and Asaro were perfectly situated to have carried out the scheme (as was Marvin). Mario was the plant manager in charge of the purchasing lists; Asaro was the vice president who approved those lists. Asaro, according to his own testimony, told Mario Mederos that he liked the plan but believed it would not work without the involvement of Gil Mederos. Because each purchasing form had to be tagged with the Gil stamp.

"Don't worry," Mario said. "I'll speak to Gil."*

A few days later Mario said, "I had a conversation with Gil. Gil will go along, and don't worry about it. We have a deal."

Over the next several years, Asaro and the Mederos brothers built a criminal network as efficient as the factory itself: phony order forms traveled from Mario Mederos to Joe Asaro, who signed them and sent them to Gil Mederos, who stamped them and sent them to the shell compa-

*All this dialogue comes from the testimony of Joe Asaro.

nies, where they were received by Asaro and the Mederos brothers, who filed them and sent phony invoices back to the factory, where they were OK'd by Marvin and sent to accounting, where stacks of Cumberland checks were signed "Marvin Eisenstadt" by the auto-pen.

The shell corporations:

Penultimate negotiated contracts with Cumberland—these were signed by the president of Penultimate, a made-up name forged by Joe Asaro—for services never rendered and billed for work never done. Here is a typical (phony) invoice:

> Replace rudder and gutter and leaders on warehouse. Install sheet metal suction to Sweet'N Low machines.

Exim Associates, another shell company, ordered bags of cream of tartar from Cumberland's European suppliers, then sold these bags to the factory at a huge markup. Or billed the factory for shipments that never existed. (This is what the government documents mean by "phantom shipments of cream of tartar.") According to court testimony, Mario Mederos's assistant, Fabio Serrano, wrote invoices for the phantom shipments. He was paid $2,500 for every truck he conjured. From 1985 to 1989, $400,000 worth of phony shipments—160 nonexistent trucks—were billed to the factory, with the invoices signed by a woman named Maria Rosen, who was in fact Mario Mederos's daughter, Marlo.

In a letter to the judge, Assistant U.S. Attorney Richard Faughnan wrote:

> *Special Agent Allan Shurack testified about how he had recovered $10,000 in cash from Gil Mederos' desk pursuant to the federal search warrant, and he further testified about how he has recovered an incriminating note attached to Gil Mederos' Rolodex. The note read, 'Fabio $5,100; truck ticket tomorrow.' This note corroborated Joseph Asaro's testimony that he and Gil and Mario Mederos had paid money to Fabio Serrano, Mario Mederos' assistant, to falsify trucking tickets for phantom shipments of cream of tartar.*

"Joe Asaro and Gil Mederos had a scheme where they would buy chemicals and sell them to Cumberland," Marvin told me. "We thought we were buying them from a chemical company that had nothing to do with people on my payroll. When I found out, I was aghast and I told my office, 'Look, you can't do that. You got a conflict of interest. You can't sell me stuff. You're working here.' I said, 'If you have a problem, let me know; if it's a money problem, I'll work with you.' I said, 'I'm going to forgive you this time. I'm not going to report you.'"

Proteus Associates, a phony real estate company, was formed to spend and launder the ill-gotten revenue. With money transferred from Exim and Penultimate, Proteus bought millions of dollars worth of property in Manhattan.

These companies were all listed at the same address: 36 Glen Cove Road, Greenvale, New York. *Guyland.* On many forms, the companies share office holders. The companies were organized by accountants and lawyers who worked for Cumberland. In other words, someone should have noticed. (Maybe someone did.) When a shell company needed an electrician or a plumber, the tradesmen usually came from Cumberland. In this way, several blue collar workers were implicated in the scandal. They wrote phony orders, issued fake receipts, postdated documents, did whatever they were asked to do. Many of these men were indicted, cut a deal, and testified against the Mederos brothers. In this testimony, each of the workers talked about how he came to work for Cumberland, giving a sense of just how small-time and wiseguyish the operation was.

Cumberland's contracting work was done by E&F Mechanical Enterprises, 50 percent owned by Frank Asaro, 50 percent owned by Salvatore Asaro. The electrical and wiring work was done by Interphase Electric Corp., co-owned by Eric Vitale, who met Joe Asaro in the 1980s at a barbecue in Asaro's neighbor's yard. Asaro told him, "We could use a good electrician. Stop by the office." Vitale billed Cumberland over $140,000. The plumbing and heating work was done by Petri Mechanical, owned by Gerard Petri, perhaps the only plumber ever asked to wear a wire.

Between 1985 and 1994, the conspirators skimmed millions of dollars from the factory. This money was deducted by Cumberland as business expenses, putting the factory in violation of tax laws. Because the factory is privately owned, it took longer than it otherwise might have for the conspiracy to be detected. There were no badgering shareholders, no angry board of directors, no irritating regulators from the SEC. A company not traded on the stock exchange is often allowed to go its own way.

Not satisfied with the money generated by the shell corporations, the conspirators also engaged in more traditional forms of skullduggery. By the 1990s, Cumberland Packing was a cesspool. For a grandson, it's shaming. It's like reading the details of a rape. If a contractor wanted to work for the factory, or to keep on working, Gil Mederos, Mario Mederos, or Joe Asaro would ask that contractor for a kickback, a taste. These demands were sometimes made of tradesmen who had done work for the factory since the days before Sweet'N Low. For such men, witnessing the changes at Cumberland must have been depressing. A contractor who gave a thousand dollars to Gil or Mario Mederos—crumpled twenties, fifties, and hundreds dirtied with engine grease and palm sweat—was told to add it to the next invoice, and in this way was reimbursed by Cumberland. Therefore, the only player to lose anything in this game was the factory itself. From 1986 to 1993, Gil Mederos was generating from a single contractor (and there were many) more than a thousand dollars a month. And it was not only money. Mario Mederos also received, among other things, electronic equipment, lawn furniture, and pool toys.

Cumberland had left the small can-do world of postwar Brooklyn and entered the underworld. There was nothing romantic about any of it. The factory was being consumed. In some of the testimony, you catch the hint of menace. One afternoon, Mario Mederos, angry that everyone had more money than he, was having a fit. Joe Asaro called Eric Vitale, the electrician, and told him to come over to Cumberland right away. "Mr. Asaro called me into his office and said Mario was complaining," Vitale testified. " '[We] do a lot of work around the factory and [Mario] is looking for some extra money.' Mr. Asaro asked if I could get cash in my business. I said I don't deal with hardly any cash. If you want me to write a check out to Mario, I will. He told me to write a check for five thousand dollars. I wrote that check and it was given to Mario."

In the memo box, Vitale wrote, REFUND. He was reimbursed by Cumberland.

On another occasion, Gerard Petri, the plumber, met Joe Asaro and Gil Mederos at the factory. Petri said he had spent beyond his means and could not pay his bills. He asked if he could borrow some money fast. He was approaching these men the way you approach the shylock under the bridge.

Why did he come to Cumberland? What did he know?

"Yeah," said Mederos. "I think we can help you out."

Gerard Petri was given fifty thousand dollars in cash,* money that came from Cumberland. He had six months to pay it back. When he failed, he was put to work: the boys recouped their debt in trade.

Cumberland had become part of the ancient criminal nation that stretches along the Brooklyn waterfront. Everywhere you look, someone is paying and someone is getting paid. Ben must have had to deal with this from the beginning: the world beyond the machines and shipping bays, the world of Socks Lanza and Albert Anastasia. In the 1950s, when Cumberland was still packing soy sauce and sea monkeys, the mob, with its protection and its kickbacks, was so prevalent in New York that it drove up the cost of consumer goods something like 10 percent. The Feds called it "the gangster tax." In the 1960s, partly in an effort to clean up the waterfront, the city took over the Navy Yard. But the gangsters never went away. They never really do. Like the poor, they are always with us. Asaro had been recommended to Marvin as a guy who could make a problem disappear. Chasing gangsters with another gangster is how people get themselves into trouble. Because after the gangster solves your problem, he stays.

The conspirators laundered their money the traditional way, investing "dirty" cash in properties and businesses that would generate revenue that was accounted for and thus "clean." They loaned, funded outside projects, and improved their own houses, hiring Cumberland workers to put in

---

*Remember that when my mother, in a moment of financial panic, had asked her father for a loan, she was told that no money was available because the factory was not "liquid."

swimming pools and tennis courts. Through the shell companies, the conspirators purchased a six-story residential and commercial building at 231 East Fiftieth Street in Manhattan in the early 1980s. According to court documents, this building cost $1.4 million,* money transferred from the accounts of Proteus and Exim. The conspirators assumed a $900,000 dollar mortgage and paid the balance. They then gutted the building. "It was a major renovation," Asaro testified. "We did all the electric, plumbing, new windows, new elevator, the corridors, renovated eleven luxury apartments and the restaurant." This work cost more than $1.6 million. Frank Asaro, one of the contractors, told the jury, "The bill was arranged to make believe the work was done at Cumberland Packing."

After Eric Vitale, the electrician who wired the building, wrote "231 East Fiftieth" on an invoice, Joe Asaro took him aside and said, "You have to show the work was done for Cumberland. Don't show any tie with 231 East Fiftieth."

The prosecutors focused mostly on the houses built by Joe Asaro and Gil Mederos in Old Westbury. A commercial building or a kickback or a phantom shipment of cream of tartar can be hard to picture, but everyone knows that a seventeen-thousand-dollar door is extravagant. Designed by the conspirators, these McMansions illuminate not just the dimensions of the crime but the taste of the criminals. That's why I drove to Guyland. That's why I circled St. Andrews Court wearing sunglasses. That's why I did a three-point turn, also known as a K-turn, and went back for a second look. That's why I sent Burke up the driveway. I see those houses in my mind, drifting through a suburban dream. I understand the provinces better than I understand any other place in the world. My clocks run on village time. The prosecutor spent some time on the house Joe Asaro built at 18 St. Andrews Court, which Asaro said, "without the land, is worth about a million-two," and more on the house Gil Mederos built at 10 St. Andrews Court.

*This seems wildly deflated; this is a big building in the middle of the city.

Because everyone else ratted and cut a deal, it was Gil Mederos's house that was taken apart and examined to show how the conspiracy worked. That's why I know so much about this house; that it was built soon after Asaro's house was completed in 1988, for example. Gil Mederos liked Joe Asaro's house so much that he wanted one of his own on the same block. When speaking to Marvin, Mederos invented a story to explain the coincidence. "Gil said he had this wonderful opportunity to purchase a house that was completely done," Marvin testified. "He said this poor guy had this house built but couldn't pay for all the construction and therefore Gil had a chance to buy it on foreclosure and get a wonderful deal. The only question he had for me was that it would be right next to Joe Asaro and would I have a problem with that? I said I have no problem, but why don't you check with Joe?"

Gil met with the contractors at the factory, approved plans, and picked materials. One after another, workmen appeared in court to explain each feature of the house. "There's three [skylights] in the kitchen," Frank Asaro told the jury, "one in the master bedroom, the Florida room, and the gallery roof."

Describing the clear cedar front door—the door that cost the factory seventeen thousand dollars—Frank Asaro said, "it's nine foot wide, approximately sixteen feet high."

An average large house is wired for two hundred amps of electricity, but this battleship was wired for four hundred amps, because Gil Mederos was running so much equipment: the security system, the closed-circuit TVs, the heated pool, the Jacuzzi, the waterfall. There were five and a half bathrooms. The master had a whirlpool and a steam room. "They were luxurious," said Gerard Petri, the plumber, who, for this work, billed the factory $150,000. Petri spoke of sitting in Gil Mederos's office at Cumberland, just a few doors from Marvin's, picking out sinks, toilets, and floor tile.

Eric Vitale described the security system: four outdoor cameras and two nineteen-inch monitors, one in the kitchen, one in the master bedroom. Pointing to a photo, Vitale said, "Here we put in some up-lights. They light the trees." He said, "I came to [Gil's] office at Cumberland. I showed him the catalogues I had on fixtures." He said, "When the frame was done, we met at the site and walked through a couple of areas." He said, "There is a closed-circuit camera on the back of the cabana facing the pool." He handed the jury a cost breakdown, which in his books shows all the work as having been done at the factory.

- Electrical work: $45,000
- Central vacuum cleaning system, Dorvac: $4,500
- Cable TV: $2,500
- Telephone wiring: $2,000
- Closed-circuit TV: $1,500
- Burglar and fire alarm: $10,500
- 182 fixture outlets
- 69 receptacles
- Intercom system: $8,500
- 93 switches, 182 fixtures
- Total: $74,500

According to an agent from the IRS, the marble in the house alone cost more than a hundred thousand dollars. The total price, not including the land, was $1.17 million, half of which was paid by Cumberland Packing.

21.

By 1988, Jeff Eisenstadt, now a vice president of Cumberland Packing, had become suspicious of Joe Asaro and the Mederos brothers, and of some of the companies doing business with the factory. Jeff had been working at the plant only for a short time. Before that, he had been a high school student in Far Rockaway, Queens; a surf aficionado; a repeat watcher of the movie *Big Wednesday*; a student at Emory University, in Atlanta; then a transfer student at the University of California at Santa Barbara, which, not unlike my own alma mater, Tulane, is a refuge for reasonably smart kids who did not work hard enough (or weren't graded fairly) to get into the Ivy League, so spent four or five or six years getting stoned at parties, or passing through the gateway drugs, and the smell of autumn, and the trippy new song by Dash Rip Rock, and the color of the sky five minutes after sundown. A perfect place for the cousin Jeffs of this world, scions of the third generation getting lost in the sticks.

Jeff went on to the University of San Diego Law School, in California, which sits on a hill overlooking the city. In the summer, when the san-

tanas blew, he would surf the morning glass. A wave rider from Queens, a redheaded Jew, skinny and freckled, eyes like the blue eyes of Marvin gone through the wash. In a sense, Jeff had gone through the wash: he was burned out, spent, fried, toasted, smashed, hammered, wasted. The hills were green, the sea was blue, and the afternoons lingered. He dated an au pair, got married. He would never come back! He was free! If he and the au pair had kids, they would never know the misery of the Jews, or the rattle and saccharin stink of packing machines.

Then I went to a wedding in New York, and there was Jeff, in a tuxedo, cocktail in each hand, double-fisted. He said, "Viking Cohen!* Get me a drink!" Then he was divorced. Then he was remarried. Then he was living in New Jersey. Then he was big time at the factory. He sought out my father in these years. He would grab my arm and slur, "Viking Cohen, where's your old man?" Whenever anyone in the extended family has an issue, they seek out my father: because Herbie is on the outside, because

---

*A nickname I had as a kid, because when I was four and five and six, I went everywhere in one of those plastic Viking helmets.

Herbie represents an opposing pole of power. I would see them standing together in a corner, Jeffrey drunk, Herbie listening.

My father told me: "When Jeffrey was drinking, he would say, 'The only reason I came back, you know—I should have stayed in California—is they made an offer I couldn't refuse.'"

San Diego was a dream; Brooklyn reached out and yanked him back in the end. Once Jeffrey had assumed his position at the factory, he changed. He became a different sort of guy. Maybe it's the price of admission: if you want to go on this ride, you have to leave your monkey at the curb. He is guarded and suspicious. In his office are pictures of him on the golf course. The move from surfing to golf is not insignificant. When I visited the factory, Jeffrey was conspicuously not there. I guess he could have been away on business, but I got the distinct impression he was not there because I was. "I trust everybody," Marvin told me. "[Jeff] doesn't trust anybody."

"He should have stayed with his first wife in California," Gladys said. "But you make your choices, and you are stuck with them. To me, Jeff is a plane crossing the ocean. Once that plane has gone a certain distance, it cannot turn back. It's too late. That's what happened to Jeff. It's a tragedy. He was never meant to be a businessman."

Jeffrey's job involved working with the Cumberland suppliers, some of whom had been doing business with the factory since the 1950s. In this way, he got his first clue that something was not quite right at the factory. It was specifically the matter of Michael Firrello, Sr., a factory supplier who had previously done as much as eighty thousand dollars worth of business with Cumberland each month. Soon after Asaro and the Mederos brothers began conspiring, Firrello, Sr., was told a fifteen-thousand-dollar monthly limit had been placed on the purchase of his products. Mario Mederos said this limit would be lifted only if Firrello, Sr., bought certain items for Mario. "He would indicate whatever merchandise he wanted," Firrello, Sr., told the jury, "appliances or refrigerators or televisions or whatever, and he would tell me where to deliver it."

Firrello, Sr., also co-owned a restaurant with Gil Mederos in Key Largo, Florida. (How this happened, I have no idea.) By 1988, Mederos, who wanted to be the sole owner of the restaurant, was pressuring

Firrello, Sr., to sell his share. Between the payoffs and the restaurant, Firrello, Sr., who was in his late fifties, was under tremendous pressure. Michael Firrello, Jr., who also did work for the factory, and was worried about the well-being of his father, decided to talk to Jeffrey.

The conspirators learned about this conversation. Either they had spies, or Jeff himself reported back. Asaro told Mario Mederos, "Next time the [Firrello] kid comes in, bring him to see me, and I will have a talk with him."

A few days later, Mario called from his office in the Navy Yard.

He said, "The kid is here."

"Good," said Asaro, "bring him over when you're done with him."

"I told Firrello to meet me on the street," Asaro said in court. "So, I came down and [Firrello, Jr., was] sitting in my car. I drove up maybe fifty yards to the parking lot and told [him] . . . I heard you been talking to Jeff and possibly to Marvin, and we are not very happy about it. If you don't say nothing, it will be better for us, and then every business will continue and everybody will be happy."

After Asaro described this exchange in court, the defense lawyer asked, "During this conversation, did you possess a gun or a weapon of any kind?"

When Asaro said, "No," there was a commotion in the courtroom. When the judge got everyone quieted down, the prosecutor said, "Your honor, it's been brought to my attention that during the testimony, the defendants, and particularly Mario Mederos, has at times audibly said, 'Liar.'"

In the summer of 1988, Jeffrey drove to the headquarters of the businesses doing so much work for Cumberland: Penultimate, Proteus, Exim. On their forms, they were listed at 36 Glen Cove Road, Greenvale, Long Island. Imagine Jeffrey—with the address scrawled on a piece of paper, a map on the passenger seat, surf music on the stereo, the theme from the documentary *Endless Summer*, say, in which two kids chase the high season around the world, refusing to put away their boards, face the winter, or grow up. He parks at 36 Glen Cove Road and finds himself before a mini mall–type retail space best suited for a Mail Boxes Etc. or a poster shop called The Great Frame Up, not the sort of industrial concern implied by all the factory supplies being billed to Cumberland. How did Marvin miss this? Or was Marvin in on it all along? Maybe Jeffrey is the sorry detective who follows the trail only to find it leads back to his own house.

Federal agents were closing in. Subpoenas had been served to Joe Asaro and the Mederos brothers for their involvement with the shell companies. This investigation had been triggered by a series of red flags that signaled graft, or possibly mob presence. The fact that so many of the companies in business with Cumberland Packing were registered at the same address: flag. The fact that each year Cumberland Packing, according to its books, bought more machinery than could possibly fit into its factory: flag. The fact that, according to its deductions, Cumberland Packing had its parking lot paved perhaps a dozen times in two years: flag.

Asaro realized the game was up: Firrello, Jr., was talking, Jeffrey was poking around, the Feds were interviewing witnesses. It was only a matter of time before the truth of the books was revealed, or the fact that, in those books, almost nothing was true. There were actually two sets of books: the phony books filed with the government, and the secret books that tracked the actual cash flow. When Marvin heard about the subpoenas, which he thought had been issued only to companies in business with Cumberland, he told his colleagues, "Let's be squeaky clean. Let's do everything right. Let's not mess around." Rather than wait to be exposed, Asaro decided to confess to Marvin.

JOE ASARO:

"I went downstairs to see Marvin in his office, which is right next door to Gil Mederos's office. I asked Marvin not to talk to him there, to walk down the block, and I want to talk with you. So we did that. We were walking on Flushing Avenue and I told him about false invoices by me, Mario, and Gil. I also told him that it was in a building that exists at 231 East Fiftieth Street under Proteus; that all the money came from Cumberland. And I also told him my house, a portion, a good portion of my house, was built from Cumberland's money. I practically told him everything."

MARVIN:

"Joseph Asaro came into my office and asked me to go out on the street with him and we started walking. He said that he had a terrible confession to make; that he, Gil and Mario were cheating the company by selling cream of tartar, one of the ingredients to Sweet'N Low, to Cumberland."

Asaro told Gil and Mario Mederos that he had confessed, and he urged them to do the same. "The best thing is to tell Marvin everything," he said. "Because he is going to find out sooner or later."

Marvin should have fired these men, called the police, and pressed charges: they had robbed his company of millions of dollars. Instead, he looked for a way to save the company and save these men their jobs. "Marvin, first he was upset," said Asaro, "then he says to me he don't want nobody to go to jail, he doesn't want to cause trouble."

"I wanted to keep it quiet," Marvin said in court. "I didn't want anyone to know because I wanted all three of those people to continue on at Cumberland. I felt that, first of all, the long association I had with Gil and Mario was something I couldn't just slough off. They had contributed so much to the success of the business."*

It's this strange turn that raised the suspicions of prosecutors. It did not look right. It did not look like the behavior of a man who knew nothing. When Marvin insisted on his innocence, the prosecutors kept asking why, when he first learned of the conspiracy, had he not called the police? Did he fire the criminals? Did he punish them? No. He struck a bargain. He aided and abetted. He paid and promoted. Where was the fury of the mugged man?

Had this man really been mugged?

As you look over the testimony and the invoices and the bills and the work orders, the houses and the pool toys and the kickbacks, you start to add. You can't help it. Your mind wants to keep score. Forty grand here, a

---

*Marvin said this on the witness stand, while testifying against the same Gil and Mario Mederos.

million-two there, ten grand here, all of it entered into the books as work done at the factory. Why didn't Marvin wonder where all that money was going? (It's not like Cumberland is a huge conglomerate. It's a modest factory in Fort Greene, the breadth of which can be walked in ten minutes.) Why didn't he ever ask, "Hey Gil, where is my giant cedar door?" "Hey Gil, where is my Central Vac?" "Hey Gil, where are my sixty-nine receptacles?" "Hey Gil, where is my gazebo?" Is it really possible that Marvin did not know what was happening? That he was so clueless? Because that is what he claims. He says he knew nothing about nothing. He was ignorant. He was innocent. He did not understand the numbers. He could not do the math. He just wanted to be left out of it. His only crime was the possession of a pure heart. He trusted too much. That's what he told the reporters, and that's what his friends and family and colleagues wrote in letters to the judge.

Gathered in a dossier, these letters were given to the court on the eve of Marvin's sentencing. I made a request in writing and within a few weeks I was reading this dossier at a federal archive on Vesey Street in Manhattan. I copied it and brought it home and read it again. I felt as if I were reading a secret diary. There were letters from business partners, colleagues, friends, neighbors—one guy referred to my uncle as "Marvelous Marv." There was a letter from Gary Carter, once a great catcher for the New York Mets, who had met Marvin through charity work. A letter from Ira, but none from Gladys or Betty. Letters from Aunt Barbara and all my cousins. In each of these letters, and in many of the newspaper stories that followed the case, Marvin is presented (perhaps as a result of a well-coordinated PR strategy?) as a man who is simply too good for this world.

Aunt Barbara: "[Marvin] is trusting to a fault, almost naïve, because he never would be anything but trustworthy himself."*

---

*Barbara suggested that Marvin's problems stemmed from a wrong decision made years before, when he first got out of college. "I believe Marvin's real interests in nature and science should have led him to being a doctor," she wrote. "In reality, I think he would have been well suited to being a doctor, but he deferred his acceptance to Lower Fifth Avenue Medical School at the request of his father to just *try* the family business." (I've not been able to locate anything called the Lower Fifth Avenue Medical School.)

Cousin Debra: "The biggest crime is that my father, a trusting man, was betrayed by people close to him and will never be able to trust in the same way again."

Cousin Jeffrey: "His trust left him vulnerable to a few selfish individuals. It is so sad that a good man's good nature and trust led him to be taken advantage of and to find himself before the court."

Michael Pedone, President of Pedone & Partners, the ad agency that handles the Cumberland account: "[Marvin] has one major flaw of being overly trusting and his problems regarding his current situation, I believe, all emanate from the single flaw."

The New York Times from April 2, 1997: "Mr. Eisenstadt will only say he trusted Mr. Asaro, and did not know what he was doing."

Crain's New York Business from July 2, 2001: "Marvin has said that he trusted Mr. Asaro and didn't know what he was doing."

How can this be?

I have broken this down and written it out and obsessed over it, and in the end, I have come up with three possible explanations for what might have been going on at Cumberland:

One: Marvin was absent. Marvin had retired. He was spending and vacationing and enjoying while the business was being run by Joe Asaro and Gil and Mario Mederos. In this scenario, Cumberland was organized like a kingdom. Joe Asaro was the prime minister, Marvin was the prince regent. He did not notice the discrepancies in the books because he did not look at the books—that was not his role. He was the figurehead. He offered the comforting (to employees, to regulators, to bankers) illusion of continuity. He didn't fire the conspirators when he did learn of their crimes because he didn't think he could run the factory without them.

Two: Cumberland had been taken over by the Mafia. A man from the cleaning service threatens to blow up Marvin and put his house on fire. Marvin goes to see Joe Asaro, who, according to *The Washington Post*, had been identified as "an associate of the Bonanno crime family." Asaro makes the problem go away. Marvin gives him an office and a title and a salary, then can't get rid of him. Cumberland had been safe as long as it had a strong leader. But once Ben retired, the walls were breached. In addition to newspaper articles and testimony, this case is made by the atmosphere at the factory—the secret meetings and threats, hints of underworld presence everywhere. The very nature of the fraud was classic Mafia. Find a business that is strong in the books, weak at the top, infiltrate it and eat it from the inside: salaries, expenses, kickbacks. Have it build you a house, buy you a car. "Joseph Asaro, as you heard from the testimony of Mr. Petri, is a pretty tough hombre, a pretty tough fellow," Irving Anolik told the jury. "He told Petri, 'Remember this, you better listen to me, and if I get into a situation where I go to jail, I'll be coming out again, and I know where you live.' Petri was frightened. He was scared to death of this fellow, and I have a right to suggest that maybe other people were afraid of him."

Most telling was the prevalence at Cumberland of what the FBI calls "walk and talks." Businessmen taking meetings outdoors on the move. Walk and talk. It's how the target of an investigation gets away from a wiretap. Give orders fast and in motion, a hand over your mouth to guard against lip-readers. In *The United States v. James Ida*, aka "Jimmy," "Little Jimmy," "The Little Guy," in testimony heard on March 19, 1997, the government argued that so characteristic is the "walk and talk" of the Mafia, this behavior alone can suggest the involvement of organized crime. Asked to describe a "walk and talk," a member of the Gambino crime family said, "Where you don't want to be heard. Whoever you're meeting with, you walk around corners; walking in the street is a walk and talk. You talk as you're walking." If a few times a month, the vice president sticks his head into the office of the comptroller and says, *Hey, Gil, can we talk outside a minute?* then the Feds see them, through their binoculars, in threethousand-dollar suits, their crushed-leather loafers in the slush and ice, walking and talking, you can assume the mob is present.

Here's an exchange between federal prosecutor Richard Faughnan and Gerard Petri, the Cumberland plumber:

FAUGHNAN: In March of 1993, did there come a time when you had a conversation about that investigation with Gil Mederos?
PETRI: Yes, I met Mr. Mederos in his office.

FAUGHNAN: What did Mr. Mederos say to you?

PETRI: He asked me to go outside to speak to him. We went outside of building number two of Cumberland Packing, outside in the street. He asked me to make up a proposal, a contract for his house and post-date it for 1991, in the amount of $85,000 or so.

FAUGHNAN: Did he say anything else to you?

PETRI: Well, that he was kind of nervous about speaking inside of their office, that maybe they were bugged.

Marvin does not fire Joe Asaro or go to the Feds because Marvin is afraid. He is being held hostage. Yes, he is behind the wheel, but the bastard in the passenger seat has a gun to his head. In this scenario, the government comes to Cumberland Packing not as an enemy but as a SWAT team. The operation is painful and embarrassing but it saves the factory from the many-tentacled grasp of the Mafia.

Three: Marvin had not retired and was not ignorant; he had not been taken over and was not being threatened by mobsters. He was simply part of the scheme: robbing his own company and the IRS and enriching himself. (Leona Helmsley went to prison for less.) In court, the prosecutors did not emphasize Marvin's role because Marvin was a witness in the case against the Mederos brothers. He had pleaded guilty to tax evasion and agreed to cooperate with the prosecution. His role was not the focus of the case. But still, it's all there in the transcripts, the pieces of the puzzle just waiting to be assembled. Yes, there was the building bought and gutted by Joe Asaro and the Mederos brothers at East Fiftieth Street, but there were two other buildings bought and remade in the same way by Marvin Eisenstadt, one at 35 West Sixty-fifth Street, another on Sixty-ninth Street between First and Second avenues.* The contractors who did illegal personal work for Asaro and the Mederos brothers did the same sort of work for Marvin and Ben and Jeffrey. Work billed to the factory was

*Here is Prosecutor Richard Faughnan explaining it to the jury: "Around the same time that Gil and Mario Mederos and Joseph Asaro were using Cumberland money to renovate the East Fiftieth Street property, Marvin Eisenstadt, Cumberland's president, was also using Cumberland money to renovate two properties he owned in

done by contractors at Marvin's house in Rockaway, at Ben's house in Flatbush, and at Jeffrey's house in New Jersey. Betty called these workers "the Little Elves," a magical swarm of fixer-uppers that would descend from the factory to remodel the kitchen or bathroom.

In his testimony, Gerard Petri makes no distinction between the members of the Eisenstadt family and the members of the conspiracy: they are just names on a continuum. He said, "I worked at Mr. Asaro's house, Marvin Eisenstadt's house, who was president of Cumberland, Ben Eisenstadt's house. He's the father. I worked at Jeff Eisenstadt's house, the son. Shelly—I don't know his last name, an employee of Cumberland. I worked at Parsoo's, an employee of Cumberland. Mario Mederos's, Gil Mederos's house."

"I met Joseph Asaro at Beach 144th Street in Neponsit, New York," Petri later said. "Mr. Asaro asked me if I could fix a plumbing problem at that house."

Beach 144th Street in Neponsit is Marvin's house, so here you have a contractor phony-billing a job not for Asaro or for Mario or for Gil Mederos but for the president of the company, Marvin Eisenstadt. "He directed me to send [the invoice] to Cumberland Packing," said Petri. "I was paid with a check by Cumberland Packing."

In three years of work on family homes, Gerard Petri billed the company "approximately $170,000."

How was it done?

Here's Eric Vitale, the electrician, who said he did personal work for Marvin "a half dozen times."

VITALE: Asaro would call up and say, "Marvin needs some work done on his house."

ANOLIK: Did you know what kind of billing you were supposed to do on the work that you did for Marvin Eisenstadt on his house?

Manhattan. Eisenstadt did this with the knowledge, approval and assistance of Gil Mederos and Joseph Asaro. Joseph Asaro supervised contractors and instructed them to submit invoices to Cumberland Packing and Gil Mederos approved those invoices for payment with his Gil stamp."

VITALE: Yes. Basically, I would just bill Cumberland Packing.

ANOLIK: Did you ever do any work on any other Eisenstadt house?

VITALE: Yes. His son. Jeff Eisenstadt.

ANOLIK: And you billed?

VITALE: I billed the company.

This was the culture of Cumberland Packing. It was how things worked. The conspirators had merely picked up on that culture and played with it and distorted it and stretched it to its logical extreme. It's the culture of Little Elves and my Cumberland bar mitzvah check. "On occasion, I would deliver Sweet'N Low to a neighborhood drugstore or momma and poppa supermarket," Marvin told the jury, "and if they paid in cash, I kept the cash." There was no distinction between business and family, factory and house: the family was the business and the business was the family. For my mother, not being given an inheritance can therefore not be explained, as Marvin and Gladys tried to do, as a business decision: *Did your mother work at the factory? Then why should she get anything?* There is no such a thing as a business decision. The business is the family, and the blood of the family is money. This is what Joe Asaro and the Mario and Gil Mederoses understood: the factory and its money are ours to do with what we want.

Marvin probably did not know everything done by his underlings. They surely took advantage of the situation and carried it to extremes, so when my uncle expresses shock at their misdeeds he is probably telling the truth. He did trust too much. He expected these men to respect the careful balance, the acceptable parameters. Marvin might have had the Little Elves build a fence around his house or fix a leak in Flatbush, but he would never have had them build a McMansion. (Would he?) Asaro and the Mederos brothers had taken the grift and run it wild. Marvin knew the men were taking liberties, because that was the culture of the corporation, but had no idea the size of the liberties being taken. When Asaro and Marvin walked and talked, Marvin was genuinely appalled. Yet he was implicated: he himself had engaged in the same fraud. If he called the cops, he would just be calling the cops on himself. Instead he got together with the conspirators and fixed the books, or tried to fix the books. This "fix" took the form of a deal, the particulars of which read less like restitution than negotiation, a dividing up of the spoils.

The terms were worked out in Marvin's office, where my uncle met with Asaro, the Mederos brothers, and a lawyer named Joseph Dornbush, who had been the counsel of the conspirators. Dornbush is like a character out of Twain, a catfish grown meaty on the trash of the river trade. He set up the shell companies, did the filings that made Exim, Proteus, and Penultimate appear legal. He did personal work for the brothers and corporate work for their companies. The guy was so involved in the criminality at Cumberland Packing that he was indicted with the rest. He cut a deal and testified. The court censured him for professional misconduct, and for a time he was forbidden to practice law.* "Marvin Eisenstadt instructed Joe Dornbush to reverse, or to do what is necessary, to make everything legal,"† Asaro testified. "He put Dornbush in charge to straighten this mess out."

In doing so, Dornbush switched sides. He had been representing the Mederos brothers. He would now be representing Cumberland Packing. It's the middle of the game and the coach changes teams. Is this a conflict? Just whom did Dornbush work for? When he testified against the Mederos brothers, it was argued that because Dornbush had been their lawyer, he was violating their attorney-client privilege, guaranteed by the Sixth Amendment. To give this switch the appearance of legality, to cover his ass, though it did him little good, Dornbush wrote an agreement, which he then had Gil and Mario Mederos sign.

*He has since been reinstated and is currently in good standing in the State of New York.

†Asaro seems to mean that Dornbush was asked to alter the books, making it appear that the stolen money and property had been salary, or gifts from the company. By "reverse," he means something like "undo" or "rewrite."

1. I have represented each of you at various points in the past, however, I am only representing Cumberland Packing Corp. in connection with this transaction.
2. I have requested that each of you obtain your own attorney, however, you have refused to do so and have advised me that you to desire to proceed with the transaction without an attorney.
3. I have advised you that a potential conflict may exist and you hereby release me from any and all claims in connection with such a conflict and in connection with this transaction.

Marvin left it to Dornbush and the accountant Marc Schreck, who had done work for the shell companies (he would also be indicted), to hammer out the terms. They spent two or three days going through the records and invoices, separating the real from the fake.

"I instructed Joe Dornbush to go upstairs, out of my office—for some reason I just didn't want to know the details—with Gil, Mario, and Joe, and work out a deal that was fair to everybody to make Cumberland whole," Marvin testified.

"All three of us told the accountant Marc [Schreck] all the invoices were phony," Asaro testified. "No work was ever done here."

"After counseling Marvin with regard to what had transpired, he indicated that he did not wish to commence any civil proceeding," Dornbush told the court. "He did not wish to inform any governmental authorities or to have these gentlemen prosecuted. He did not want me to tell the other shareholders of the corporation, which are his family. Marvin's concern, as he said to me, was bad publicity for the product. He didn't want anything to affect the good name. He wanted to keep everything in house, and he retained me to, as he said, make a fair deal with the three individuals."

THE FAIR DEAL:
a. The building at 231 East Fiftieth Street would be given to Marvin Eisenstadt. Dornbush later said that the conspirators would be "turning over the Proteus property inventory to Marvin Eisenstadt

in exchange for Marvin Eisenstadt not firing them or going to the authorities about embezzlement of funds."

b. The money stolen by Joe Asaro and Mario and Gil Mederos would be reclassified as salary, loans, and gifts.

c. Cumberland would forgive all loans and gifts:
- $100,000 for Joe Asaro;
- $95,000 for Gil Mederos; and
- $120,000 for Mario Mederos.

d. As a result of this newly declared "income," the conspirators would owe thousands of dollars in taxes. Marvin agreed to pay these taxes and all other expenses incurred by the conspirators as a result of their crime. Marvin would give Joe Asaro seventy-five thousand dollars in cash, and the Mederos brothers around the same.

e. Gil Mederos would be given ownership of the company car he had been driving—a 1986 Mercedes.

f. Mario Mederos would be given cash value for the same car.

g. Gil Mederos would be made the chief shareholder of the Nine Kings Corp., a Navy Yard printing company (owned by Cumberland) that made the packets used by the factory.

h. Joe Asaro would be promoted and given a raise. In addition to being the factory's vice president of governmental affairs, he would also serve as an outside consultant. He had been making fifty thousand dollars a year. He would now make more than a million dollars a year.

In agreeing to this deal, Gil and Mario Mederos acted as if they were giving up something they were entitled to, something they had earned, and so wanted something in return. Even after the deal was struck, the brothers continued to press for better terms. "Gil and Mario came to me and actually pleaded poverty," Marvin testified. "They said that [231 East Fiftieth Street] was their only real asset and therefore it wouldn't really be fair if this was the whole deal because Fiftieth Street was worth much more than they were being given, and I made a subsequent deal with them."

The terms of the deal—as a result of their crime and confession, the conspirators actually appeared to benefit—seemed to confuse even the judge. You just can't study the particulars without thinking, "Marvin and these guys must have been partners all along," or, "These guys must have had something on Marvelous."

Here's a courtroom exchange between Irving Anolik and Joe Asaro:

ANOLIK: Shortly thereafter, you got an agreement to be hired for a million dollars a year as a consultant, is that correct?

ASARO: Yes, in 1989, my retainer was increased.

ANOLIK: They were so proud of you that they gave you a million dollar contract?

ASARO: I don't know if proud, I took more responsibility and I got a five year extension that I never had before, running all the international, and Marvin thought I should make more money.

ANOLIK: Even though you told Marvin you had been stealing from the company, that is correct?

ASARO: That's correct.

At one point, the testimony was interrupted by Judge Sterling Johnson:

JUDGE JOHNSON: Just a second. That's a big leap. I understand he was making $50,000 a year. And then I heard testimony that he was to be paid a million dollars.

ASARO: Not a salary. It was consulting.

JUDGE JOHNSON: Did you get a million dollars a year compensation?

ASARO: That's right, consulting.

JUDGE JOHNSON: Who agreed to pay you a million dollars a year?

ASARO: Marvin Eisenstadt.

JUDGE JOHNSON: Why did he agree to pay you that?

ASARO: Because he thought I was worth it. I produced.

And then, once the bad moment had passed, once the investigation that set off the confession and the deal seemed to be winding down, the shenanigans continued as before. "We stopped for a while," Asaro explained. "And then everything was quiet and so everything went back as usual."

The conspiracy picked up right where it left off. It was only *after* the confession and the deal that Gil Mederos built his house in Old Westbury. For this story to track, the conspirators had to cheat and hide and lie to Marvin, confess and pay back and "feel terrible," then — without Marvin noticing or checking the books, without Marvin having learned a single lesson — start cheating all over again. "As the ink on this agreement with Marvin Eisenstadt was drying," the prosecutor told the jury, "as the federal grand jury was just beginning to examine this tangled web of shell corporations, false invoices and diversions of corporate funds, the defendants and Joseph Asaro resumed their conspiracy."

22.

On February 23, 1993, twenty-four federal agents gathered outside of Cumberland Packing. They were divided into three assault teams, each consisting of eight members. At 8:30 a.m., the team leaders banged on the doors, flashed their warrants, and overran the factory. G-men raced down the corridors. Some carried handcuffs and side arms, some carried walkie-talkies and cameras, some wore jeans and windbreakers. On the factory floor, the ladies in hairnets looked up in confusion. *Hola, Marvin?* Agents blocked the exits and cut the phones. You could not get a call into the factory for three days. The hold music ("Sweet and low, sweet and low, wind of the Western seas") had been replaced by a recorded message.

Neil Gillon, an IRS agent who worked in Brooklyn as a member of the Business and Securities Crime Task Force, later explained the particulars of the raid: how each team was given a specific area of the factory to search, how agents went through all the closets and desks, examining and photographing. An agent named Allan Shurack searched the office of Gil

Mederos, where he seized ten thousand dollars in cash. "On the desk was foreign currency," he testified. "It was underneath a scale."

At some point, Gil Mederos sent a message to Amel Falcon, a sixty-eight-year-old Cuban-born maintenance man. Falcon later said Mederos told him "to go down to his office to pick up an envelope, so I could hide it for him." As Mederos handed over the envelope, he said, "It would be better for you if you don't look inside." Falcon then gave this envelope to his son, Alan Falcon, who was also a maintenance man at the factory. "Gil had given [my dad] the envelope to put away," Alan Falcon told the court. "Gil told him he would be better off not looking inside. My dad had another job, so I took the bag to our shop and opened it. [Inside were] corporate papers and ledgers and stocks, stuff like that. I put it in a black garbage bag and went upstairs with one of my workers, Jairo. We opened up a hole in one of the walls behind the window and put it back there and then I closed the wall up again."*

As I have said, there were two sets of books at Cumberland: the fake books and the real books. The real books were now inside the wall.

During the raid, the police booted Marvin out of his own office. A federal agent, while sitting at Marvin's desk, then interrogated the top officers of Cumberland. The office with the fish tank and the pictures of Barbara and the family had been turned into the headquarters of the takedown. What a blow! The scandal and the newspaper articles—that is not what broke my uncle. It was the federal agents kicking him out of his own office. Marvin had been waiting to occupy the big chair for his entire life. Ben finally steps aside, and it's seized by the Feds! This sent Marvin into the kind of exile from which you never return.

Why did the government go in with twenty-four agents? Why did they shut down the phones? Why did they go through the factory like Glen

---

*When Alan Falcon cut a deal, he turned over the hidden papers. "On a Saturday, I met the government at Cumberland and I took them up to the fourth floor and showed them where I had put the papers," Falcon testified. "I opened the wall and took the papers out. There were FBI agents and IRS agents. One of them was videotaping and the other one was standing next to me."

and Alice Zimring going through the drawers in their son Clay's room* looking for weed? Why were the doors locked? Why did the men with the guns linger? Why did they photograph everything? When Joe Asaro and Gil and Mario Mederos were arrested, why was bail set at a million dollars? What did the Feds think they would find? Why was this such a big operation?

For starters, Sweet'N Low is a world-famous product. The fact that you could wrap all these white-collar crimes in that magical phrase—Sweet'N Low—made the case sexy and possibly career-making for a young prosecutor. Such a prosecutor might say he is going after Sweet'N Low because Cumberland Packing has been engaged in criminality, or he might say that because Sweet'N Low is so well known, the prosecution will serve as a powerful deterrent to other corporate wrongdoers. But, really, the pink packet just made a swell target. "Once you develop that magical brand, nothing can touch you," Marvin told me. Well, this was the flip side of that coin: Sweet'N Low is a movie star, and as any hack from *The National Enquirer* can tell you, the only way to become a movie star is to kill a movie star.

Then there was the business with the Mafia. According to *The Washington Post*, "Asaro has been identified as an associate of the Bonanno crime family in a prosecution memo." Asaro's actual criminal history is, of course, irrelevant: the prosecutors *thought* he was a mobster working out of Cumberland, which made the factory, as far as they were concerned, part of the web of organized crime. The case against the factory may well have been a piece of a much larger case against the thugs who ran the waterfront. The federal agents went in heavy in hope of scaring the conspirators and causing some of them to panic and flip.

This is a theory. I can't prove it. Much of the information has been blacked out of the government documents. But I believe it to be true. Like most good theories, it makes sense of several otherwise senseless facts. Why did Marvin and Asaro serve no prison time? Why did the government go to such expense to prosecute Gil and Mario Mederos, in the

---

*A friend's big brother, a burnout who on more than one occasion came to blows with his father, a Chicago commodities trader who used to call me "Scrawny Ass."

process freeing Marvin Eisenstadt and Joe Asaro? Why, when Marvin Eisenstadt and Joe Asaro confessed, was there a delay in sentencing?

If the Cumberland investigation was part of a more ambitious prosecution, if the real targets were bigger, more mythical, and offscreen, the pieces fall together. Why no jail time for Asaro? Because Asaro was cooperating against his real bosses.

The other reason the Feds went in so heavy is shocking. I hear it in the voice of a high school friend explaining why a previously top-drawer student suddenly fell off the charts: *druuuuuuuugs!* Cumberland was suspected of trafficking cocaine. I heard this from prosecutors, from law enforcement officials, from defense attorneys. A late-night disc jockey told me that, when he used to buy crack in Harlem, it came in pink Sweet'N Low packets—he was probably on crack when he said this. I heard it from experts in narco traffic and waterfront crime. I heard it but thought I would never repeat it because it's so awful, because drugs are beyond the pale, because I had no real evidence.

Then, as a result of a Freedom of Information Act request, I received a document that surprised me. I had sent requests to the FDA, the Justice Department, the U.S. Customs Service, and the DEA asking for any information they had on Cumberland Packing, which, by law, they are required to turn over, and do turn over, slowly, with the majority of the good stuff blacked out. For the most part, the documents I got back were not very interesting: a report by the Health Department on infestation at the factory; a (minor) Sweet'N Low recall in 1993 because of discoloration caused by "nonviable mold;" a tampering case at a Shoney's in Cape Girardeau, Missouri.* I read each of these documents three or four times.

---

*A man ordered a salad and sweetened his ice tea with Sweet'N Low. When a waitress came to freshen his drink, she noticed that the tea had a "cloudy appearance." The man said the drink was fine and asked for a refill, to which he added still more Sweet'N Low, then noticed—because of sunlight coming through the window—that several packets of Sweet'N Low had been opened and resealed with Scotch tape. He was rushed to the hospital. He was running a fever and could not focus his eyes. Tests showed that the Sweet'N Low packets were filled with insect poison. According to the FBI, "a kind of poison used on tomato plants in backyard vegetable gardens." The agents got fingerprints off the tape, but did not pursue the case: they thought the victim had poisoned himself in hopes of generating a lawsuit. There had been a similar

Whole paragraphs had been blacked out. I held these passages to the light, or tried to feel the shape of the letters, like Braille. Nada. Nothing. Zero. But looking through an investigation report from the U.S. Customs Service, I noticed some sentences I had previously missed. Probably because they were scattered amid so much Magic Marker. As if the hand of the censor had slipped and I was seeing information meant to be hidden. It mentioned Cumberland and Nine Kings, the business then owned by Cumberland, that makes packets for the factory.

> Queries related to Cumberland Packing revealed the following results: [censored] revealed a Customs record for Cumberland Packing Corp with [censored] record identification number [censored]. This record shows the subject company as being suspected of money laundering and cocaine smuggling.

The operation of the company, with its tons of white powder, its mixing rooms, its packing machines, its worldwide distribution, would be perfect for shipping cocaine. This warrant gave new resonance to the testimony of the IRS agent Allan Shurack who talked about his search of Gil Mederos's office, during which he seized ten thousand dollars in cash, foreign currency, and a scale. When Ben died, *The New York Times* called him, "A Sweetener of Lives." *You bet!* When I asked Marvin about all this, he stammered and said, "Well, the Brooklyn—what they . . . what—the government initially thought that we were doing drugs at the Brooklyn Navy Yard, that these canisters of dextrose were really drugs. I mean I had this whole crazy thing. But all that was disproved.* But of course it was— it was terribly stressful for me, obviously. And I was embarrassed at my stupidity, and I swore that I wouldn't be a good guy anymore. In fact, I have a sign outside my office. It says, NO MORE MR. NICE GUY."

---

case at a Shoney's in Cookeville, Tennessee, where a woman put Sweet'N Low in her ice tea, said she felt sick, went to the bathroom, came back, drank more ice tea, then went to the hospital. She sued the restaurant for a quarter of a million dollars. The man in Cape Girardeau threatened to bring a lawsuit against Shoney's, but refused to take a polygraph test, then dropped the whole thing.

*As far as I can tell, no drugs were found as a result of the search.

23.

Marvin told me it was not really drugs the government was after. Nor was it false deductions, or McMansions, or corporate crime. It was Alfonse D'Amato, the (then) Republican senator from New York. D'Amato had done a lot for Cumberland over the years: Cumberland was a successful business in his state, a source of manufacturing jobs in an area bleeding such jobs. But the prosecutors wanted to prove that D'Amato had been bought. They wanted to kill his career, and so make careers of their own. The case against Cumberland was, suggested Marvin, just an elaborate effort to nail the senator. "I don't have a high regard for the government," Marvin told me. "They wanted me to put dirt on D'Amato, even if it was true or not true. If we did that, they would forget about us." It was this relationship (senator, factory boss, and the man employed by the boss to influence the senator) that generated the eye-catching headlines. Without D'Amato, the scandal would have been one of those middle-of-the-paper business stories clipped by the researcher who does legwork for Elmore Leonard. With D'Amato, it became part of a running scandal picked up by newspapers around the country.

Alfonse D'Amato had been described on a wiretap as a guy "on the take," "a guy you can relate to." (This was during Abscam, the federal investigation in which FBI agents, dressed as Arabs, tried to bribe elected officials.) When D'Amato won his first statewide primary, a victory party was thrown for him at a nightclub in Island Park, Queens. It was the sort of place where you go in search of New York types, wiseguys and torpedoes two deep at the bar, saying stuff like *Shut up, I wanna hear da broad sing!* The owner of the club, Philip Basile, served as the master of ceremonies. He was a "close associate" of Paul Vario, a Lucchese family captain known on the street as "Big Paulie," the real Paulie behind the movie Paulie played by Paul Sorvino in *Goodfellas.* In 1983, when Basile was indicted for conspiracy and racketeering, D'Amato, then a U.S. senator, was the only character witness at his trial. He called Basile "honest, truthful, hardworking, a man of integrity." Basile had himself gotten a drug dealer out of prison: Henry Hill, played in the same movie by Ray Liotta. In 1986, Mark Green, a Democratic candidate for Senate, said D'Amato had "a pattern of receiving gifts from members of organized crime."

Green also said, "His vote was for sale."*

According to the defunct *New York Newsday,* "Dozens of contractors and garbage haulers contributed to the 1980 [D'Amato] campaign. More than thirty of these [contributors], from whom D'Amato accepted more than $30,000, have since been indicted or sued by state or county officials for allegedly profiting illegally from public projects."

Such information appeared regularly in the New York newspapers, where tracking D'Amato's misdeeds became a kind of whale watching. In articles—because of his name (Al-*fonse*), because of his swagger, because of the sting operation in which he and his friend Rudolph Giuliani dressed as "drug users," Giuliani in a leather vest, D'Amato in an oversized coat, a baseball cap, and aviator shades, D'Amato was known as "The Fonz." In the 1980s, while Giuliani, then the U.S. Attorney for the Southern District of New York, was waging a war against organized crime, D'Amato placed a few calls that make you think of shady doings

---

*I owe a reporting debt to *Senator Pothole, The Unauthorized Biography of Alfonse D'Amato,* by Leonard Lurie (Secaucus, N.J.: Carol Publishing Group, 1994).

in some below-ground, smoke-filled social club. In those calls, D'Amato, according to *The Village Voice*, asked Giuliani to go easy on Mario Gigante and Paul Castellano, gangsters who were being prosecuted by the Southern District.* If you are not familiar with mob lore, it's hard to convey the menace of these names. D'Amato at first denied the entire incident. "I never called anyone about it," he told the *Daily News* in 1989. "I never heard of it." Because this seemed ridiculous, he then said, okay, yes, he had made the calls, but only to address "the concerns of community leaders." He then told a reporter that he had called Giuliani just to pass on a plea for leniency from Louis Gigante, brother of Mario Gigante. "I am concerned about the fairness of the sentence," he explained. "And I hoped I could convey that. I never asked Mr. Giuliani to do anything to affect the outcome."

When his actions were described as "naïve," D'Amato said, "I accept that. I'm not happy with this. Hindsight is a wonderful teacher."

"Would any other senator have lifted a finger, much less made calls, to help two leaders of organized crime, like Paul Castellano and Mario Gigante?" asked Mark Green at the time. "Senator D'Amato says he was innocent and uninformed. You don't make a phone call to help a convicted felon unless you know who he is and why you're calling. He claimed that he didn't know who Paul Castellano was. It's like a public leader saying he doesn't know who John Gotti is. Assume that's true. Then why did he make the call? D'Amato's answer is that a lawyer asked him to do it. Well, who was the lawyer? D'Amato's answer: Roy Cohn. Roy Cohn is not any old Cohn. He is the sleaziest lawyer of the modern era. Which is documented by his disbarment by the New York Bar in 1987."

In America, there are two types of politicians, two species. The good-looking and the ugly, the coiffed and the uncombed. By good-looking I do not mean handsome. I mean put-together. I mean built for a life before

---

*The article, which appeared in *The Village Voice* on October 25, 1989, was written by Dan Collins, who had gotten the scoop while interviewing Giuliani for a proposed biography.

the cameras. Such politicians trail a cloud of hairspray. Get too close with an open flame and they go up like flash paper. POOF! They exist within the context of no context chronicled by George Trow in his book of that name, in the make-believe world of television. They are either homey politicians in the way of the TV show *Matlock* (Lindsey Graham), tough politicians in the way of *Law & Order* (Rudy Giuliani), or deep-down decent politicians in the way of *The West Wing* (Al Gore). As Hemingway said of the cardboard books in the Sherry Netherland Hotel in New York, "Phony, just like the town."* With such politicians, you wonder if their colorful backgrounds are really just backstory cooked up by a hack on contract at Warner Bros. Turn them ninety degrees and they disappear.

The ugly politician, on the other hand, reeks of the real. He is the creation of a particular neighborhood or block, the product of a long local history of crime and deals. As a rule, politicians of this type, because they cannot skate across the camera lens, need some special skill. For Mario Cuomo, it was the soaring rhetoric. For Paul Simon, the big-eared senator from my own state, it was the aura of integrity. For Al D'Amato, it was the street sense and the knowledge of how things actually get done. Fonzy knows politics as the tough knows the high school hallway. He was not our senator: we were his people. He chose us. He was the image of city politics, the art of give-and-take. His hair was combed over, his skin as pale as a snake's belly. He had the lazy-eyed look of the bully the moment before he delivers the charley horse. Even in photos, he is so real you can smell the Barbasol. He was elected to the Senate in 1980, reelected in 1986. The longer he stayed, the more power he amassed. The more power he amassed, the better his ability to deliver. The better his ability to deliver, the longer he stayed. It's the song of the system, the whirr of the fake rabbit as it whips around the dog track.

D'Amato took questionable contributions, and he took contributions over the legal limit. He was accused of rigging bids for government housing contracts that, according to *The Wall Street Journal*, were then awarded to his friends from Queens. He took thirty grand in contribu-

*This quote comes from the great Lillian Ross profile of Hemingway that appeared in *The New Yorker* in May 1950.

tions from Wedtech, then helped that company score a fifty-five-million-dollar contract to build an artificial harbor. While preparing to introduce a bill on junk bonds, he was feted by Michael Milken's Drexel Burnham Lambert, the company that mastered the junk bond. His brother Armand D'Amato was convicted on seven counts of mail fraud for using Fonzy's office to raise $120,000 illegally from a company that sought the senator's influence. At times, it appeared the senator made his action on legislation conditional on a favor or a contribution. In 1986, Al Sharpton endorsed D'Amato for reelection. A month later, Sharpton won a half-million-dollar grant for his National Youth Movement. "It's raw, distasteful," a lobbyist told *Time* magazine in 1995. "Al's guys reach right through the phone and say, 'We're helping you, you have to help us.'"

The Senate Ethics Committee investigated sixteen allegations against D'Amato. Twenty-five of the fifty-six witnesses took the Fifth. The committee ruled that Senator D'Amato had "conducted the business of his office in an improper and inappropriate manner" by allowing his brother to use it for personal business. They dropped the other charges and let him off with a lecture. "D'Amato operates within the law but goes up to the very edge," Bert Neuborne, a law professor at NYU, told *The New York Times*. "He understands power and the way politicians can wield power and the relationship between politics and power and money. He doesn't break the law. He understands it and exploits it to the very edge."

For years, D'Amato hosted a poker game in his government office every Thursday night. Most of the players were lobbyists with legislation before the Senate, including a man on the payroll of Cumberland Packing. A story about the game ran on the front page of *The New York Times* on October 26, 1995, under the headline "High-Stakes Poker Put Lobbyists Close to D'Amato's Ear." On the senator's calendar these games, marathons that often went into the early morning, were listed as "The Fellas." "They ate Chinese food, smoked expensive cigars and told bawdy stories into the night over pots that reached hundreds of dollars," according to *The New York Times*.

One of these lobbyists told my friend Burke that, yes, a game could go on all night, yes, the Fellas sometimes ate Chinese food, but more often D'Amato had corned beef and pastrami shipped in from a deli in New

York; and yes, the senator tended to win. "Alfonse was an extraordinarily lucky card player." According to *The New York Times*, D'Amato did indeed take most of the big pots, the implication being, I think, that the games were a back door through which a lobbyist could kick the Fonz some extra green. The air filled with cigar smoke and corned beef steam. D'Amato talking big as the lobbyists lose—American politics in action. They played six and seven card games, variations of Stud, Draw, and Hold 'Em. They called one of these games Seven Card D'Amato, a pretty good name for the bigger game D'Amato had been playing since he first entered politics.

The saccharin ban and the moratorium on that ban, which came up for renewal every two years, had dogged Cumberland since 1977. It had to be managed at great expense, with nonstop lobbying, fund-raising, and glad-handing. The factory officers had worked the political process into their routine, like sealing the boxes or stirring the mix or performing quality control. In the course of this process, Ben and Marvin participated in a behavior characteristic of the modern corporation: they gave to both sides, Democrat and Republican, incumbent and challenger. A bet placed on neither black nor red, but on the continued existence of the casino itself, or on the system that underlies the casino. That way, even when you lose, you win.

When the scandal broke, the newspapers printed a list of politicians to whom Cumberland had contributed money through third parties, violating the prohibition against corporate donations.

- Senator Lloyd Bentsen: $10,000
- Senator Quentin Burdick: $30,000
- The Bush-Quayle campaign: $7,000
- Senator Bob Dole: $10,000
- Congresswoman Geraldine Ferraro: $9,000
- Congressman Thomas Manton: $31,000
- Various Democratic and Republican campaign committees: $69,000

By the 1980s, the focus of Cumberland's lobbying had become Alfonse D'Amato. Partly because D'Amato was from New York and so had a legitimate interest in protecting the factory, partly because, as the man told the fake Arab during Abscam, D'Amato was "on the take." To deal with the senator, Marvin promoted Joe Asaro to the office of vice president of governmental affairs.

This contractor, this Sicilian-born construction worker, who in a few years, had climbed the beanstalk—what were his qualifications? Connections. He knew everybody, could handle anything. If you are Marvin, if you are banned but still alive, you need a guy who can get to the guy who can fix the thing that causes the pain. "He did protect us with his influence," Marvin told me. "I don't know how he did it. I guess he paid everything off with our money. But I was unaware of this."

ANOLIK: What was your title?

ASARO: Vice president of governmental affairs.

ANOLIK: What governmental affairs were you involved in?

ASARO: Well, see, in 1978, the government, the FDA, banned saccharin. And the government, prior to me getting involved with Cumberland, the moratorium, other people did it before me, and then I got involved in 1982. So I handled that to make an extension on saccharin every two years.

ANOLIK: Were you registered as a lobbyist in Washington?

ASARO: No.

ANOLIK: Well, what impact did you have with the government?

ASARO: Well, I knew a lot of politicians. Besides, I had lobbyists working for me in Washington. Former Congressman Leo Zeferetti. I had another lobbyist, Bruce Ray.* I knew Leo Zeferetti for many years when he was in Congress. His father came from the same home town I came from in Sicily, and I was very friendly with him.

Through Asaro, Marvin connected the factory to the vast network that

*Bruce Ray had previously worked as Senator D'Amato's legislative director.

runs just beneath the system, the subterranean grid where politics and business and crime overlap, where things get done. By having Asaro handle the ban, Marvin also maintained what the spooks call "plausible deniability." *I don't know how he did it. I guess he paid everything off with our money. But I was unaware of this.* Marvin was like the head of the record label who hands a promoter a bag of cash and says, "I don't want to know how you do it. I don't care. Just get the song on the radio."

In 1995, as the scandal was breaking, Doreen Carvajal profiled Asaro in *The New York Times* under the headline: "Executive's Social Acumen Masked His Political Agenda":

> The owners of [Cumberland] were particularly pleased with Mr. Asaro's po-
> litical skills after he arranged a personal introduction with President Reagan.
> Company officials were also impressed when Mr. Asaro escorted several
> Congressional visitors to the plant, including Representative Geraldine Fer-
> raro. Martin Auerbach, a lawyer representing the company, said, "This is a
> man who, despite his humble origins, was a very effective communicator. I
> think he really had the appeal of a self-made man. I think that people in
> Washington respond to that."

For Asaro, there was one big challenge: once you have gotten to the key politicians, how do you give them the kind of money that makes a difference without running afoul of the campaign-financing laws?

Two bedrock rules had to be skirted. First, corporations are banned from any political giving. Second, private citizens are limited to gifts of a thousand dollars per candidate per election. Because the second rule had been broken so often, Congress added an amendment. "No person shall make a contribution in the name of another person, or knowingly permit his name to be used to effect such a contribution, and no person shall knowingly accept a contribution made by one person in the name of another person."*

The scheme Asaro came up with is so common—no one said he was

---

*See *Campaign Finance Reform: A Sourcebook,* edited by Anthony Corrado, Thomas E. Mann, Daniel R. Ortiz, Trevor Potter, and Frank J. Sorauf (Washington, D.C.: Brookings Institution Press, 1997).

an original thinker—that the Federal Election Commission has given it a name: bundling. Since the company itself could make no contribution, and since the most a private individual could give was a thousand dollars, Asaro went from family to family (Asaro, Mederos, Eisenstadt) gathering from many members a personal check for a thousand dollars. When the papers printed a list of D'Amato's contributors, it included Ben Eisenstadt, Marvin Eisenstadt, and Gladys Eisenstadt.

Asaro also went to the contractors and the suppliers in business with the factory, gathering from many a personal check for a thousand dollars. When Asaro had gathered thirty or so of these dog-eared, grease-stained checks, he rubber-banded them into a bundle, which he handed to Senator D'Amato's office as if it were a single contribution from Cumberland Packing. In this way, D'Amato and the other politicians Cumberland gave to were able to maintain their innocence. Each donation had been a legitimate, below-the-limit personal check.

Up to this point, Cumberland itself had broken only the spirit of the law. The line was crossed when the contractors and the suppliers, who, at the insistence of Asaro, had written checks to Senator D'Amato and other politicians, entered these contributions on their invoices, in a phony way, as work never done, and were then reimbursed by the factory—the same method that Asaro and the Mederos brothers were using to fix up their houses and reimburse the contractors for kickbacks. It might have been a hundred personal checks, but in the end all of the money came from Cumberland, which violated rule number one: corporations cannot contribute. The mechanics of the scheme—"I asked the contractors to submit false invoices and to use the difference to make contributions," Asaro testified—violated the amendment to rule two.

According to *Newsday*, "Cumberland and people associated with the company contributed $76,500 to Sen. Alfonse D'Amato."

According to *The Los Angeles Times*, "Over $200,000 dollars was drained from the company using a false invoice scheme."

According to *The Associated Press*, "The maker of Sweet'N Low pleaded guilty to funneling more than $200,000 in illegal contributions to political campaigns to try to head off a ban on saccharin, the sugar substitute's key ingredient."

The object of all this giving was not merely to secure the continuation of the moratorium on the ban but also to get the length of each moratorium extended, then, it was hoped, to get the ban lifted altogether. In 1987, D'Amato did indeed sponsor legislation that changed the parameters of the moratorium, which had come up for renewal every two years. It would now be reviewed every five years, an adjustment worth far more than the seventy or so thousand dollars Cumberland had funneled to the senator. Of course, there is no way to prove quid pro quo. Maybe D'Amato really did think that a review every two years was wrong, the way Jim Crow was wrong. But all that maneuvering fit a pattern the senator had established in the course of his career: you pay, you play. I laugh when people say the system does not work. Of course the system works. It works beautifully.

24.

In the spring of 1993, Marvin Eisenstadt, Joe Asaro, and several other Cumberland Packing employees and contractors were arrested and charged with tax evasion and criminal conspiracy by the U.S. Attorney's office for the Eastern District of New York. The real news came a few years later, in the spring of 1995, when many of the conspirators pleaded guilty: Marvin Eisenstadt to "knowingly filing false tax returns and conspiring to impair the operations of the Internal Revenue Service"; Joe Asaro to "one count of conspiracy to defraud the Internal Revenue Service, one count of causing false documents to be filed with the Federal Election Commission, and one count of witness tampering."* Because this story had so many great tabloid elements (Sweet'N Low, a family for-

---

*As reported in *The New York Times*, April 13, 1995. This article ("Guilty Plea on Donations to Politician") went on to say: Marvin Eisenstadt "could receive a prison term of up to six years and a fine of $500,000"; "the Cumberland corporation pleaded guilty to one count of conspiracy to defraud the Internal Revenue Service and agreed to pay a fine of $2 million." "[Joe] Asaro could receive up to 20 years in prison and a fine of $750,000."

tune, kickbacks, indictments) it broke big, and was reported in, among other places, *The Wall Street Journal*, the New York *Daily News*, the *New York Post*, *The Washington Times*, and *The New York Times*.

On April 12, 1995, the story appeared on *ABC World News Tonight*, the martial theme music fading to a shot of Peter Jennings, who introduced reporter Catherine Crier, who told the story of the Cumberland scandal over a series of images: the boat that took Asaro and some of his supporters on a cruise around Manhattan; a document said to connect Asaro to the Bonanno crime family; a shot of D'Amato; a shot of Asaro with D'Amato; a shot of the factory in Fort Greene; a shot of the warning label on the Sweet'N Low packet; a shot of records compiled by the Federal Election Commission. D'Amato denied his involvement in the scandal the same way he had tried to deny making the phone call for Paul Castellano and Mario Gigante. He told the press he knew nothing about any illegal contributions from Asaro. ABC followed this denial with a clip from a video made in 1989 at a fund-raiser for a charity established by Asaro called the Foundation for a Brighter America. On the video, D'Amato introduces Joe Asaro, saying, "My friends, I am privileged to present to you our friend, our host, our benefactor, the benefactor to so many good causes, Joe Asaro."

For D'Amato, it was the beginning of the end of his life as a politician with a future. (He lost his next Senate election to Charles Schumer.) The scandal somehow embodied all the others. I went back and looked at what else was going on with D'Amato as the scandal broke; it was a bad week. He had been spotted in public with Claudia Cohen, the New York socialite. It was said that he loved Claudia Cohen but her parents did not want their daughter running around with the goyim. He was catching hell for his appearance on the radio show *Imus in the Morning*, during which he had done an off-color World-War-II–era-Jap (*me so sowwy*) imitation of Judge Lance Ito, who was then presiding over the O. J. Simpson trial. In the middle of the week, he checked into St. Francis Hospital complaining of chest pains.

In her column in the *New York Post*, Cindy Adams wrote:

Al D'Amato's chest pains weren't from a heart attack. They were from heartache. Heartache over being in love with a woman whose parents don't approve of him. Heartache from the woman's ex-hubby who's threatening a nasty custody fight over religion. Heartache from upstate voters who don't like his new brand of Catholicism. There has been lots of speculation since D'Amato was hospitalized about all the stress he has been under recently. There have been Japanese insults, investigations, elections and his father's recent stroke.

It was a strange time. I was working at *The New York Observer*, a newspaper printed, once a week, on pink paper. When the scandal broke, a fellow reporter, who never did like me because I was young and maybe not very smart, looked at me in a knowing way, as if this new information—that my uncle was apparently mixed up with the mob and with the Fonz—finally explained just who I was and just where I came from: D'Amato, Bonanno, saccharin. It was unpleasant, but also a thrill. I was learning about the world, how, when the jackals suspect cancer, whether you have cancer or not, they will find its evidence everywhere.

It must have been hell for Ben. His family was a mess, one daughter estranged, one daughter housebound, one son absent, one son indicted. The factory was all he had. It was his life and legacy. Now it was being dragged through the mud. Even worse, Marvin was intimating—to me and my parents, anyway—that he was taking a hit for the old man. When I asked my mother if she thought Ben had been involved in the conspiracy, she thought for a moment, then said, "Grandpa once told me and your father a story: Grandpa started delivering newspapers when he was seven years old. His father died when he was eight. One day, he took something from a porch. I don't know what it was. And his father marched him back there and made him ring the bell and tell those people, 'I stole something from you.' That's why I don't think my father would do anything like what Marvin said. Because he always remembered that story. He followed a code. He believed in right and wrong."

Soon after the scandal broke, Gladys called my mother in a panic. "That's when Gladys and I became friends again," said my mother.

Gladys said, "Marvin is in trouble."

Gladys said, "Marvin might be going to jail."

Gladys said: "Marvin came over in the middle of the night. He had a hundred thousand dollars in cash. He said, 'Hide it because they're going to search my house.'"

"I did not want my brother to end up in jail," my mother told me. "I had no desire for that. I talked to your father. We both felt, hey, if we could help Marvin, we would. I sent your father to New York to speak to Marvin."

Herbie: "Why did I go? Was it because I was nosy? Yes. Yes. Yes. It's a big weakness I have. Curiosity. Being very curious. It's my problem. And your mother asked me. She said, 'Marvin could go to prison, and this would be terrible.'

"So I called the factory. I talked to Marvin. I said, 'Maybe I can help.' He says, 'Oh, thank you.' And I went over there."

My father took the Delta Shuttle to LaGuardia and hired a town car for the drive to the factory. The streets, the stoops, the Dumpsters, the alleys—he had not made this trip in twenty years. Marvin met him on the curb. The factory reared up behind him like a monster. The machines rattled, the walls shook. It never stops. Marvin gave one of his jaunty waves. At such a moment, such a greeting is an act of courage. Herbie was witnessing his brother-in-law's disaster. "Marvin was nervous," my father told me. "He was complaining about the government and what they had done to him. He told me that in one year the company had made some astronomical amount of money in profit. He said, 'We worked our ass off all these years and now we have a windfall and we deserve it and did not feel that we should be paying it all to the government.'

"I listened to this and I didn't say anything."

"He told me how the government had ransacked the place, took the files away. How they closed the factory for three days. He told me that he was really taking the rap for his father and that Ben knew everything.

"He said, 'Well, what do you think I should do?'

"I said, 'Let's go outside. I want to smoke a cigar.'"

Before my father made this trip, he had come to the conclusion that the factory might be bugged. If you are going to say anything you don't want read in court, he told himself, go out in the street.

So Herbie let Marvin talk and talk for the microphones, then, when it was time to answer, he reached into his bag, pulled out a Cohiba, and said, "Let's go outside. I want to smoke."

Walk and talk!

If you live long enough, you see everything. You see Marvin the millionaire prince and you see Marvin hunted by the Feds. "Well, maybe your father did try to help me, but I had my own counsel," he told me. "And I was very, very, very embarrassed about the whole thing, 'cause I was so stupid about how I had trusted these people. I was embarrassed and I didn't want his help."

"No, Marvin did not want our help," said my mother. "He was in with some very bad people. My father at that point was eighty-four, eighty-six. I cannot believe he knew about it even though my brother wanted us to know that he was protecting our father."

"So we went outside and I smoked," said Herbie. "I said, 'Look, Marvin, get yourself a good fuckin' lawyer.' I said, 'Get a lawyer involved in the federal system. A prestige guy. A guy like Arthur Liman. A guy who's had many cases, who knows the inside players. This is very serious. You got to recognize the potential and be careful.' And that was all I said to him."

25.

I started researching this story in earnest shortly before my first son was born, but I have always known I would write it. (I have been writing it in my head my entire life.) It tacked on my horizon like a yacht. I studied the old patents and the newspaper articles archived in the New York Public Library. I stared at the pictures of Ben and Marvin that ran with these stories. I examined photos in old family albums. I talked to defense lawyers and lobbyists and scientists and prosecutors. My mother gave me copies of the will, family letters, and legal correspondence. It is a personal story, a version of which exists in the head of every member of the family, yet in just a few months of research it generated a mountain of paper. I sent away to a federal record center in Georgia for all the boxes and files on the Cumberland prosecution, which I examined over several days at a building in Manhattan. If I had been an anonymous reporter, I would have thought, "Gold mine!" As it was, I felt like a stalker lurking in the weeds behind my uncle's house.

I interviewed Marvin and Gladys. I interviewed my sister, who, because she is older than I, refers to our mother as "my mother" and our father as "my father," as in "my mother had a difficult relationship with my grandfather," causing in me a sensation that is not entirely unpleasant. I interviewed my parents, the red light of my tape recorder glowing like an eye. After leading me through a well-crafted narrative, my father said, "I urge you to be suspicious of everything I say." I called my uncle Ira, the youngest child of Betty and Ben. Ira said yes, he would talk to me, but not now. Because he had to take care of the cats. He told me to call back later, when his wife was in town. When I did so, he said, "Sorry, still can't talk. Cats." I called my cousin Jeffrey. To me, Jeffrey is the summer and surfing, and I had this idea that when I called he would invite me to his house in New Jersey and we would sit on lawn chairs and drink cervezas and talk about the family and stare at our toes. In his slurry way, he would say, "So that's how it was, Viking Cohen." Then we would go surfing. As we sat on our boards, rising and falling on the tide, he would talk about the wind and the temperature of the water, using his hands to demonstrate the curl and break of a wave, in the same way that Ben once spoke about his idea for a packing machine. So here you would have these two pictures—Ben in the factory; Jeffrey on the waves, riding an ocean that, to his ancestors, had been nothing but a terrible obstacle—that, taken together, would capture the entire arc of our history, not just the family history but American history, the move from heavy industry to the economy of fun. But when I called Jeffrey, he blew me off even more efficiently than Ira had. Jeffrey said he could not meet me because he never comes to the city. Then, when I said, "Great, I will come see you," he said, "Well, you see, I can't because I'm in the city almost every day."

I often felt the thrill of a private detective. When you uncover the crucial piece of hidden information, the charge pops in your brain like a whippit and you cannot wipe the stupid smile off your face. My research was full of such moments. I kept coming across creepy details buried in the documents. It's addictive. The more you find, the more you want to find. I had become an obsessive repeat watcher of the David Lynch movie *Blue Velvet*, in which the hero explains why, at great risk to himself, he tries to unravel a conspiracy. "I am seeing something that was always hidden," he says. "I am involved in a mystery. I am learning. And it's all secret." I clipped a passage from the Walker Percy novel *Lancelot* that captured my mood perfectly:

> I can only compare it to the time I discovered my father was a crook. It was a long time ago. I was a child. My mother was going shopping and had sent me up to swipe some of his pocket money from his sock drawer. For a couple of years he had a political appointment with the insurance commission with a "reform" administration. He had been accused of being in charge of parceling out the state's insurance business and taking kickbacks from local agencies. Of course we knew that could not be true. We were an honorable family. We had nothing to do with the Longs. We may have lost our money, Belle Isle was half in ruins, but we were an honorable family with an honorable name. Much talk of dirty politics. Maury, I *told* you not to get into it! (my mother). The usual story of the honorable man besmirched by dirty politicians. The honor of the family won out and even the opposition gave up. So I opened the sock drawer and found not ten dollars but ten thousand dollars stuck carelessly under some argyle socks.
>
> What I can still remember is the sight of the money and the fact that my eyes could not get enough of it. There was a secret savoring of it as if the eye were exploring it with its tongue. When there is something to see, some thing, a new thing, there is no end to seeing. Have you ever watched onlookers at the scene of violence, an accident, a killing, a dead or dying body in the street? Their eyes shift to and fro ever so slightly, scanning, trying to take it all in. There is no end to the feast.
>
> At the sight of the money, a new world opened up for me. The old world fell to pieces—not necessarily a bad thing. *Ah, then, things are not so nice*, I said to myself.

26.

Where was Ben?

This question arises naturally. Because, in these years, when Cumberland, the reputation of which mattered greatly to my grandfather, was coming to be known in law enforcement circles as a dark planet, Ben was going into the factory only two or three days a week. Maybe he could not stand to see what had become of his company: taken over and strip-mined by hooligans.

As Ben aged, he looked more and more the way he had always looked in my mind: gaunt, otherworldly. Time stripped away the inessential, revealing his true face. He looked like the old Tolstoy, an insane mystic, emitting old-man smell like a radar signal from beyond. He looked like a guy we called the Bird Man, who used to go through the public trash bins in my town. It was all about longevity. Outlive the bastards. Survive. He went on and on. A bad driver at forty, he was still driving at eighty-five. To me, he is a mystery, a shadow. What did he care about? What did he want? He loved Betty. That you can see even in pictures taken when both of them were very old. My grandfather hugs my grandmother in some of these pictures, and she looks so fragile as she smiles and grabs the flesh under his chin. He wanted a simple life. A piece of grapefruit. Something sweet in his tea. And he did not want to be bothered, and did not want to hear his children fighting. Mostly he wanted Betty to be happy. But Betty wanted a lump sum. And that fueled everything.

Did Ben know about the dirty dealings at the factory, the graft and the illegal campaign contributions and the phony tax returns? Marvin told me that it was Ben who hired Asaro, and he sometimes gave the impression that he had cooperated with the prosecutors to protect his father. Ben did have work done on his house billed to Cumberland. And his name did turn up in the evidence. But I think Ben's graft was small-time. He dipped into the corporate accounts the way he might have dipped into the cash register at the cafeteria when Betty had seen something nice in a window on Avenue M. By the time Ben might have realized that Avenue M in Flatbush led to St. Andrews Court in Guyland, he was too old to do much about it. Too many decisions had been made, or left unmade. In some sense, the corporate scandal was the result of certain family dynamics put into play many decades before, the outcome of the immigrant longing and immigrant fear: the death of Abie, the sorrow of Bubba, the shame of Betty. The weakness that led Marvin to rely on (or trust or conspire with) Joe Asaro is the result of her "love is finite" parenting style. There had always been someone to throw a sheet over the tank when the fish started to die. Because Ben grew up without a family and did not understand the ways of family life, he left the domestic politics to Betty. I think he realized his mistake in the end. You see this in pictures taken of him after the factory had been raided. His eyes are filled with a question he cannot bring himself to answer. He radiates sadness and confusion, the melancholy of the boy who has spent a summer day building a sand castle only to see the battlements collapse with the first wave of the new tide.

The father of a girl I once dated told me his goal was to have it said at his funeral, "Here lies a man who got fifteen pounds into a ten pound sack." Well, that was Ben. Not a bad goal, really. But it kept him working long after he should have retired. When Ben finally did step aside, it was too late. Marvin had been kept waiting too long; he had become a kind of man-child. The wall was quickly breached and the scum of the Yard

flowed in. Ben, too old and too weak to fight, retired deeper into Brooklyn. He spent his final years as a fund-raiser and an administrator at Maimonides Medical Center, engaged in the sort of philanthropic work that bleaches away the stain of scandal.

Ben started at Maimonides as a patient. In the late 1970s, he was admitted suffering from an intestinal virus and exhaustion. He was seventy years old and working five days a week. As he recovered, the gears started to turn. That's what it means to be alive, the hum that tells you the machine is up and running. He noticed that the hospital was understaffed. Over the next decade, he made the hospital his cause. On August 23, 1987, *The New York Times* ran an article headlined "Hospital Patient Becomes Its Patron":

> Mr. Eisenstadt was recuperating in Maimonides when a junior administrator stopped at his bedside for a chat, and Mr. Eisenstadt announced, "You people here need help."

Maimonides* is the sort of second-tier hospital where you go for

---

*The hospital is named after the Jewish sage Maimonides, a royal physician to the king of Egypt who, in 1190, wrote *The Guide for the Perplexed*. I happen to know a lot about him because he was the subject of my bar mitzvah speech. I know, for example, five stitches, or else to die. Ben wanted to remake it into a world-class destination. He was soon working there three days a week. For Maimonides, Ben must have been like manna from heaven. He raised funds and interviewed personnel and helped build new facilities. He invested the hospital's money, guaranteeing any losses out of his own pocket. He donated a million dollars to start the Maimonides Research and Development Foundation. He took out a life insurance policy and named Maimonides as the beneficiary. He gave another million dollars to start a nursing school. He was a member of the board of directors and later became its president.* "I'm not a religious man in the conventional sense, because religion depends usually on the family into which you happen to be born," he told the *Times*. "But when I got to be about 65, I said to myself: 'Mr. Eisenstadt, you have made quite a bit of money. This community has been good to you. If there is a God, he put you in this world for a reason.' Am I here to have a good time? The most pleasure I get is from helping other people. I can't solve all the world's ills. But . . ."

One afternoon in July, on the hottest day of the year, with the sky going green at the fringes, I went to Maimonides to talk to Edna Palozzolo, who had worked for my grandfather and is now president of the research foundation. I had clipped the notice Edna placed in the newspaper when Ben died:

---

that Maimonides wore a turban, and wrote parts of the Talmud and Midrash. He believed there were two Bibles, one on the page for everyone to read, and another hidden in a code that could be understood only by an elite. Most of my speech had actually been written by my father, including the line, "Can there be such a thing as a holy hermit?" I guess the idea was that to be holy, you have to get mixed up in the ugliness of the world.

*An interesting source on the hospital is a book written by Dr. Joseph Estrin (with Barry P. Moskowitz): *An Uncommon Commitment: My Reflections on the History of Maimonides Medical Center* (Brooklyn, N.Y.: Maimonides Research and Development Foundation, 2003). The book is dedicated to "the memory of Benjamin and Betty Eisenstadt."

Mr. Eisenstadt, the last of the giants, will remain forever in the annals of history at Maimonides for his vision, his intellect, his philanthropic contributions. It will be a long time, if ever, before we see his breed again. His light of life will shine on all those whose lives he touched.

I caught a 1 train at 110th Street, transferred to the express at Ninety-sixth Street, rode to Court Street in Brooklyn, wandered around the platform examining the underground display of freaks and cranks, faces washed out in the dim underground light, then caught an M train deeper into Brooklyn. I stared at the walls and stations rushing by, at my own reflection. I thought about Betty and Gladys and Marvin. I thought about my parents and where you go when you die. In college, when I was studying in England, feeling marooned and forgotten, I wrote Ben a letter. By that point, he and my mother were already having problems. In one letter, he had told her to die and go to hell. But he was my grandfather, and I missed him. Because of Ben, I like ketchup on everything. I was writing long letters that year, letters in which I tried to communicate not just the news of my life but also the nature of my soul. I waited weeks for a reply. When it came, it was not from Ben but from Marvin. It began, "Grandpa was happy to receive your letter. Unfortunately, it is a busy time and he has asked me to respond."

At some point, the M train turns into an elevated. You are cruising through the tunnels and then, *ka-chunk*, the wheels screech and the train climbs and you are above the aerials and chimneys near Bay Ridge, gliding over check-cashing joints and taverns and flower shops. Everything out the window was a wonder to me. I saw a man reading a book on a bench. I saw a woman with big hair talking to a skinny guy on a stoop. I saw a Hasid in a beautiful blue prayer shawl. It was as if the train had carried me back to the ancient city where my parents are still children and where Ben is still young and still hustling, as if I had finally reached the headwaters, the source of Brooklyn. I got off at Fort Hamilton Parkway. The tracks curved away in the distance. I went down the steps and walked through the shadows. When a train went overhead, the sound was tremendous. I said to myself, "Remember where this station is you fool! You don't want to get lost and have to make camp out here!"

The street was desolate. There were liquor stores and rows of identical houses that must have once seemed like a great idea for the working man. There was a pink building of Hudson River brick with a mansard roof. A gull cleared the roof and headed for the harbor—from up there, it must be a world of water—and for a moment, as in a dream, the old city rebuilt itself around the building, the omnibuses and streetcars and coffee shops and newsstands.

I took a right on Forty-ninth Street and went uphill into the hospital traffic—Jews and Latins and Italians, many in colorful shirts; Indians and Pakistanis, many in turbans; West Indians with gaudy accents; and people so old they had aged beyond ethnicity and stereotype. It was a carnival. It was a dream. On one hand, these people were off to bury their dead. On the other hand, they themselves were not dying or dead, and so were allowed to leave the hospital whenever they wanted.

They were free!

There were two big buildings with a driveway between them. At first these buildings were in the distance, then they closed over me like a wave. They blocked out the sky. The building on the right had steel letters that said, BENJAMIN AND BETTY EISENSTADT MEMORIAL PAVILION. The building on the left had steel letters that said, ABRAHAM GELLMAN WING. It was as if the ghosts had taken physical form.

I met Edna Palozzolo on the second floor of the Ben and Betty building in what had been Ben's office. Edna has left it largely unchanged, a shrine to the old man. There are inspirational sayings, cartoons, and awards on the wall.* "Marvin has given me special permission to keep these," said Edna. She sat in a desk in an antechamber, leaving the big desk as it had been left by Ben, the chair pushed aside as if he had just gone out for a cup of coffee. On her desk was a framed portrait of my grandfather, his face broad and fleshy.

---

*It reminded me of a wall in my Grandma Esther's condo—a personal hall of fame—covered with plaques and certificates marking even the smallest accomplishment of her children and grandchildren. Displayed with equal pride was the diploma awarded to my cousin David Blumenthal by Cornell Medical School and a certificate issued to my father by the state of Illinois for going three years without a moving violation.

Edna's hair was whipped into a pompadour, her clothes blowsy, her makeup heavy, her glasses tinted. She looked like Sun God Elvis, like Vegas Elvis, like take-horse-tranquilizers-and-die Elvis. She was nice. She told me she had been born in the hospital when it was still called Israel Zion, that she had worked there since 1966, that she was married and lived in Bensonhurst, that, in her mind, Ben and her father were like one person.* She said she knew about the trouble in my family, that Ben talked about it and it saddened him. She told me that I looked like Ben, but that was just chitchat. (I don't.) She told me that Ben used to drive home to make lunch for Betty and Gladys. She told me that after I had called to arrange this meeting, she called Marvin (he is on the board at Maimonides) and asked if it was okay.

Marvin said, "Meet him, but don't say anything bad about me or my parents."

Edna said, "I can't believe a grandchild would ever say anything bad about a grandparent."

She then told me, "Marvin is no Ben."

Edna said there had been three great tragedies in Ben's life: the early death of his father; the asthma that tormented his mother ("He used to pray she would die," Edna told me), and the death of Marvin's twin. "Your grandfather thought better medicine could have prevented all these tragedies," she told me. "That's why he gave so much of his time and money to the research foundation."

When the president of Maimonides was killed in a car crash, Edna nominated Ben to fill the post. The first choice had been an Orthodox Jew, but Edna argued that such a man might not appeal to Christians, atheists, Muslims, secular Jews, Hindus, and miscellaneous. Once Ben was made president, he began spending a great deal of time and money at the hospital. He built a new auditorium and refurnished the office of Rabbi Friedlander. He told Edna, "Money is to be used for good things."

*Edna Palozzolo died in July 2005. A paid notice, which was signed by Marvin Eisenstadt, among others, recognized her for "39 years of devoted service to the hospital, culminating in her role as president of the Maimonides Research and Development Foundation."

Then Edna took me on a tour. In the auditorium, a doctor was explaining the symptoms of heart valve failure. Edna asked if I wanted to stay and listen, but I said no because I am extremely suggestible, and hearing about these symptoms might cause me to suffer them, resulting in many weeks of doctor visits and echocardiograms. We walked to the administrative offices and tried the door, but it was locked. When I pressed my face to the glass, I could see portraits inside of men in business suits. Edna said these portraits showed the various presidents of Maimonides in chronological order. The oldest were of bearded Jews in yarmulkes, some with thousand-yard I-see-God-but-you-don't stares. Others showed men from the crew cut era, the sideburn era, the big-on-top era. The portrait of Ben looked like a painting by Max Beckmann, a study of a mercantile Jew. He is smiling in his curt way, as if a big smile would be wasteful, indulgent. Save your smiles, save your pennies. He wears the sort of suit made by Joey the Heeb or Max the Yid, some ancient Polish tailor who outfits you for a big night in Krakow. The backround in the painting is rich and blue; Grandpa Ben before a flawless sky, up in the heavens, as if the God of the Jews has been replaced by the factory owner.

We went downstairs and across the street into the lobby of the Abraham Gellman Wing. In the emergency room, behind scratched-up Plexiglas, is an exhibit that honors Uncle Abie. There is a picture of him in uniform, with soft features and a myopic stare; there is a detailed description of his death in the Pacific. His Purple Heart and Silver Star are hung up like movie props. There are the letters Sarah received from the secretary of war and President Truman. The doctors and nurses hustling through the room, and some of the patients, who, God knows, had problems of their own, seemed irritated that I was lingering before the display, as if I were missing the point of the place, which is to exist in the boldface present of EMERGENCY. In other words, this shrine built to my great uncle is mostly ignored, which makes sense. Because Abraham Gellman is a key to this story not in his presence but in his absence. The absence of Abie determined everything. It was Abie's absence that broke Bubba's heart and sent her to the roof, which broke Betty's heart, which made Betty certain to break Ellen's heart. Had Abie lived, everything might have been different.

27.

The trial began on November 10, 1997. In his opening statement, Richard Faughnan, the assistant U.S. attorney in charge of the case, told the jury, "Ladies and gentleman, this trial is about a criminal conspiracy to defraud the United States, formed and carried out by the officials of the Cumberland Packing Corporation, which is located right here in downtown Brooklyn. Cumberland was founded by Benjamin Eisenstadt in 1947. After the company invented Sweet'N Low, it became a multimillion-dollar corporation with sales throughout the United States and in foreign countries as well. Although Cumberland became a very profitable enterprise, it remained a family owned business run entirely out of its Brooklyn offices."

Seven people had been indicted in the scandal, Cumberland employees as well as outside contractors who paid kickbacks, faked invoices, and made illegal campaign contributions. Most of these men cut deals and testified. Marvin filled whole legal pads with what he knew. As did Asaro. In return, the U.S. attorney's office asked the judge for leniency.

Marvin was given one-year probation, and the company was fined more than two million dollars. Marvin has since turned the operation of the business over to his son, Jeff. Asaro, who also got probation, works with his sons, the makers of a sugar-free candy, who are still in business with Cumberland. In the end, the only men tried for the crimes at the factory were Gil and Mario Mederos. "My clients are being used as scapegoats," Irving Anolik told the jury. "The people who made the money, the people who ran this company, have all pleaded guilty. Not one of them, so far as I know, went to trial. Gil Mederos was woefully undertrained and underqualified for his job. How convenient for Marvin! Now ask yourself whether these two men, Gil and Mario, were leading millionaires like Marvin Eisenstadt, running a $110-million-dollar corporation, around by the nose: 'Oh my God, look what they did to me!' "

Marvin appeared before the jury only as a witness. He was on the stand for two days. The transcript runs to several hundred pages. For Marvin, who has organized his life to avoid just such situations, it must have felt like an eternity. He talked about the company, how it was built, how it was run. As the prosecutor went through Marvin's biography, the judge cut him off, saying, "He's married, he lives in Queens, before that he lived in Brooklyn. That's enough background." Marvin told the jury that it's wrong to think of him as the boss of the factory. "You have to understand that when you say [Gil and Mario] were employed by me, I started the way they did. From the bottom." He explained how, following the raid of the factory, he finally fired his colleagues, or saw to it that they *were* fired. "Marvin indicated he would prefer not to terminate [Gil and Mario]," Joseph Dornbush testified. "He asked if I would do it."

And though the brothers were fired, they were, in another sense, not fired. Marvin gave them a controlling interest in the Nine Kings Corporation, which made the packets used at the factory. In this way, even after the brothers were indicted, Cumberland guaranteed their income. Irving Anolik seemed to suggest this was a payoff. In return for Nine Kings, the brothers would keep quiet. "Sir, isn't it a fact that Gil and Mario Mederos were never fired," Anolik asked Marvin, "but that they went into another business that continued to do business with Cumberland?"

"I grew up with them," Marvin explained. "Whatever happened, they were Gil and Mario, so we continued doing business. It was a decision that I made after discussing it with my father and my brother."

In his closing statement, Richard Faughnan presented Marvin as an ineffectual dupe, pushed around by his own employees.

Gil and Mario Mederos and Joseph Asaro stole nearly three million dollars from Cumberland. They used part of that money to purchase and renovate their building at 231 East 50th Street. To avoid being fired as a result of their act, they then negotiated an agreement with Marvin Eisenstadt where the only thing they gave up was the building they had purchased and renovated with Cumberland money, the money they stole. They then managed to get Marvin Eisenstadt to pay them additional compensation in the form of forgiveness of their personal loans, and additional compensation to pay any taxes they would owe for the forgiveness of their loans, and then additional compensation in the form of a company car for Gil Mederos, and money to buy a new car for Mario Mederos.

Now, you tell me, who was running Cumberland during this period? Was it Marvin Eisenstadt, the man who signed this absolutely ridiculous one-sided agreement, or was it those two men and Joseph Asaro, the men who negotiated this extraordinary deal when they were on the brink of ruin?

From the same facts, Irving Anolik built a narrative in which Marvin is crafty and cruel, in which he set up the Mederos brothers like a couple of patsies with big-title jobs they couldn't perform. That way, if the conspiracy unraveled, the brothers could be blamed. "Gil Mederos, according to the prosecutor, was in charge of approving or disapproving business and whatnot," said Anolik. "But his only training was that of a mechanic. He has not one minute of training as an accountant. This mechanic they put in charge. They said approve or disapprove. He made the mechanic his controller, and all he has experience in is mixing chemicals or mechanics. He's sent out to clean a fish tank. He works on mixing machines. He works on fixing cars. That's the controller of a company making over

$110 million a year? Maybe he's a good mechanic, but he's not any genius. He's not a bright fellow in that respect. I'm not trying to denigrate him. But this is way over his head."

The jury heard fourteen witnesses and looked at almost two thousand exhibits. The Mederos brothers were charged with, among other things, tax evasion and obstructing justice. "The testimony of Joseph Asaro, we respectfully submit, is coming from a person who everybody, I believe even the prosecution, considers to be a crook of the highest magnitude," Anolik told the jury. "You remember the story that Joseph Asaro tells. He asked Mr. Eisenstadt to come out of the office. 'I want you to come out in the street,' he says. This is real cloak and dagger stuff. Mario Mederos was told, 'Well, we're going to put you in charge of purchasing.' Then, when he reports cheating, Marvin Eisenstadt says, 'Just forget about it. Don't pay attention.' It's even possible that Joseph Asaro might have conjured up the whole thing with Mr. Eisenstadt. Mr. Eisenstadt ended up with something very valuable [the building on Fiftieth Street]. Worth far more than what was stolen from him. I think he said at one point it's worth five million dollars. On top of that, shortly thereafter Asaro is hired at a million dollars a year to do something in Washington. For what? A million dollars a year plus his $50,000 salary, plus expenses. That's a pretty hefty piece of change. You have a den of iniquity here, ladies and gentlemen. You have even the president of the company deeply involved in criminality. He got a pretty good break in this case."

The Mederos brothers were found guilty, Gil on one count of obstruction of justice and Gil and Mario on one count of conspiracy to defraud the United States and two counts of income tax evasion. Mario was sentenced to ninety-seven months in prison. He was sent to Fort Dix Federal Correctional Institution. Gil, who was then about fifty-eight years old, was sentenced to ten years. He was sent to Fairton Federal Correctional Institution, in Fairton, New Jersey. As I write, on a sunny day in August 2004, he is still there.*

---

*According to the website of the Federal Bureau of Prisons (www.bop.gov), the scheduled release date (the last time I checked) of Mario Mederos is May 18, 2005. The scheduled release date of Oswaldo "Gil" Mederos is February 14, 2007.

28.

One evening in the fall of 2002, when the wind was on the river and the trees were turning and the leaves were as crunchy as Jiffy Pop, I went to meet Irving Anolik, who lives on Long Island but was staying at the Millennium Hotel. Because I had read all of his court memos and letters, his opening and closing statements, his objections and his stabs at eloquence, I felt I already knew him. What came through in the transcripts was his sense of outrage. Everyone stole and everyone schemed, but only his clients, because they were lowly and had no good information to trade, took the hit.

The Millennium Hotel is across the street from what had been the World Trade Center. The hotel was damaged in the September 11 attack and had reopened shortly before we met in the restaurant on the second floor. I looked out the big windows at what had been the World Trade Plaza, now a construction site, cranes and backhoes and dump trucks and flatbeds rumbling and digging and grinding through the rubble, men in hard hats climbing on the machinery, floodlights illuminating everything. I thought about the rush of time and the past and how it gets blown up and buried and something new is built in its place. Anolik shook my hand. He was straitlaced and stern. He was wearing the kind of big class ring I sometimes imagine opening a cut beneath my eye. He told me that his clients had been badly treated by my uncle: Joe Asaro was living in the mansion paid for largely by Cumberland and Marvin Eisenstadt was making more money than ever, while Gil and Mario Mederos grew old in prison.

While going through the court files, I had come across an affidavit and a letter that Mario and Gil Mederos sent to the judge and the prosecutor. In my mind, the Mario and Gil of these panicky prison-house documents appear on a split screen, with Marvin on the tee green addressing a Titleist, drawing back his club: *Ka-bam!* When you hit the ball just right, it becomes a speck in the sky, an imperfection in the iris of the Lord.

> During the course of the trial, we were shocked when we learned that the court was going to permit our lawyer, Mr. Dornbush, to testify against us. At no time did we understand that Mr. Dornbush was no longer our attorney after we allegedly signed certain documents wherein he testified we knowingly, willfully, and intelligently released him as our attorney and that he was free to act in a conflict and antagonistic situation with respect to us from that point on. We continued to regard him as our attorney and consulted him on many, many occasions and paid him bills for his services not only to us personally but to the corporation in which we were principal stock holders. We submit that Mr. Dornbush is a liar and a perjurer by his own testimony if he says anything to the contrary.

In the letter (I have included only part of it) dated March 22, 2000, Mario offered the prosecutor his cooperation in return for a reduced sentence and also suggested his frustration with the trial.

From Mario Mederos
Unit 5910
Fort Dix, NJ

TO: *Richard Faughnan, AUSA, Brooklyn*

Dear Mr. Faughnan,

    I was very upset and saddened to learn from my attorney, Irving Anolik, Esq., that you did not feel you should give me a letter pursuant to Federal Rule 35 (b) of the criminal procedure rules* because of the fact that I tried to be helpful to the government . . .

    I recall that you apparently became very upset with me when I told you that I felt that the evidence that some of the witnesses gave against me at my own trial was untrue, but I want to make it clear that I am well aware of the fact that I have been found guilty and I am not in any way, shape or form accusing you of being aware of the fact that these witnesses may have lied.

    I want to assure you that all I have been saying to you is true and that I recognize that I was wrong in being part of what created the case for which I was convicted and sentenced . . .

Sincerely,
Mario Mederos

Anolik implied that his clients had not testified at their trial because a deal had been struck with Marvin. The brothers would keep quiet, and would be taken care of in return, a trick accomplished via the Nine Kings Corporation. (The brothers had not counted on the severity of their sentences.) As long as Sweet'N Low was sold in packets, Gil and Mario Mederos would do fine.†

Anolik said his clients were now in a state of extreme agitation. It

---

*A letter from the prosecutor to the judge, urging time be taken off a sentence in return for cooperation.

†Anolik seems to be referring to the "fair deal" that had been worked out earlier by Marvin, Joe Asaro, and the Mederos Brothers, in which the brothers were, among

seems that Jeff Eisenstadt, who now runs Cumberland, had been shopping for other packet suppliers. Maybe Jeff did not know Marvin had made a deal, or maybe he did not care. Maybe he looked at the Nine Kings invoices and said, "We can do better." Maybe Marvin thought, with the brothers in prison, he was free to do whatever he wanted.

Anolik asked if I knew why Jeff was backing out.

I laughed.

Anolik told me it was okay, Gil and Mario would take care of themselves.

When I asked Marvin if he was nervous about what might happen when the men were released from prison, he said, "A little afraid, yeah. I am a little afraid. But what can I do?"

---

other things, made controlling shareholders of Nine Kings in return for which all parties agreed to release one another from legal liability. Of course, Nine Kings remained valuable only as long it was patronized by Cumberland Packing.

29.

Meanwhile, water flows; stars collapse and burst into novas; people are abducted by aliens, probed, and returned to their houses; good sons become delinquent and fall in with a bad crowd, try drugs, and go to prison; supermarkets stock, sell, restock, and sell again—time passes. So you wonder: what was going on in the rest of the industry as Cumberland was lost in this thicket? Because you go into the movies in the afternoon, but when you come out it's night.

While Marvin and Ben were tangled in scandal, the market was being remade by the saccharin ban. It was the ban that chased my uncle into the cul-de-sac: not a dead end, because there are money and McMansions in culs-de-sacs. It was the ban that caused my uncle to lose the horizon and focus only on the ban itself. It was the ban that opened the industry to competitors, big behemoths that, in the course of a decade, would drive Cumberland Packing out of its position of dominance.

Following the saccharin ban, there was no FDA-approved artificial sweetener on the market, no "safe" alternative to sugar. The moratorium was passed as a consequence of this, as a lesser of evils for diabetics. In other words, at the very moment that my uncle turned his attention to managing the ban, a void had opened. The result was a race like the race for the moon. Who will find the alternative to the alternatives? Who will plant the flag? Because it had long been the market leader and the owner of the most famous brand, Cumberland would have had a great advantage in this race. They would not have been starting at zero. They would have been building on their existing dominance. Nor would they have had to devise a clever way to introduce a strange product from the laboratory. They could instead have sold any new sweetener as new and improved Sweet'N Low, in the same way that Coca-Cola introduced its new formula as "New Coke." But when Cumberland ducked out of the race, or did not even realize that a race was under way, and instead directed its time and resources to saving saccharin, the market opened and the conglomerates flowed in.

In 1977, GD Searle, an Illinois-based chemical manufacturer, brought in squinty-eyed Donald Rumsfeld to restructure the company and get its chemical sweetener, aspartame, approved by the FDA. The company had been founded by Gideon Daniel Searle, who, in the years just after the Civil War (he was a twice wounded, shell-shocked veteran) built a chain of pharmacies in Omaha, Nebraska, then opened an elixir factory in Illinois, where he made his first fortune with Dramamine, a motion-sickness pill perfectly suited for the new footloose travel-happy American middle class. In 1925, Searle moved his company to McHenry County, Illinois, then to Skokie, Illinois, where, in 1965, aspartame was discovered by accident.

A chemist named James Schlatter had been searching for a formula to treat ulcers and heartburn when the potion bubbled onto his hands. He licked his fingers: EUREKA! It was two hundred times sweeter than sugar and could be used in quantities so small as to amount to no calories. Aspartame is made of two amino acids: phenylalanine and aspartic acid, which, when they enter your system, produce methanol, which, according to *Merriam-Webster's Collegiate Dictionary*, is "a light volatile flammable poisonous liquid alcohol."* Aspartic acid is sometimes classified as an excitotoxin, a family of chemicals that excite the nerves and pathways in your brain—think of the old footage of a carpet of cluster bombs lighting up the jungles of Vietnam. In 1966, the *Journal of the American Chemical Society* described the new formula as a result of "an accidental discovery of an organic compound with a profound sucrose (table sugar)–like taste. Preliminary tasting showed this compound to have a potency of 100–200 times sucrose depending on concentration and on what other flavors are present and to be devoid of unpleasant aftertaste."

Sweeter than saccharin; no aftertaste.

The executives at Searle saw the commercial implications immediately; these were hard to miss. Yet they had a terrifically hard time getting their new compound approved by the FDA. In every test, something came out wrong. Over time, a sinister aura grew up around aspartame that has never been entirely dispelled. Just go to the Internet and look up all the freelance nutters who have attached the compound to a conspiracy that traces a line from Donald Rumsfeld to Ronald Reagan to airplane crashes to early death: it does freaky things to your brain, knocks you for a loop, blows a hole in the cortex. They claim the FDA has received more than ten thousand aspartame-related complaints. They sing of headaches, seizures, blackouts, memory loss, lesions, slurred speech, mood swings, anxiety attacks, coma, extremity numbness, and loss of limb control.

"We were running a [aspartame] test product here and the girls, some of the girls, just couldn't run it because they would get hives," Marvin told me. "The dust. Some people are allergic to it and it affects their vision."

The FDA rejected aspartame in the 1960s and rejected it again in the

---

*According to www.aspartame.net, "Methanol is a natural and harmless byproduct of many foods we eat every day. . . . The amount of methanol in the human diet is nowhere near the levels that cause toxicity. You would have to drink about 675 to 1,690 cans of diet soft drink at one sitting to reach the toxic level."

1970s. Because of certain discrepancies. Because of certain worrying patterns in the tests. Since the market was already well served by cyclamate and saccharin, there was no reason to introduce a questionable new compound into the food supply. Then cyclamate was banned. Then saccharin was banned. Then Congress received a hundred thousand angry letters: *Do not take away my fake sugar!*

It was a scientific study commissioned in the late 1970s that finally convinced regulators that aspartame was safe. According to the study, the compound is indeed a danger, but only for the tiny sliver of the population that suffers from a hereditary disease called phenylketonuria (PKU), an enzyme deficiency in the brain that, if acted on by phenylalanine, can send a sufferer into seizures and damage the brain. Babies with PKU exposed to aspartame can suffer mental retardation. (Diet Coke cans carry a warning for those with PKU.) With this new study, the bad early tests had been explained: it was just a few people with a disease you've never heard of. In 1981, after twenty years of controversy,* aspartame was approved.

There tend to be two explanations for this approval: (1) executives at Searle, knowing their product was good and true, pressed on, searching for and then finding the reason for the occasional seizure; and (2) executives at Searle surely suspected that their wonder chemical left a wake of blinded, jittery, panicky amnesiacs, but pressed on anyway, because that's corporate America, until just the right cards were dealt—a cyclamate ban, a saccharin ban, a fat-obsessed nation, a market without an unbanned artificial sweetener, and, most important, a Republican administration. For two decades, aspartame failed to win approval. Then Ronald Reagan was elected president and Donald Rumsfeld, while keeping his position

---

*The NutraSweet Company responded to these rumors and complaints on its website www.nutrasweet.com. "The overwhelming body of scientific evidence clearly demonstrates that aspartame, even in amounts many times what people typically consume, is safe and not associated with adverse health effects. The FDA has investigated alleged complaints since 1982 and states that there is no 'reasonable evidence of possible public health harm' and 'no consistent or unique patterns of symptoms reported with respect to aspartame that can be casually linked to its use.'"

at Searle, worked on the president-elect's Interim Foreign Policy Team. On January 21, 1981, the day after Reagan was inaugurated, Searle reapplied for approval of aspartame. Within a few months, largely because Reagan had named a new head of the FDA, the chemical got the green light. Rumsfeld had correctly recognized that Searle's problem was not scientific; it was political.

Many aspartame-is-going-to-kill-you websites include a quote from a former Searle salesperson named Patty Wood-Allott, who remembers Rumsfeld telling the sales force just before Reagan took office that, if necessary, "he would call in all his markers and that, no matter what, he would see to it that aspartame would be approved that year."*

"There were a lot of questions about brain damage in rats on aspartame," Martin told me. "People have gone blind. The formulation of aspartame is very much like MSG. It's not going to kill you, but some people are allergic and they get reactions. I know I'm allergic. I get a terrible headache. If there's MSG in Chinese food, the next day I've got an awful headache."

At some point during Searle's struggle to get aspartame approved, an executive from the company called Cumberland and arranged a meeting with Ben and Marvin. "We went out there and met them," said Marvin. He told me that, while meeting in Searle's sprawling corporate office in Skokie, Illinois, a public company filled with MBAs, he experienced culture shock. At Cumberland, when you look out the window, it's red brick and iron. In Skokie, it's parking lot and highway. "It was strange," said Marvin. "I went into this big office—and when I say me, I also mean my father; we were like Mutt and Jeff or the Shadow and Lamont Cranston in those years—and I remember, this guy was practicing golf in his office, putting."

The executives at Searle wanted to buy Cumberland Packing. They

*This was reported, among other places, in "History of Aspartame," by Alex Constantine, Gregory Gordon, and former FDA investigator Arthur M. Evangelista, and posted on www.wnho.net, the website of the World Natural Health Organization.

made an offer that Marvin described to me as "extremely generous." Millions and millions of dollars, perks and extras, probably much more than the factory was actually worth. By buying Cumberland, Searle would, in one stroke, have eliminated its biggest competitor, become the market leader, and saved millions of dollars in marketing and advertising. "They wanted to buy us out and call their new product Sweet'N Low," Marvin explained. "We tried to convince them, 'Let's merge somehow. Let us keep our independence.' But they wanted to buy us out. They said they would make me vice president and give me stock."*

As he says this, Marvin pauses, loses focus, seems to be thinking or remembering, then says, "But we didn't want to do it, so we turned them down."

If Marvin had made this deal, he would now be an incredibly wealthy man. He would have cash from the sale, plus the GD Searle stock, which, with the success of aspartame and the later sale of Searle to Monsanto, and then Monsanto's success with genetically engineered crops, increased in value tremendously. When I asked Marvin why he had turned down the deal and the other offers made over the years, he talked about the importance of being independent. If he had sold the company, he told me, he might have had to fire longtime employees, which he could not stand to do because, as he told a reporter, "I have to sleep at night."

While Marvin and Ben were hunkered down in Wallabout Bay, Searle created a new division, the NutraSweet Company, to market aspartame, the first new sweetener on the market in twenty-five years. The company registered two trademarks: Equal, the tabletop sweetener (fake sugar) it would introduce in 1981, and NutraSweet, the food and drink additive it would introduce in 1983.

"I was told we were going to lose our business," Marvin said. "I was not panicked for two reasons. One, I felt that we'd been in the market for such a long time people would not desert us. Two, there were questions

*The NutraSweet Company did not respond to my requests for an interview.

about Equal, health things. Three, taste. For people used to Sweet'N Low, [Equal] wasn't sweet enough."*

The launch of Equal and NutraSweet was brilliant, not Harvard Business School or Wharton brilliant, but Sun Tzu or Von Clausewitz brilliant. It was a military campaign. It was a slaughter. Searle, not just content with a good debut, wanted to overwhelm the field.

In 1983, Searle sent a gum ball sweetened with NutraSweet to millions of homes. It was like the drug dealer giving the kid on the playground a taste of cocaine saying, "Pass it around, let 'em all try it. You know where I am if you want more." That summer, kids talked about the new miracle product the way Columbus once spoke of the antipodes. Here I speak not as a historian or scholar but as one who was lucky to be young at the time, who went to the mailbox expecting to find bills and fliers and instead found a gum ball in a clear envelope. The gum balls came in red, yellow, green, blue. Some kids tried to collect them all, lining them up like trophies, eating them all at once, then, through all that gum, pontificating on the mysteries of taste. By introducing aspartame as a gum ball, Searle was not presenting itself as the lesser of evils. The people who eat gum balls are not, after all, the same people who count calories. Searle was taking on sugar itself.

In 1984, Searle made deals with Coca-Cola and Pepsi and many other companies that sold diet foods. These companies would be sold Nutra-Sweet at a tremendous discount. In exchange, they would carry the Nutra-Sweet trademark (a swirl) on their labels. The swirl became part of the Coke can, the most famous piece of packaging in the world. Aspartame, long troubled by its bad reputation, remade itself in the trusted image of Coke and Pepsi. In December 1984, Robert Shapiro, then president of the NutraSweet Group, told a reporter from *The New York Times*, "Sugar is in trouble. The industry will have to adjust to that reality. They can't do anything to improve the product."

By the time NutraSweet was introduced as a sweetener, the ground had been well prepared. The mothers had been targeted. The kids who

---

*Though aspartame is sweeter than saccharin, the formula in which aspartame is sold (Equal) is not as sweet as Sweet'N Low.

ride backward through the supermarkets and make all the decisions had been brainwashed. It was called Equal. It carried the swirl. It was sold in a light-blue packet because white is nothing and pink is for girls but blue is rational, blue you remember, blue stands out, blue is progress, blue is ocean, blue is sky. Nothing was accidental. Unlike Sweet'N Low, Equal was marketed not as a "sugar substitute" but as an "alternative sweetener." Executives at Searle had apparently determined that, when attached to a food, the word *substitute* (why were they the first to realize this?) is like poison. Also, as sugar is among the most beloved products of the earth, consumers are skeptical of vainglorious efforts to create a facsimile. With "sugar substitute," you get people who want to be thin and don't care how. With "alternative sweetener," you get everyone.

In 1985, Equal outsold Sweet'N Low. The swirl had become the number one brand in America. Aspartame sweetened 27 percent of all soft drinks sold in the country, 87 percent of all diet drinks. Searle reported annual sales of $132 million. Cumberland's were less than half that, around $67 million. Sweet'N Low had been pushed out of the top spot it had occupied since the early 1970s. By the end of the year, Searle and its NutraSweet subsidiary had been sold to Monsanto for an astounding $2.7 billion.

After the first success of Equal, Marvin and Ben fought back. This was a time of advertising wars, lawsuits, dirty tricks, and corporate espionage. "[NutraSweet's] CEO promised me he wouldn't bring up health with his product against Sweet'N Low 'cause we had the warning label," Marvin told me. "Then he goes behind my back at various supermarkets and tells them, 'You don't want Sweet'N Low on your shelves. It's going to kill you. You want Equal.' The supermarkets called me . . . And I called Shapiro. I called him every name under the sun. He denied it. He said it was an assistant who didn't know what he was doing. I explained to Shapiro, 'What you're doing is hurting the whole industry. 'Cause if you talk bad about one product, you're talking about all the products. They're going to stop using Sweet'N Low, they're going to stop using Equal.' "*

---

*Robert Shapiro has since retired. I tried to reach him for an interview, without success.

In 1988, a subsidiary of Cumberland called the Stadt (as in Eisen*stadt*) Corporation, introduced Sweet One, an artificial sweetener sold in a blue packet virtually identical to the Equal packet. Marvin calls this a *me-too* product, as in *I make that too, I sell that too!* Monsanto sued for the violation of its trademark, claiming that Sweet One was so close in appearance to Equal that it would confuse consumers. You think you have walked out of the store with a box of Equal, but realize when you get home that you have bought something called Sweet One. (The legal precedent was the 1961 case, *Polaroid Corp. v. Polarad Electronics Corp.*) Monsanto's case made it to the U.S. Court of Appeals, where in 1990 a judge decided in favor of Cumberland. Monsanto then appealed to the Supreme Court, which agreed with the lower court that "mere color" is not entitled to trademark protection. Otherwise, if there were a boom in the industry, within a few years the makers of artificial sweeteners would run out of colors, which would discourage competition, the opposite of the law's intent.

In the 1990s, when Monsanto lost its patent on aspartame—a "use patent" lapses, depending on the nature of the discovery, after fourteen to twenty years—Cumberland introduced a me-too aspartame sweetener called NatraTaste, a cheap Equal knockoff sold in a blue packet. A few years later, when Monsanto introduced a low-cost aspartame product of its own, also packed in blue and called NutraSweet, Cumberland sued, arguing that NutraSweet would confuse consumers who meant to buy NatraTaste. To prove its (ludicrous) case, Cumberland furnished the court with an internal Monsanto* memo in which an executive says he hopes NutraSweet will "beat the pants off NatraTaste." According to Marvin's lawyers, this memo proved "bad faith." In his decision, the judge wrote, "Competition is not bad faith."

Sweet'N Low, which had been the industry leader for decades, eventually dropped into a distant third behind Equal and Splenda, an artificial tabletop sweetener (it comes in a yellow packet) introduced by Johnson & Johnson in 2000. Yet, amazingly, Cumberland has made almost twice as

---

*In 2000, Monsanto sold its food-sweetener business to private investment firm J. W. Childs for $440 million, and its tabletop sweetener business to Merisant, which now owns the trademark for Equal.

much money annually in recent years as it did thirty years ago, when Sweet'N Low was the top brand. By bringing artificial sweeteners into the mainstream—people drink Diet Coke not because they are on a diet but because they prefer the taste—Monsanto supersized the market. In 2004, artificial sweeteners generated sales of $343 million, of which Cumberland Products represented 19.4 percent, or about $66.5 million.* "Equal opened up the market," Marvin told me. "And though our share went down, the market got much bigger. Let's say, for example, someone that would never use saccharin decides, because he is bombarded by their sales pitch, to try Equal. He tastes it and says, 'Well, it's okay.' Then he goes to a restaurant and they only have Sweet'N Low, so he says, 'Okay, I'll try it.' And it tastes even sweeter. So he begins to buy Sweet'N Low."

In July 2000, the National Institutes of Health removed saccharin from its list of carcinogens. "Much ado about nothing." Or as a girl I dated in college who found a ticket stub in my pocket asked, "What is this Mexican play? Muchado about nothing?" Because all of that money and worry was used to fight a ban that in the end was lifted for the same reason it had been passed: science. A new study showed that, yes, saccharin does cause tumors in male rats. But it also showed that these tumors resulted not from saccharin alone but from the way saccharin reacted with the monster amounts of acid in male rat urine. As Samuel Cohen, a scientist at the University of Nebraska, explained, "Saccharin as a cause of cancer is both rat specific and high dose specific."

Or as Lyn Nabors of the Calorie Control Council told *The Wall Street Journal*, "Man is not a big rat."

"The Sprague dory rat has a particular protein in his urine which, taken with the sodium in saccharin—it wasn't even the saccharin, it was

---

*Despite this dramatic increase in sales over the decades, Cumberland's overall sales actually declined between year-end December 2002 and December 2004, from $72.8 million to $66.5 million. During the same period, sales of Sweet'N Low alone dropped from $55 million to $52 million, as the market was eaten up by Splenda. These numbers come from Information Resources, a market research group based in Chicago.

the sodium—creates stones," Marvin told me. "And the stones irritate the bladder and that's what caused the cancer in those fourteen male rats. If you follow the logic, you have to ban salt, because sodium is what killed the rats. With saccharin you can give them all they want, because you don't metabolize saccharin, it's pissed out. That's why it has no calories."

The congressional legislation that removed the warning from Sweet'N Low and other saccharin products was called the Sweetest Act. It passed on the Senate floor and was signed by Bill Clinton in January 2001—great news for the factory, of course, but in a sense, it came too late. The saccharin ban was like a piece of bad intelligence from which every other bad decision had followed. It corrupted Marvin, it made Joseph Asaro vice president for governmental affairs, it brought the company into an association with Alfonse D'Amato, it spurred the FDA to approve aspartame, which remade the entire industry. Fourteen rats get cancer, and nothing will ever be the same.

The artificial sweetener market is currently dominated by Splenda, the only product in this book not discovered by accident. Splenda is part of the scary effort to get into the toy box and tinker with the grains and spices of the earth. We are in the age of the genome and the genetic code, the double helix twisting toward the sun. The age of the accidental discovery is over. Known in the lab as sucralose, Splenda is the result of a Holy Grail–like search for a sugar that behaves like saccharin, that leaves no trace in the gut, ass, or hips. It was discovered in 1976 when a scientist at the British sugar company Tate & Lyle rearranged the sugar molecule, replacing its three hydrogen-oxygen groups with three chlorine atoms, resulting in a compound that is something like a mirror image of sugar; it looks and tastes like the real thing, yet, because it's so strange, goes unrecognized by the body. It slips right past the turnoffs and checkpoints on its way to the toilet. As if it were never there. As if that Weight Watchers cake never existed. Splenda is not just another sweetener. It is sugar remade, a molecule stolen from God, put up on blocks, painted, and thrown back on the market.

Of course, you read this and think: ball game. Or *Tilt*! Because how can fake sugar compete with a variation of real sugar that has no calories?

But there are drawbacks to sucralose. As a result of the success of Sweet'N Low and Equal, some people actually prefer the fake to the (sort of) real, as some men prefer fake blondes. There will always be a market for the phony and supersweet, as there will always be a market for Cheez Whiz. Also, because it results from an intricate process of infinitesimal tinkering, Splenda is much more expensive to make than saccharin or aspartame.

In 1998, when Johnson & Johnson—they had bought the sucralose patent from its inventors—was planning the release of the product, executives at the company, which makes medicine, not food, offered to resell the patent to Cumberland; they wanted Marvin to buy out the entire line.* With sucralose *and* saccharin, Cumberland could have secured years of dominance. "It's a good sweetener," Marvin told me, "but we couldn't afford it. The equipment to run this stuff goes into millions of dollars."

In 1998, sucralose was introduced in diet foods and soft drinks.† In 2000, it was released as a tabletop sweetener called Splenda.

The packets appeared first on the West Coast, then bled east. At the Brown Palace Hotel in Denver, Colorado, where I was staying after several days of altitude sickness and vomiting in a nearby mountain town, I conducted a taste test, laying packets of Sweet'N Low and Equal and Splenda on a cloth-covered table in the cocktail lounge as a three-piece band played "Everything Happens to Me." I opened the packets one at a time, carefully pouring the contents of each onto my tongue, swirling and tasting the sweeteners as if they were tumblers of Scotch,‡ then jotting down some notes.

That notebook is before me now:

Sweet'N Low: Wow, that mother kicks! Tastes like cancer. Those poor rats! The aftertaste drags you to the mat. Like the balloon payment that comes at the end of the financing plan. Was the Camaro really worth it?

---

*My request to Johnson & Johnson for a factory tour and an interview went unfulfilled. However, I did receive a folder stuffed with Splenda PR materials.

†Johnson & Johnson sells sucralose through a division called McNeil Nutritionals.

‡I chewed ice between each packet to cleanse my palate.

Not bad in coffee, or cereal, but all alone it's a mother. Remember the time we were kids and Alex Trumble, thinking it was sugar, poured a pack of Sweet'N Low — maybe one of the specialized packs Ben made for Sharon's bat mitzvah, the ice cream cones on front — into his mouth and seized up and dry-heaved?

Equal: Not as sweet, which, if you ask me, is a good thing. No kick in the ass going away. No wonder they beat the pants off Marvelous.

Splenda: The yellow pack makes me think of dog pee in snow. Does it taste like sugar? Not quite. Something is chemical and off. Maybe it's been so long I forget what real sugar tastes like. I'm all hopped up. Sugar isn't sweet enough for me. I'm a Diet Coke fiend. Maybe I'm projecting all that lab work onto the product. But it's close. No aftertaste, smooth. Cumberland is going to get crushed.

Within two years of its release, Splenda had passed Sweet'N Low as the number-two selling brand. By the time of my taste test in the summer of 2003, Splenda had passed Equal. During the twelve-month period ending December 2004, Splenda had reached $173 million in annual sales. According to Information Resources, Splenda then had 51 percent of the market, Equal 19 percent, and Sweet'N Low 15 percent.* "Splenda came out with an ad saying that they're the number one sugar substitute in the world," Marvin told me. "But they're number one only because they are so expensive. Dollarwise, yes, they're number one. But in this country, industry doesn't go by dollars. If you are going by dollars, you would have to say Rolls Royce is the number one car. It's not. It doesn't sell more cars than Ford. Beer is the same. You go by volume. As far as [volume] goes, we are very fortunate and we are very lucky. We are number one.[†]

*In February 2005, Coca-Cola announced the coming release of a Diet Coke sweetened with Splenda. Pepsi said that it, too, would mix a Splenda-sweetened drink to be called Pepsi One.

[†]In 2003, when I interviewed Marvin, Cumberland was indeed the leader in volume sales, selling 133.6 million ounces of Sweet'N Low, or 30.5 percent of the market, in

He then said, "They made a dent, yes. It tastes pretty good. It's in a yellow packet. But it still has that flat aspartame taste, and it's even more expensive than Equal. They say it's from natural sugar—that's one of their slogans. It does come from sugar, but they change the molecule from carbon to chlorine. Chlorine is a poison, by the way. So it's not sugar. It's rearranged sugar. It's like if you take your DNA and changed it so that you have fifteen eyes. You're not human anymore, you're something else. So that's misleading on their part."*

He then said, "Oh yes! They got money. They spend and spend and spend. So there's always threats out there, but we have this established name, so that, you know, we don't feel threatened."

In the beginning, sugar was valued because it offered a treasure of calories and energy in a small dose. Sugar accordingly fueled the growth of the modern city, the modern workforce, and the modern nation. It powered the slave trade and made possible the rise of the mercantile class that overthrew the kings. It fueled the revolutions that gave birth to modern democracies and modern wars. The spread of sugar led to the plagues of obesity and diabetes and tooth decay that generated a need for alternative sweeteners realized with saccharin and cyclamate and aspartame, which, by *their* success and the resulting health concerns, created a need for a new kind of sugar. "Sugar is in trouble," said Robert Shapiro. "They

---

the previous twelve months. (Because it's cheaper than the competition, Sweet'N Low is favored in the same sort of restaurants that carry Hunt's instead of Heinz.) But by the end of 2004, Splenda had passed Cumberland in this category, too, climbing in just one year from a 23.3 percent to a 36.8 percent market share. Sweet'N Low had by then fallen to a 26.1 percent share of volume sales. (These statistics come from Information Resources.)

*In 2005, the Sugar Association, a trade group made up of various sugar manufacturers, filed a lawsuit against Splenda's marketer, McNeil Nutritionals, over this very issue, specifically the claim printed on its packet that Splenda is "made from sugar so it tastes like sugar." Jeff Cronin, a spokesman for the Center for Science in the Public Interest, was quoted in *The Seattle Times* saying, "We consider [Splenda] safe. But it happens to be a synthetic chemical cooked up in a flask somewhere. That doesn't mean it isn't safe, but people should know [what it is]." The makers of Splenda countersued, claiming that the Sugar Association was involved in a "malicious smear campaign" against their product.

can't do anything to improve the product." But that's exactly what happened. By scrambling the molecules, the scientists replaced an ancient food valued because a little gives you a lot with a designer spice valued because a lot gives you nothing—no calories, no energy. A buffalo nickel, a check on an overdrawn account. An old friend returned to us lobotomized, a big fat zero, millions spent to unmake sugar, or remake it with no value. It's the story of the age. *Taste without content. Food without value.* By the late 1990s, sugar had lost 70 percent of its market to high fructose corn syrup (HFCS), saccharin, aspartame, and sucralose. In 2004, the Domino refinery closed its doors in Brooklyn. With the invention of sucralose, the story of sugar comes to an end.

PART THREE

TO GRANDMA BETTY, LOVE WAS FINITE, LOVE WAS COAL;
THERE WAS A SHORTAGE, AND THERE WOULD NEVER BE
ENOUGH TO GO AROUND.

30.

In this section of the story, my family gets disinherited. Imagine it introduced like a chapter in *Don Quixote*: XXX . . . *Wherein Old Ben Gets Sick and a Terrible Injustice Befalls Ellen and Her Issue*. The events leading up to the disinheritance follow like the events in a dream, in which every development seems at once random, nonsensical, and inevitable. As if this is where the story had been heading from the moment Herbie approached Ellen in the NYU cafeteria, or from the moment Marvin and Gladys got away with taking Ellen's quarter at Coney Island.

Is this the way it had to be?

In the summer of 1995, Ben checked into Maimonides complaining of dizziness and nausea. He was sent for tests. Betty waited in his room: the empty room was a picture of her future. Ben's heart was failing. Not just the arteries; one of his valves would have to be replaced. The doctors said they would operate the next morning. As a precaution, Ben was given an antibiotic. "He was either given penicillin by mistake, or else was administered a drug called vancomycin too quickly and he went into ana-phylactic shock," said Gladys. "He almost died."

By this time, Betty had gone home to Flatbush to rest. When the cri-sis came, only my brother was on the scene. "Steven was there alone," my sister told me. "He was making the decisions. Then Betty came back and she was very upset, and he took care of her. It was totally weird for Steven to be in that situation."

Ben recovered.

Within a few days, he was off the respirator and sitting up in bed. But the bypass and valve-replacement surgery had been postponed indefi-nitely. The shock from the antibiotics and the ensuing illness had weak-ened him severely. He had gone into the hospital with a bad heart, had been given antibiotics that almost killed him, recovered from the shock of the antibiotics, and was sent home with the same bad heart that had brought him to the hospital in the first place.

My parents were staying on Long Island for the months of July and August. They had rented a house in the dunes east of Amagansett. It was off Route 27, where the road makes a run across the flats to Montauk. The island is narrow there. You can see water on both sides of the road. Sand blows across the pavement. That summer, I was dating a girl I had dated in high school. Being with her was like being back in my town. We were living together for the first time. There was no longer a plane to catch or a train steaming at the end of the platform. I soon realized that she did not like me. She told me that by its nature, being a writer is selfish. Because I grew up in a town full of businessmen, I agreed. If I did not do something, I knew I would marry this girl. It would just happen. Then I would be married to a person who did not like me. I left her the keys to my apartment in the city and moved to the house on Long Island, where I planned to stay until she returned to Chicago at the end of the summer.

When Ben got sick, my parents chartered a plane at the East Hamp-ton airport and flew to New York. They sat with him in the house in Flat-bush. He was gaunt, going away. Did my mother impose herself on Ben, or was she asked? It's a stupid question; a daughter trying to help her dying father is only good. "She wanted to come back here and save the day," Gladys later told me. "Your mother wanted to be the hero."

"I was horrified by how they had treated him at Maimonides," my mother told me.

"They said there was nothing more they could do, and sent him home," said my father. "It could be six months or a year, but he would become weaker and his heart wouldn't function and he would die. He didn't want that life. He asked your mother to help get him to a doctor who would do an operation."

My mother had an inside track to one of the best cardiologists in the city, David Blumenthal, who happens to be my cousin, the oldest grandchild of Morris and Esther Cohen. ("If you are such a brilliant doctor," Esther had once asked David, "why are you bald?") David last appeared in these pages several thousand words ago, at the wedding of my parents. He was the skinny bucktoothed ten-year-old sitting next to Uncle Ira. In one picture you can see Ira and David on the right laughing together as my mother and father walk down the aisle. *One day this monkey boy is gonna carve you open, Ben!*

David is affiliated with New York Hospital–Cornell Medical Center, where he tends to the heartsick famous. Each year, his name appears in the *New York* magazine list of the city's best doctors. He often works in tandem with a physician named Wayne Isom, who is considered among the best heart surgeons in the world. Dr. Isom operated on David Letterman and Larry King. Marvin speaks of him dismissively, saying, "Your mother took my father to this Dr. Isom, who advertises on radio."

David put Ben through his paces: electrocardiogram, Vaseline, suction cups–the needles dancing, sketching the hidden topography of his chest; echocardiogram, the TV screen where his heart squirmed like a hamster; blood-pressure cuff and stethoscope. *Hold it, hold it, breathe!* David Blumenthal told Ben what he had already been told at Maimonides. His arteries were clogged, his valve failing. The blood could hardly get through. David held up a pencil and pointed to the tip and said, "This is the size of the opening."

Ben was eighty-eight years old, an age at which many doctors, fearing

complications and lawsuits, refuse to operate. He had been weakened by the ordeal at Maimonides. There were many risks. But he was strong and in relatively good shape. David thought that with Isom operating, Ben's prospects were excellent. Without surgery, there were no prospects at all. "[Ben] was told by Dr. Blumenthal that if he didn't have the surgery within a week, he would be an invalid," Gladys said. "He didn't want to be an invalid. I asked David, 'Is my father too old for the surgery?' And he said, 'Your father has the body of a fifty-year-old.'"

"Maimonides felt it was too soon after the anaphylactic shock, and he was in a weakened condition and should wait," said Gladys. "But my dad was an impatient man and he did not want to wait, so he followed what Dr. Blumenthal said and he went to Cornell Medical Center."

"[The doctors at Maimonides] begged him not to go to Cornell," Marvin told me. "It was too soon. Wait, wait, wait. But he wouldn't. This Dr. Isom convinced him that he should do it now, as well as your cousin. They convinced him. My dad wanted to be back to his old self. Didn't want to feel weak. Wanted to get it done. Everyone told him no. I told him, 'Go to North Shore [Hospital] and get another evaluation.' He turned it down. Didn't want to do it. So he got the best, Dr. Isom, with the reputation, and your cousin, David."

Go to any hospital and look at the board. Bypass surgery has become routine. They schedule them like flights. The surgeon cuts the veins from your leg and grafts them into your chest, *bypassing* the gunked-up arteries. A quintuple bypass is five new lanes to carry the blood to your ticker, capital city. Most of the trauma comes not from the surgery itself but from the aftereffects of deep anesthesia, the pain of reentry: to get to your heart, they break you open like a clam. The doctors stand over your open ribs like gearheads in Guyland standing over the engine of a Chevelle. Valve-replacement surgery is more complicated. The doctors hook you up to a heart-lung machine, which pumps your blood and breathes for you as they pull out your heart and lay it on a tray and cut away the bad valve and replace it with a pig valve or a titanium valve. A titanium valve lasts much longer—if you look in my father's coffin in a hundred thousand years (he had the same surgery), you will find teeth, bone, and titanium—but it has a tendency to clog.* A pig valve, which does not clog, breaks down after about ten years. Once the new valve is stitched into your heart, your heart is stitched into your chest and started up the way, on a cold morning, you jump a dead car—shocked, until it kicks over and roars.

Ben came through the surgery well. I visited him in intensive care. There were flowers and the ping of a heart monitor. My mother was sitting on the edge of his bed. She said, "Grandpa is going to be fine." I always had this idea that when you get old, you no longer care much about dying or not dying. Looking at Ben, I could see this was not true. He was holding my mother's hand and looking triumphant. He was clearly happy to be alive. He said, "It's my grandson." When I asked him how he was doing, he reached for a contraption a nurse had left behind. It looked like a toy. You blew into a tube at the top and a red ball danced. The harder you blew, the faster the ball danced. Ben was supposed to do this exercise

---

*People with this valve spend the rest of their lives taking a blood thinner called Coumadin.

several times a day to clear his lungs. But now he was doing it for fun, or showing off. I watched the ball dance, and it was as if it was his soul, scooting and jumping, or else his breath was his soul and the ball proved his continued existence.

Ben went home five days after the operation. My mother went with him on the ride to Flatbush. East on Sixty-eighth Street on the way to the FDR, south along the river, past the jagged shoreline once crowded with sugar refineries. As he looked out the window, he said to his daughter, "I am sorry, Ellen. I am sorry."

31.

I went with my parents to Flatbush a few days later. We sat in the kitchen. The mood was one of convalescence, as if the house itself had returned from surgery and was shaky on its pins. I was drawn to Ben. I wanted to sit near him and look at him and touch him. He was weak. All the color had drained from his face. He looked like a snow cone after you have sucked out all the flavoring. He ran a pale hand along his leg and said, "Come into the living room. I want to talk to you."

As I followed him through the house, I thought, "It's happening at last."

A few years before, when I was getting ready to graduate from college, my sister called me and told me that Grandma Esther was going to give me a check for a thousand dollars. My sister called this "the big check." I said to myself, "Maybe I will travel to South America with this big check, or maybe I will start a magazine." But the big check was more than money. It was a legacy. It was Esther blessing me. It was Esther telling me that I counted as much as my brother and sister and cousins. I was her sixth-born grandchild, but Esther did not judge by birth order. She

arranged it that, when I hit certain life markers, big checks would be issued even after she died. (A family joke had me getting five hundred
bucks when I got married, a thousand if the girl was Jewish.) A few hours
before the ceremony, Esther said, "Come, I want to give you something."
I followed her into a hallway. She smiled. I could see she loved me. As she
reached into her purse, she said, "At a time like this, you can forget to
eat," and handed me a bag of American Airlines peanuts. (The check
came a few weeks later by mail.)

Now it was happening again—the walk to the living room, the look in
Ben's eyes, how I felt like I already knew what he was going to say.

You are my grandson.

I know.

I love you.

I know.

*Even when we did not talk, even when I did not answer your letter,
I thought of you as my grandson.*

I know.

*I never did forget about you and have watched you from a distance,
from the shadows.*

I know.

We are the same, you and me.

I know.

But Ben did not say anything. He looked like he wanted to, but could
not get the words out. We stared at each other dumbly. His eyes went all
over me and he smiled. I asked him about the new television set. He gave
me a technical answer. Then we went back into the kitchen.

Two weeks after surgery, Ben returned to the hospital for an exam. The
fog had begun to lift. He was stronger every day. But when the doctors examined his scar, they noticed a popped stitch. The wound gaped open. It
was infected, and the infection had spread. It was destroying his heart
muscle. Ben had probably been infected during surgery. Because of what
had happened at Maimonides, Dr. Isom had operated without antibiotics. In many cases, such an infection can be quickly killed with a

megadose of vancomycin. Ben's allergy made that more difficult. An allergic reaction would be just as dangerous as the infection itself. Dr. Isom decided to open up Ben's chest and clean out the infection by hand. Within a few hours of his arrival at the hospital, Ben was back in the operating room.

David Blumenthal began experimenting with low doses of antibiotics, searching for a combination Ben was not allergic to. He soon discovered that Ben was not in fact allergic to vancomycin. His bad reaction had probably come from the way the drug had been administered: too much, or too fast. The infection was soon beaten back, but it was too late. Under the stress of the infection, Ben's body had begun to break down. He slipped into a coma. "He went down to that surgery strong, talking, walking, and ready to come home," Gladys said.* "He came back up on a respirator and in kidney failure. You could never talk to him after that."

Afternoons at the hospital. I used to go two or three times a week. I would speak to my mother in the hallway. She was there almost every day. My father, too. He would check in on Ben, talk to David, then phone Gladys. "My brother-in-law would call every morning after he saw my dad," Gladys said.

What was my mother thinking?

She had tried to help, and the whole thing had blown up in her face. " 'Dr. Isom said they had to cut out the infection,' she told me. "It was destroying him. So he had the second operation and he never woke up, and now they blame me."

"My father was at Maimonides and they suggested a certain type of treatment," my uncle Ira said. "Ellen and Herbert came to the rescue, sent him to a cardiologist who impressed them, who was their nephew. My father went into the hospital, had surgery by a world-renowned sur-

---

*All the Gladys and Ira quotes in this section come from the depositions my aunt and uncle gave a few years later, when my mother was exploring the possibility of contesting her mother's will.

geon and eventually died. Now, they say don't shoot the messenger, but just based on that, it might be enough for some people to say, 'To hell with her. I'm not leaving her anything. She killed my husband.'"

"You want to know my mother's words?" said Gladys. "'Your sister killed your father. She sent him to that hospital.' We all felt that way."

Here is the sound Ben used to make: *Go check those damn boxes!* *Do you love him here, here, or here?* *Don't talk to me when I'm driving!* *You know? No, I don't know. Why don't you tell me?*

Here is the sound he made now: *Ping, ping, ping. Ka-cooosh. Ka-cooosh. Ka-cooosh. Ga-ga-ga-thunk! Ga-ga-ga-thunk!*

Though he was in a coma, a nurse said he might be able to hear us. I stood next to his bed and talked about what was happening in the world. My brother and I bought a transistor radio and tuned the station to classical music and put the headphones on his ears. His arms were full of needles. His face was ashen. His body looked huge. Following the second surgery, the doctors, fearing they might have to go back in, did not close his rib cage. It was flung open like the hood of a car. I would stare at him. Nose, mouth, ears. I wanted to pull back the sheet and look at his innards. Now and then, his eyes would laze open, the way the eyes of an antique doll— blue and calm and glassy—laze open if you tilt its head back. The first time this happened, I ran for the nurse, shouting, "He's awake!" She shined a light into his pupils, then said, "No, that's just something that happens." It amazed me that this man who built an empire had ended up in this bleak place, this room where we're all heading, where you hang between this world and the next. He lived so long and worked so hard and got in so early and stayed so late and had no fun, and look where it got him.

Betty was at the hospital every day. She would stand over Ben and talk. She would say, *Come back, Benny.* She would say, *I need you, Benny.* She told me that Ben was Odysseus trying to get home to her. Everyone looked away when Betty said this, but it spooked me, her dogged belief that comatose Ben was at the helm of a square-rigged sailing ship, tormented by pride, tacking across a secret Mediterranean as Betty stood knitting on the shore.

———

Ben was in a coma for five months. During that time, Gladys kept track from her bed of every member of the family. She would call the nurses' station, the intensive care unit, the cell phones of each relative. She would ask, "Is Ellen there? Who is she talking to?" She was gathering evidence against my mother, my siblings, and me. She said we were not there, or not there enough, or not there in the right spirit. "My mother went every day," Gladys said. "My brother Marvin was always there. My nephew Steven Eisenstadt took my mother every Sunday. My nieces came. My nephew Jeffrey came. My sister came on occasion."

Of course, Gladys never went herself. "I couldn't walk down the front steps of my house," she explained. Asked why she didn't just get help, she said, "I didn't want to see my dad like that. He wasn't speaking. He was on a respirator. He wouldn't have known I was there."*

Because she is a shut-in, Gladys has become an artist with the telephone. She can play it like Dizzy Gillespie played the horn, dazzling riffs ending in a slow fade, or the crisp percussion of a slammed receiver. She can reach out with the telephone, or punish. To my aunt, the telephone is a blood-swelled part of the anatomy, the antenna that feels out the world. This is suggested by the house itself, which looks like every other house on that sad street but for a massive television dish that straddles its pitched roof.† With the right kind of eyes, you can almost see the billions of radio waves cascading into the house from the satellites that circle in low earth orbit. When you describe most people, you start with hair color, or height, or weight. With Gladys, you start with her voice, because it's her voice you remember and imagine. It's deep and breathy, the voice of an all-night DJ. Her conversation is wide open and free, like she has all the time in the world. She is curious and well read and charming and smart. She can talk about the Mets, or O. J. Simpson, or Michael Jack-

*Uncle Ira, who was living on West Eighty-eighth Street, a few minutes from the hospital by cab, hardly ever visited. "Three, four, five times total," he said. "It's just something I don't enjoy doing. And I try to make my rare trips as good as I can possibly make them so that someone can savor it for a while. It's just the way I am."

†The last time I was at the house, the satellite dish had been removed, apparently replaced by the more efficient broadband cable.

son, or J. D. Salinger, or anything. While Ben was sick, Gladys expressed herself through hundreds of calls made to family, to doctors, to experts, to laypeople, to nurses and the like, through which she gathered information and tried to shape the course of events. If it had been possible, my aunt would have rolled up her sleeves and operated on Ben by phone.

She called the doctors and nurses ten, twelve, fifteen times a day. Because he was the cardiologist on the case, because he was my mother's nephew, the brunt of this fury fell on David Blumenthal. This must be the hardest part for a doctor. You have advised a certain course of action, and it has failed. What if the patient is a relative? What do you tell the family? Do you feel guilty? But good doctors have a way of sloughing off even the worst turn of events. It's how they stay confident enough to keep recommending high-risk treatments, I guess. They must teach this to them in medical school: the moment to get on the phone and answer all the questions, the moment to stop taking every call, the moment to become unreachable.

> ATTORNEY: What information was it that your sister gave that you that you thought was inaccurate?
> GLADYS: I don't think it was inaccurate. I know it was inaccurate.
> ATTORNEY: Okay.
> GLADYS: She had said that her husband's nephew, Dr. Blumenthal—and really, more it was her husband who told me this—that he and my sister, Dr. Blumenthal and my sister were very, very close and that she had like a personal hot line to him and that he would report everything to my sister and that they were on very, very close terms . . . and the reason we agreed [to go to New York Hospital] was because my sister said she had this relationship with Dr. Blumenthal . . . She had no relationship with Dr. Blumenthal. He didn't even want to talk to her.

To me, this exchange is useful in the way when you wake up from a long nap, a look at the clock is useful. It gives a sense of the objective reality. Because I don't know what goes on at New York Hospital and I don't know why Ben did not want to take money from Morris, but I do know my mother and I do know my cousin David and I do know that in this instance Gladys sounds crazy. She speaks of the machinations of Ellen as certain other people speak about the machinations of the Freemasons, or the Illuminati, or the Jews.

Have you ever been in a hospital and walked by the nurses' station and the phone is ringing and ringing and no one picks it up? Well, that's my aunt Gladys calling, searching, digging, inquiring, probing. She talked to doctors from Maimonides, friends, experts, and know-it-alls. She gathered every statistic and story of malfeasance associated with New York Hospital. Because she had never visited the hospital herself, it became to her an abstraction, a dark star. She talked about Andy Warhol and his death at the hospital. She talked about Libby Zion, the daughter of the newspaper columnist Sidney Zion, who, admitted to the hospital and treated for cardiac arrest, had an adverse reaction to a drug given to her and died. "I wanted to call Sidney Zion and say, 'Look, you have clout and you hate that hospital. They took your daughter. They said it was cocaine, they said it was this, said it was that,'" Gladys told me. "'And we need you. We don't want the money. We just want to expose them.' I mean, Andy Warhol died in that hospital."

Gladys can catalogue the various miscues in the treatment of Ben. "In cardiac care, they mixed up the tubes, and so instead of giving him oxygen, he was taking in carbon monoxide and emitting oxygen.* When I spoke to Dr. Blumenthal about it, he said, 'Well, these things happen.' And I thought, 'Well, not to my father.' Well, all right. Then they were feeding [Ben] through a tube in his stomach and the medication went into his lungs and he got pneumonia."

Asked how she came by her information, Gladys said, "I spoke to doctors. I spoke to a nurse there. Donna. I spoke to my brother, who knows a lot about medicine. I spoke to Dr. Isom. I spoke to an infectious-disease doctor."

---

*I think this would have made Ben a plant.

She said the hospital was rank with germs. As proof, she cited a call she made to the nurses' station that was answered by a woman who "had laryngitis."

"Your cousin was wonderful," Marvin told me. "I don't blame him for my father's death. The operation was a success. It was just that the antibiotics they gave were second rate. And if the operating room was sterile, he wouldn't have gotten the infection in the first place."*

In April 1996, when Ben had been in a coma for around five months, my parents flew to Paris. My father was working for a bank and my mother was working with him, as she often does.† It was a business trip that had been scheduled for over a year. Betty did not want my mother to go, but my mother went anyway. According to Gladys, my mother had been warned by doctors that Ben had only a few days to live. If it had been Duluth or Akron, probably no one would have made an issue of it. But it was not Duluth or Akron. It was Paris. "You cannot go to a place like Paris when your father is in the hospital," said Gladys, who, in all of those months, did not once visit her father.

Shortly after my parents arrived in France, they got word that Ben had died. "His heart split in two," Gladys said.

A few weeks later, when David Blumenthal sent his bill to the house in Flatbush, Gladys scrawled a sentence across the top and sent it back.

It said, "You killed him. You collect from him."

The funeral home was on the edge of Brooklyn, out where avenues are huge and desolate and the buildings are two stories. Everyone was there but Gladys, who, in her place, had sent her friend Sherry. Though Gladys was not there, she made many of the arrangements, scheduling the burial for the earliest possible moment, less than twenty-four hours after

---

*When complaints made by my family members were presented to New York Hospital, a spokesman responded by email, "It would be inappropriate for us to comment."

†When my father gives a seminar or speaks to a group about negotiation, my mother travels with him to manage the crowd, hand out materials, work the door, and deal with bills and expenses, among other things.

Ben's death. Gladys did this, some of us came to believe, to make it impossible for my mother and father to make it back in time. In the end, my parents decided to take the Concorde—it was the only way—reaching the mortuary just before the prayers began. My mother looked devastated. As long as Ben was alive, there was always a chance for another chapter, another page. Now everything had been frozen, and the world after Ben had begun. The rabbi spoke less about Ben than about the generation he was said to represent: Americans born at the beginning of the last century, who came through the wars and the Depression, who knew how to make things, who were tight-lipped and stoical.

We drove in procession through the empty streets of Brooklyn. We got onto the Belt Parkway. We went under viaducts. We merged onto the Long Island Expressway. My mother was with her siblings in the first car behind the hearse. I was in another car, with my father, my brother, my sister, and my father's sister, Renee Blumenthal. The clouds were dark and the rain was coming down. The weather was so endless it seemed it must be raining everywhere, even on the moon. We passed little suburban towns that seemed to swim in the rain like sad little islands.

I asked my father how old Ben had been.

"Eighty-nine," he said.

I said, "Eighty-nine. That's old. That's almost a hundred."

"It sounds old," said Renee, "but when you reach our age, it suddenly does not sound so old anymore."

My father, who was staring out the window, said, "Bullshit. Eighty-nine is old."

The rain had let up by the time we reached the cemetery. We stood around as the workmen lowered the coffin into the ground. The rabbi said prayers, and then some men stepped forward to say Kaddish, the Jewish prayer for the dead, but you need ten men to make it official, and there weren't ten who knew all the words, and some who said they did know all the words were faking. You could just tell.

32.

Betty went home and went to sleep. She did not come to the phone, did not talk, did not eat. Ben's death was like the death of a star that makes the planets go wobbly. My grandparents had been married for close to seventy years. Betty slept for weeks. It was the sort of all-encompassing coma-like sleep in which the sleeper dreams only of sleep itself. She was mimicking the behavior of Ben, willing herself into a coma, willing away her consciousness so she could join her husband in nowhere. During the last hours in the hospital, she sat in a chair saying to herself, "He is going to die. He is going to die. He is going to die."

My mother learned the details of Ben's will at the shivah in Flatbush that followed the funeral; she and her children had been almost entirely excluded. Gladys later said, "I said to my friend Sherry, '[Ellen] is never going to come back to this house again.' I just knew that she would be very angry and very upset and that she would not come back."

I have since come into possession of the will, which I have deconstructed and frisked for hidden meaning.

Last Will and Testament of Benjamin Eisenstadt*

September 21, 1992

ARTICLE THIRD:

If my wife, BETTY EISENSTADT, shall survive me, I give and bequeath to her all of my personal and household effects and all other articles of tangible personal property, together with all policies of insurance covering such personal property owned by me. If my said wife fails to survive me, I give and bequeath all of said property to my daughter, GLADYS EISENSTADT. If my said daughter fails to survive me, all of the said property shall be distributed to my surviving issue.

ARTICLE FOURTH:

If my wife, BETTY EISENSTADT, shall predecease me, I give and bequeath the following:

A. The sum of One Hundred Thousand ($100,000) Dollars to my daughter ELLEN E. COHEN, if she shall survive me.
B. The sum of Fifty Thousand ($50,000) Dollars to each of my grandchildren who shall survive me.
C. The sum of Twenty-Five Thousand ($25,000) Dollars to the UNITED JEWISH APPEAL—FEDERATION OF JEWISH PHILANTHROPIES OF NEW YORK, INC, New York, New York.
D. The sum of Twenty-Five Thousand ($25,000) Dollars to ADRIAN FALCON, if he shall survive me.

*This is not the entire document, only the parts that seem relevant.

ARTICLE FIFTH:

I give and bequeath all shares of Class A Common Stock (Voting Stock) of Cumberland Packing Corp., owned by me at the time of my death, as follows:

A. If my wife, BETTY EISENSTADT, shall survive me, I give and bequeath such stock as follows:
    - One (1) share thereof to my wife, BETTY EISENSTADT.
    - One (1) share thereof to my grandson, JEFFREY R. EISENSTADT.
    - Three (3) shares thereof to my son, MARVIN E. EISENSTADT. If my said son shall predecease me, said shares shall pass to my grandson, JEFFREY R. EISENSTADT, if he shall survive me.

B. If my said wife shall predecease me, I give and bequeath such stock as follows:
    - Six (6) shares thereof to my son, MARVIN E. EISENSTADT. If my said son shall predecease me, said shares shall pass to my grandson, JEFFREY R. EISENSTADT, if he shall survive me.
    - One (1) share thereof to my grandson, JEFFREY R. EISENSTADT. If my said grandson shall predecease me said share shall pass to my son, MARVIN E. EISENSTADT, if he shall survive me.

In the past, Ben had spoken to Ellen about his estate and he had made certain promises. He told Ellen that she would share equally in his legacy. Marvin and Ira would get the business, Gladys would get the money, Ellen would get the property. She had instead been tossed a scrap. It might look like Ellen had been given a hundred thousand dollars while everyone else had been given nothing. In fact, Ellen had been given a hundred thousand dollars (or would have been if Betty had died first) while everyone else would end up with millions, because Ben had tied up the vast majority of his money in the corporation, then, before and after he died, divided the corporation among Marvin, Ira, Jeffrey, and Betty. The stock that was passed on to Marvin and Jeffrey over the years is worth perhaps a hundred million dollars. Ira had been taken care of long before, having been given close to half the company by Ben. Still, in this document you see the workings of primogeniture: Marvin and Jeffrey, the oldest son and the oldest son of the oldest son, were given the class-A voting stock, while Ira and Steven Eisenstadt, the youngest children in each of their respective nuclear families, were given nothing. Gladys was left a fortune in property (the house) and cash. According to Ben's will, the grandchildren, the Eisenstadts and Cohens, would each get fifty thousand dollars, so were seemingly equal in the eyes of Grandpa Ben. And yet, because the big money is all controlled by Marvin, the Eisenstadt grandchildren will, in all likelihood, inherit the millions of dollars accumulated over the years by Ben, while the Cohen grandchildren will get nothing. By shorting Ellen, Ben shorted my sister, my brother, and me. The old man spanked my brother Steven when he was six; now he was spanking him again.

My mother felt that she and Ben had reconciled. She stepped in when Ben had been sent home from Maimonides; she found him a cardiologist and a surgeon; he had even apologized on his way back from the hospital. (No one knows for what.) Over the years, he had made certain promises. In addition, my mother had been told by Ben that, for other reasons, he wanted to disinherit Jeffrey. Yet none of this was reflected in the will. In fact, Jeffrey came out very well. And Ben was the sort of man who would amend his will when circumstances changed. Yet this document was dated from 1992, four years before he went in for surgery. The date seemed suspicious. Wouldn't Ben have reviewed the document before facing the knife? For these reasons, my mother wondered if this was in fact her father's last will.

Maybe there had been others?

When I asked Marvin, he told me Ben basically died broke, and had no money to give my mother or anyone.

It's true. Ben's personal accounts were depleted. At the time of his death, his liquid assets amounted to only five hundred thousand or so. In his last years, he had even borrowed seven hundred thousand from Cumberland Packing. Of course, this means nothing, because most of Ben's money was plowed back into the business. In this way, it was kept safe from the government, from the IRS, and from my mother.* If Ellen came to challenge, Marvin could merely shrug and say, "My father basically died broke."

Soon after my mother read the will, she received a letter from Pearl Polifka, a tax and estate lawyer. The letter broke down Ben's remaining assets, many of which had been turned over to Marvin and Gladys and Ira before Ben died.

- Large cash accounts
- The factory buildings
- New York real estate
- California real estate
- Cumberland stock:
    - Class A: Voting stock (valued at $27,620 a share)
        - Ben: 5 shares
        - Betty: 5 shares
        - Marvin: 5 shares
    - Class B: Non-voting stock
        - Marvin 49.87%
        - Ira: 49.87%
        - Jeff: 0.26%
- Ben's personal stock:
    - RJR Nabisco, 10,000 shares
    - Con Edison, 800 shares
    - Entourage International, Inc, 20,000 shares
    - Rite Aid Corp, 1200 shares

---

*I learned some of these techniques from a book called *How to Disinherit Your Son-in-law . . . and Stiff The IRS*, by J. Dan Recer (North Little Rock, AR: Afri Publishing Division, 1997), which includes the chapters "He Wanted His Father-in-Law . . . Dead," "Wiping the Smile Off the Son-in-Law's Face," and, "Turning His Smile to a Grimace."

- Carolina Power & Light, 1100 shares
- Chase Manhattan Bonds, 25 K
- State of Israel Bonds, 6 K

Polifka asked each of Ben's children to sign a waiver agreeing not to contest the will. "The waiver merely says that you consent to the filing and admission of the will with the court. It is typical for family members to sign a waiver and I hope you will do so since that will save time and legal fees."

What did my mother do?

Nothing.

She did not sign and she did not refuse to sign. She waited. She let the days go by. She did not want to contest the will, but she was not yet ready to relinquish her rights.

To the Eisenstadts, Ellen not signing the waiver was of major importance.

"Mom was very upset by the will," my sister told me. "She was not upset about the money, but by the idea that she had been kept completely on the outside. She was upset that her father had left her nothing. And as she is trying to deal with this, Gladys keeps calling and saying, 'How can you be upset? Why should you get anything? What do you deserve?'"

"It wasn't enough for them to leave her nothing," my sister explained. "They also wanted her to say it was okay that they had left her nothing."

I learned about the will and the waiver not from my parents—they had not told me their plans, if they had any, and I had not yet realized that the past of your family is your past, too—but during a call from my cousin Debra Eisenstadt, who over the years had become a close friend of mine. I think members of the extended family found hope in this friendship. It was the innocence of children. It was Israelis and Palestinians playing Twister. As far as I was concerned, it depended entirely on an unspoken agreement that we not talk about the family. If we started talking about it, we would end up taking sides. This was harder after Ben got sick. On one occasion, Debra imitated my mother's voice in a way that made me bristle.

As soon as Debra called that day, I knew it was not going to be one of our normal talks. Her voice was hard, direct. She had worked herself up for a confrontation. She wanted to know why my mother would not sign the waiver, why my parents were threatening to contest the will, and why my father had called her father a "felon."

I remember where I was when Debra said all this. I was in the living room of my old apartment on West Eleventh Street looking down Washington Street at the Twin Towers, which stood at the foot of the island like double exclamation points.

I told her I did not know what she was talking about. I had heard nothing about the will. I said, "If we are going to be friends, we cannot talk about this. It's my mother and my father and my brother that you are talking about, and soon I will feel the need to defend them and you will not like what I have to say."

As soon as I got off the phone, I called my father. I asked him about the waiver and the will.

He said, "It's your mother's decision."

When I told him what my cousin had told me about my father having called Marvin a felon, he said, "Well, he *is* a goddamn felon."

In the end, my mother did not contest the will. She did not want to take the bad moment and live in it and extend it indefinitely. It was too painful. I think this decision had something to do with my sister and me. We begged her not to challenge the will. I said it would be a mistake. She would have to relive the pain under oath. She would have to tear open her chest for the world. Who wants their stupid money, anyway? If the money from the estate is the cost of getting away, consider it money well spent! My voice broke as I said this, and I spoke fast, with tears in my eyes.

Even after my mother dropped any notion of contesting Ben's will, Gladys continued to call. She was a tongue probing a sore. When my mother stopped taking these calls, Gladys started calling my sister.

"How can your mother possibly feel entitled to anything?"

"Why doesn't your mother call Grandma Betty?"

"Why is your mother angry?"

Gladys rambled, reminisced, argued, left messages, hung up, and called back. "She kept telling me how ridiculous it was that my mom was upset about not being left anything," my sister told me. "She said, 'No one got anything, Ben had no money.' I would try to get off the phone but she would not let me go. She said, 'Betty got the house, Betty got everything. Does your mother think she should get more than Grandma?'

"Finally, I said, 'Aunt Gladys, is that really true? Ben set up a trust for you which has God knows how much money in it. Marvin and Ira got the business.' And she says, 'You're saying your mother should get the business? Marvin and Ira founded the business and spent their lives working for the business.' Then she says, 'Your mother is the richest woman in the country. She goes to Paris. She has diamonds all over. She stays at the Plaza. She buys designer clothes. She flies on the Concorde. Where do we go? What do we do?' Then she started telling me these ridiculous stories about how Ben and Betty offered to help Mom at times and Mom had said, 'No, I don't need your help,' stories that bear no relation to the real world.

"By the way," said my sister. "Gladys was totally supportive of O. J. Simpson. She is sure O.J. didn't do it.

"Then she told me that Ben and Betty had in fact paid for everything Mom and Dad had over the years. She said that Ben and Betty paid for our houses and our vacations and had given Mom and Dad like a hundred thousand dollars and all these things."

My sister was so shaken by this call that she immediately phoned my father and told him everything, and he flew into a rage and called Flatbush and got Gladys and Betty on the phone. "You told my daughter that you gave me all this help and money? You gave me nothing! You gave me less than nothing! You say you gave me a hundred thousand dollars? Prove it! There would be records or tax returns! If you show me any evidence, I will give you a hundred thousand dollars right now! But if I prove you never gave me nothing, you give me a hundred thousand dollars! How about it?"

"The last time he spoke with my mother, my brother-in-law, he was yelling and screaming at her," Gladys said in her deposition. "I took the phone away. My mother sat there, she looked cowed and I cursed, I said—I used a word I never use, a four-letter word, and I hung up on him."

Gladys had been deeply shaken by the prospect of a will contest. In her worst nightmare, Betty dies and Ellen challenges the estate, and the trusts and the house itself get tied up in court, or, worse, the house ends up in the possession of my mother. In the months after Ben's funeral, Gladys expended great amounts of energy trying to get Betty to change her will. Gladys wanted the house and the money from the trusts given to her while Betty was still alive, or immediately upon Betty's death. Because Betty's health was failing, this became a race against the clock.

And so it comes to this, all the twists and turns lead back to Flatbush, where these two women, one ancient and stooped, the other crippled and house-bound, struggle and wound and manipulate in the final battle over the gold.

"We tried to do crossword puzzles," Gladys later said.* "We watched Jeopardy, we watched television. [Betty] did a lot of sleeping. She spoke on the telephone. I would read to her."

In these months, the relationship between Gladys and Betty, which had always been complicated, grew into a tortured epic.

"She was angry," said Gladys. "She was offensive. She never said anything nice."

"She said, 'You don't love me.'"

"She said, 'You didn't love your father.'"

"She said I wanted her to die, that I prayed for her to die."

According to Gladys, Betty's psychiatrist told Gladys that she (Gladys) was, "living in a concentration camp."

"Now, that's a little bizarre," said Gladys, "since I was being fed and there weren't dogs and gates. I asked him what he meant. He said what he meant was that I could be expected to be beat up, figuratively, every hour by my mother."

*Much of this information and all of the quotes come from the depositions that Gladys, Ira, and the estate lawyer gave under oath after Betty died.

LAWYER: Were there times when Betty declined to speak to you?

GLADYS: Yes.

LAWYER: How long would those periods last, on average?

GLADYS: Three or four days.

LAWYER: Were there periods of time when Betty refused to visit you in your room?

GLADYS: Many times. I'd say to her, "Why can't you come in." And she'd say, "I just can't."

Betty was heavily medicated, the doses kept increasing, and the medication was controlled by Gladys. "In the morning, she took Toprol," my aunt testified. "She took a potassium supplement. She took furosemide, which is Lasix. She had drops for macular degeneration. B_{12}, Zoloft, 81 milligrams of baby aspirin, and Ocuvite, a multivitamin for free radicals. In the evening, she took Vasotec. She was depressed. She was angry. She was non-communicative. She took Ativan and Xanax. The doctor said 50 milligrams [of Zoloft] would be a panacea. Then it was upped to 100 milligrams. It wasn't a panacea. He upped it to 150 milligrams."*

Betty was cared for by nurses, by my aunt's friend Sherry, who when Ben began to deteriorate, moved into a vacant room on the second floor of the house, and by Gladys herself, who demanded a salary for this work, because she made calls, handled pills, dealt with taxes and real estate. At the end, Gladys was being paid three thousand dollars a week. In this way, she earned three hundred thousand dollars. "My mother knew I loved her," said Gladys. "She wasn't sure about anybody else except my dad, maybe. She could depend on me for everything."

If Ellen called Betty, Gladys had Sherry listen in and report back:

LAWYER: Did you ever listen in on any of the phone calls that your mother received?

GLADYS: Once in a while I had my friend Sherry listen. I didn't listen in because, well, there's a mute button on the phone and if

*In her deposition, Gladys said Betty had also been given Thorazine during a stay in the hospital. Thorazine, a favorite in mental institutions, is used to treat, among other things, schizophrenia. It is sometimes called the chemical lobotomy.

you press the mute button you can't hear the other person breathing. My hands weren't good enough to press the button.

LAWYER: Why was anybody listening to those calls?

GLADYS: I wanted to see what my sister's attitude was, if there was any hope that there could be some kind of reconciliation and how my mother responded to her and how I was supposed to, you know, go about discussing my sister with my mother.

In the last weeks, an effort was made to reach out to Ellen. "My mother preferred my sister's company to mine," explained Gladys. "My sister made her laugh. Ellen had an outrageous sense of humor. My mother needed that."

I don't think Betty was reaching out because my mother made her laugh. I think she was reaching out because she was trapped. Gladys was drawing a salary and had moved her best friend into the house and was controlling the medicine and listening to the phone calls and managing Betty's every contact with the outside world. When Betty refused to talk to Gladys, or go into Gladys's room, my aunt became infuriated. *Betty won't go into Gladys's room? Fine! Gladys will observe Betty as Gladys observes the rest of the world.* She had a surveillance camera mounted in the room where Betty slept—a bed had been moved into the living room so Betty would not have to climb the stairs. Gladys said she did this to keep an eye on the nurses, but I think she was translating Betty into the format she understood best: television. The tapes are now stored in the basement in Flatbush: old lady sleeping, old lady walking, old lady taking pills. "And I would watch," said Gladys. "I spent many nights awake watching."

Near the end, Gladys assaulted Betty.

LAWYER: Do you know whether Gladys ever struck your mother during the period that the two of them were living together and Ben was not in the house?

IRA: Gladys told me once that it got physical between my mother and her . . .

LAWYER: Did Gladys ever tell you that she had physically restrained your mother?

IRA: She told me that she stopped [Betty] from trying to get up. If you want an explanation for why one would do that, one only had to see the fact that my mother had problems and needed help walking. So if you were in a chair there and you wanted to get up and you shouldn't go somewhere without someone helping you, I would probably try to restrain you if I cared about you.

LAWYER: Do you know that Gladys restrained your mother in ways that made it impossible for her to get up?

IRA: As I just explained, if you want to go outside, and, for example, say you were drunk and you wanted to drive, I would do my best, if I cared about you, to stop you from driving. If you couldn't walk properly without assistance and I couldn't assist you in walking, I would do my best to stop you from walking until someone else could help you walk.

LAWYER: Did you ever strike your mother?

GLADYS: Well, physically, my hands at the time and probably now, too, were bent. You know, they were like, Steven—I can't ask Steven* —so that I couldn't possibly strike anybody.

LAWYER: Are you saying that you never struck your mother?

GLADYS: I'm saying that I never inflicted any harm on my mother because my hands were incapable of doing that. I'd been told over and over by Dr. Lipkowitz, by my therapist, by Adrian [Falcon] that my hands couldn't hurt anybody.

LAWYER: But did you ever put your hands in contact with your mother?

GLADYS: I had physical contact with my mother, yes. In an angry way, yes.

LAWYER: Did you kick her out of frustration?

GLADYS: No. First of all, physically I cannot kick anybody. I have one fused leg.

LAWYER: Did you ever throw coffee at her?

*Gladys was calling out to my brother, Steven, who was in the room for the deposition but stayed in the background.

GLADYS: I threw cold coffee at her, yes.

LAWYER: And why was that?

GLADYS: She was going on about what a non-wonderful person I was, and I couldn't stand it anymore, and I got angry. And I had cold coffee there and I threw it at her. I'm not proud of it.

LAWYER: Did you ever tell Betty you would have her institutionalized?

GLADYS: When I was angry I did, yes.

LAWYER: Don't you remember complaining to Dr. Lipkowitz that he wasn't backing up with Betty your threat that you could have her institutionalized?

GLADYS: No. My father would have come down and killed me if I ever did it. And it would have killed my mother. I certainly did not want to kill my mother.

LAWYER: Then why were you threatening to have her institutionalized?

GLADYS: Because she was driving me crazy. I was getting sick.

LAWYER: Did you ever tell Dr. Lipkowitz that you hated your mother?

GLADYS: If I did, I was lying.

LAWYER: Did you ever exercise any form of restraint over Betty? Did you ever forbid her from leaving a room, or something like that?

GLADYS: Forbid her? You didn't forbid my mother.

LAWYER: Did you tie her to a chair?

GLADYS: Well, she would sit in the chair in my room and then turn away from me and I was afraid that if she decided to get up by herself she would fall. So what I did, I put one leg on one side of her and one leg on the other side of her and tried to keep her in the chair. If I really wanted to do my mother harm, I would have helped her get up.

More than once, Betty threatened to disinherit Gladys.

"I was angry," Gladys told the lawyers. "Then, as she repeated it, I was offended, because I didn't believe she would do that."

Asked why she didn't believe Betty would disinherit her, Gladys said, "She certainly knew that my brother didn't need [the money], she knew that my other brother didn't need it, and she knew that my sister didn't need it."

When confronted by Gladys, Betty said, "How could you believe I would do a thing like that. I'm not a monster. I would never do that."

Perhaps realizing that this was an admission by Betty that disinheriting a child is awful, the lawyer underscored the point by asking, "So on further reflection, when she discussed threats of taking you out of the will, [Betty] would describe that as monstrous?"

Just why were Ellen and her issue disinherited? Because Ellen brought Ben to the doctors at New York Hospital and those doctors killed Ben, because Ellen flew off to Paris when Ben was in a coma and he had only a few days to live, because Ellen did not visit often enough after Ben died, because Ellen did not sign the waiver regarding Ben's will, because Ellen married too young, because Morris wanted to buy Herbie into the business, because Ellen left Flatbush for Bensonhurst and Bensonhurst for the world, because Ellen's son wrote about Herbert's family but not about Uncle Abie, because, in his own book, Herbert acknowledged Frank Sinatra but not Ben and Betty, because if Ben loved Ellen how could Ben love Betty, because Ellen tried to steal Ben away from Betty, because Gladys was there and Ellen was not, because Sherry moved in and Gladys doled out the pills and threw cold coffee on Betty? It's like infinity. If you think about it too deeply, you go crazy.

Betty made changes to her will in 1996 and finalized those changes in the fall of 2000. The meeting that resulted in the final changes, attended by Betty and an estate lawyer named Alan Halperin, took place around the dining room table in Flatbush. In my imagination, this meeting is on permanent display, a diorama in a museum of exhibits that tells the story of the family. I enter through the big front doors and buy a ticket. I poke around the gift shop, looking at figurines of Ben, the red-haired Betty dolls, the replica of Uncle Abie's officer's cap, portraits of Asaro and D'Amato, Sweet'N Low refrigerator magnets, a model of a packing machine, a dollhouse version of the house in Flatbush complete with a miniature hospital bed that actually goes up and down. I buy a map and head down a wing marked LATER YEARS. I pass dioramas that show wax scientists injecting saccharin into taxidermic rats, lobbyists playing a hand of Seven Card D'Amato, the Concorde inbound from Paris, speeding my parents to Ben's funeral. If you stand on your toes, you can see a skyscape painted on the far windows of the jet, the clouds and the curve of the earth, New York in the distance, a fake Herbie, with realistic tobacco leaves scattered on his shirtfront, dozing in the aisle seat. And here, just before a display that shows the grave of Betty, is the diorama in which I am being disinherited. A psychiatrist is giving Betty a competency test. "Do you know your name?" he asks. "Do you know your address?" He makes Betty say she wants to leave Ellen nothing in her will. And here are Betty and Alan Halperin at the dining room table in Flatbush. "I asked [Betty] if she is absolutely sure she does not want to leave anything for either Ellen or her children or grandchildren," Halperin testified. "And she said absolutely. She does not wish to leave them anything. I had to make substantial changes in pen, then I read them all back to her and she signed it and we executed the will."

> LAWYER: Did you know that Gladys physically restrained Betty from time to time during the period that they were co-habiting after Ben died?
>
> HALPERIN: No.
>
> LAWYER: Do you know what psychotropic medication Betty was taking during the period from July 1996 until she died?
>
> HALPERIN: No.
>
> LAWYER: Would her being on psychotropic medication change your view of her being of sound mind?
>
> HALPERIN: No.
>
> LAWYER: Under no circumstances?
>
> HALPERIN: Not under these circumstances.

LAWYER: These circumstances being what, Mr. Halperin?

HALPERIN: Betty Eisenstadt, my observation of her, my discussions with her.

LAWYER: Would you consider somebody who is severely depressed to be of sound mind? Is that your opinion, your view?

HALPERIN: My view is that somebody who is severely depressed may certainly be of sound mind for purposes of executing a Will.

LAWYER: Well, when you talked to Betty to determine whether or not she was of sound mind, did you ever ask whether she was on medication?

HALPERIN: No.

LAWYER: Why not?

HALPERIN: I don't know.

LAWYER: Did you know that Betty was in the care of a psychiatrist during any of the period between 1996 and 2001?

HALPERIN: I learned of that fact certainly after Betty died.

LAWYER: Were you aware of the fact prior to Betty's death that she had been hospitalized several times during the period from 1997 to 2001?

HALPERIN: No.

LAWYER: And I take it that wouldn't have had any impact on your view about the soundness of her mind?

HALPERIN: Correct.

LAWYER: Even though you don't know what she was hospitalized for?

HALPERIN: Correct.

LAWYER: Well, certainly Mr. Halperin, if she was hospitalized because she was delusional or if she had attempted suicide, that would have had an impact on your assessment of her soundness of mind, wouldn't it?

HALPERIN: I don't know. I can just tell you that unequivocally I am convinced that she was of sound mind.

LAWYER: Were you aware of the fact that Gladys was in fact receiving remuneration from Betty in exchange for taking care of some of Betty's needs?

HALPERIN: I was not aware of that.

LAWYER: And if I were to tell you that there was substantial dependence by Betty on Gladys and that Gladys from time to time struck Betty or physically restrained Betty, would that alter your view about Betty's capacity to make a free choice with respect to her will?

HALPERIN: No.

I saw Betty at a party at my cousin Jill Eisenstadt's house in Park Slope. The rooms were open and filled with light. Prospect Park was just a few doors away. You could not see it but you knew it was there. You could feel all that green space the way, as you head east on the interstate, you can feel the approach of the ocean. I wandered through the rooms, dazed, thinking, So this is how it ends, this is how the cousins grow apart, this is how the members of the family have children and you have children and the children grow up as strangers, who have children, until any connection is lost. So this is how the planet is populated. This is how Brooklyn continues.

About an hour into the party, Betty walked up the stoop and into the house with the help of Sherry. "My niece Jill made a housewarming," Gladys said. "She invited my mom, Sherry, her sister Debra, her father and mother, and Ellen's children, Sharon, Steven and Richard. My friend Sherry called me and said, 'Your mother's not happy.' I said 'Why isn't my mother happy?' 'Because Steven Cohen was not speaking to her.' I called the house and I first spoke to my sister's son, Richard. Then I spoke to Steven Cohen. I said to Mr. Cohen, 'Today is not about the past. It is not about the future. It is just about today. Speak to your grandmother. She's very upset that you're not speaking to her.' He said, 'OK, I'll speak to her.' And then he never did."

I sat with Betty in the living room. I held her hand. She was weak, frail. I could see something of my mother in her, an essence, the thing that never ages. You had to sit close to hear her voice. It was full of gravel. Her hair was done up carefully and she had a lot of makeup on. Makeup on an old lady always makes me sad. I don't remember what we talked about. It was the last time I saw her. One morning a few months later, she told Gladys that she was not hungry for breakfast. Then she was not hungry for lunch. Then she was not hungry for dinner. She refused to eat. She wasted away. In September 2001, she was admitted to Maimonides, where she died.

33.

Soon after Betty's death, my mother decided to challenge her will. Or at least to investigate the possibility of a challenge. This would mean deposing the lawyer who had written the will, Alan Halperin, and the executors of the estate, Gladys, Marvin, and Ira Eisenstadt. My brother, Steven, and attorneys from the firm in which he is a partner represented my mother. My sister and I were told about the suit only later, when the action was well under way. Maybe we had not been told earlier for fear that one of us would get on the phone and beg our mother to drop the whole thing. My father told me about the contest as the lawyers were preparing for depositions. We were driving through the Hudson River Valley, crossing a beautiful ramshackle bridge. I looked through the beams and cross-hatchings at the shadows on the water and at the river curving through the cliffs toward the city. Whenever I am in the river valley, I imagine the first white sailors who ventured this far north, the masts of their tall ships passing above the Palisades, the Indians naked and free, the spooky wilderness. My father said this was something my mother had to do, a gesture of defiance, a protest, or something.

Marvin later told me he knew that I had not been involved with the lawsuit, which is why he agreed to talk to me. It's true; I did think the lawsuit was a mistake—there are some kinds of injury that cannot be redressed in court—but my feelings wavered when I read Betty's will. It stirred me to anger, for my own sake and on behalf of my mother. It was not just whom Betty left out (us), but whom she included, the nurses, maids, and drivers. If Betty had left my mother a ring, or a memento, or a photograph, or even a note . . .

But her will reads as if its real intent was to injure:

I bequeath all articles of personal or household use or ornament that I may own at my death, including (without limitation) china, furniture and furnishings, together with any insurance covering these articles, to my daughter GLADYS if she survives me. If my daughter GLADYS does not survive me, I bequeath my tangible personal property to my sons MARVIN and IRA, if they both survive me.

I bequeath the sum of fifty thousand ($50,000) dollars to each of the following grandchildren of mine who survives me: STEVEN EISENSTADT, JEFFREY EISENSTADT, JILL EISENSTADT and DEBRA EISENSTADT.

25 thousand to the United Jewish Appeal
25 thousand to Sherry Meyer
25 thousand to Adrian Falcon
10 thousand to Rita Anthony
5 thousand to Sara Romero
10 thousand to Judy-Anne Ramoutar
5 thousand to Hazel Prince

I hereby record that I have made no provision under this WILL for my daughter ELLEN and any of ELLEN'S issue for reasons I deem sufficient.

Marvin had known that my mother was going to be disinherited. He even told me that he said to Betty, "Maybe you should leave Ellen something." Yet he did nothing. Nor does he know why he should have done anything. He says the disinheritance of his sister is none of his business.

In deposing Ira,* the lawyer asked how anyone could possibly blame my mother for Ben's death.

LAWYER: Do you think that is a rational view?

IRA: I'm not going to really judge that. I really can't judge that.

LAWYER: You can't judge whether it is rational or irrational to hold Ellen responsible for your father's death?

IRA: I really can't.

LAWYER: What is it that prevents you from reaching that judgment about whether or not that is rational?

IRA: Because I consider myself rational, and I blame things on people that other people don't think it is rational for me to blame them for.

LAWYER: That is the very reason why you are in a good position to assess whether you think it is rational to blame Ellen. Do you think it is rational to blame Ellen for Ben's death? I am not asking you what other people think.

IRA: No, it wouldn't be rational for me to blame Ellen for my father's death.

The deposition of Gladys is strange beyond description. It is July 30, 2002. My brother, Steven, is back in the house of his aunt, only now he is a grown man and a lawyer and accompanied by another lawyer, a stenographer and a videographer. My brother's colleague asks Gladys if she will turn down her fan. The roar makes it hard to hear. My brother getting his aunt to turn off her cold air might be the point of the entire exercise—by warming the icebox, he will throw Gladys off her stride and defeat her at last. But she refuses. And the machine stays on. And the blades whirl

---

*In his testimony, Ira presented himself as a free-spirited nutty professor type; when asked his age, he said, "Fifty-five, I think." When asked when his siblings were born, he said "Exact years, I don't know."

away. Now and then, during her testimony, she addresses my brother directly, as if to say, "Steven, look what you have done to your aunt Gladys!"

On the day of the deposition, Gladys had taken pills. "Two Mylanta," she told the lawyer. Four hundred milligrams of Motrin. "And I took a Valium. Five milligrams. I took it around 8 this morning. An Atenolol. I also take Zoloft."

"Are you taking Zoloft now?"

"Yes."

My father believed that Gladys would be terrified by the prospect of such an encounter: strangers violating the sanctity of her room. He believed she would settle rather than face a deposition. But in playing chicken with Gladys, he had badly misread her character. The deposition must have been the most fun she had had in years. What could be better? The TV cameras had been reversed. The world had come into her house. My brother had to sit and listen as my aunt spun out her theories and trashed our mom. "[Ellen] was always angry," said Gladys. "She was angry at my mother. She was angry at my father. She was angry at Marvin."

My mother had no stomach for any of this. After the first depositions—when it became clear that David Blumenthal would be deposed, spreading the contagion to the other wing of the family—she dropped the case.* When I go back and look at these events, I can come to only one conclusion: Gladys won.

---

*My brother speaks of the decision clinically, as a matter of costs and benefits. In a recent letter to me, he wrote, "So why not pursue the suit? The problem was (1) it was making Mom a wreck, (2) if we won, we'd get 150–200g, (3) it was getting very expensive."

34.

When was Betty's funeral? It was on a Tuesday or a Wednesday. It was in the middle of one of the many hundreds of weeks I have used up and forgotten. I caught the 2/3 train to Brooklyn, got off at Clark Street, and walked past the brownstones of Brooklyn Heights. In New York, everything is so compressed. Go right, and you are at Ellis Island. Go left, and you are at the factory. Go straight, and you see Manhattan across the water. I walked to Willow Street and rang my brother's bell. He had offered to drive me to the funeral. I waited on the stoop. We were late. He wanted to stop for a cup of coffee, which made us later. He talked to a client on his cell phone and drank his coffee as he drove. He ran a red light, and the cars in the intersection braked, creating a kind of gauntlet. He spun the wheel, stepped on the brake, sipped his coffee, and continued talking as the car skidded right, then left, then right, leaving an S of burnt rubber.

Because I am getting to the end of this story, it seems like a good place to go through some of the characters, who, after I am done, will still be my relatives, and tell you what happened to them, where they are now. Ben is dead. Betty is dead. Uncle Abie is dead. Bubba is dead. Morris is dead. Esther is dead. Ira is alive. My parents are alive. Marvin has served his probation, and the company has paid its fine. Jeffrey is running the factory, which has fallen into third place but goes on churning out pink packets. Since the death of Betty, Gladys has gone out into the world. She had surgery on her hip, which has made her more mobile, and a car specially fitted to carry her around. She has been liberated by the death of her parents, for so many years the focus of her energy. Gladys could not grow up as long as Ben and Betty were alive, and so she just stayed in her room — a sick day that lasted almost thirty years. She goes on drives with Sherry now, and out to eat. She told me about her lunch at the Old Homestead in Manhattan (Axl Rose's favorite restaurant), where she ordered the Kobe beef hotdog. Spreading her arms, she said, "The thing was so big it was obscene."

By the time my brother and I got to the funeral, the testimonials had begun. Marvin was talking about Betty and her uncanny ability to take on the pain of others. His face was haggard and his shoulders stooped, but he still looked boyish. He likened Betty to a creature from *Star Trek* called an Empath, an extraterrestrial who, with a mystical laying-on of hands (or claws), not only feels your pain but removes it, actually taking it onto its own shoulders.

My mother was seated in the front row with her siblings, probably for the last time. I could see the backs of their heads (Marvin, Ellen, Ira) all bending in the same direction, like flowers toward the setting sun. I felt like I was playing out a scene in an old script. *This is the part where I meet a girl, this is the part where I get married, this is the part where I go to a funeral.*

Afterward, we stood near the cars. My mother spoke to distant cousins.

"Can you believe she left the house?" my sister asked me.

"Who?"

"Didn't you see her? Aunt Gladys is here."

It was my aunt's first appearance in public in decades. "The last time she was out of the house was for Jeffrey's bar mitzvah," Marvin told me. "Jeffrey is now forty-two years old."

Why did Gladys have such a need to attend Betty's funeral?

"Ben and Gladys had arguments, but they got along," Marvin told me. "It was different with my mother. Gladys had a tremendous love for my mother, and my mother never gave it back. Maybe she thought in death my mother would see how much she loved her."

I decided to go into the chapel and say hello to my aunt. I had not seen her since Ben died. She was slight and frail, standing with a cane, hair dark and coarse, cheeks rouged, face red and shiny. She knew I was there, but did not look at me. I said, "Aunt Gladys. It's me, your nephew, Richard."

Then she looked at me. Her eyes were cold. She said, "I have no idea who you are." And turned away.

The mourners got into their cars and drove to the burial ground. *Guyland.* Past the Levittowns and outlet stores and McMansions of Old Westbury. I would like to say I know all this from personal experience, but I did not go to the cemetery. My brother was my ride. He had to get back to the city. He said, "Come," and I went. So I tell this as my sister told it to me. It was sunny and cool. At the cemetery, the mourners stood by a freshly dug hole. The workmen, in their jeans and hard hats, stood over their shovels. The coffin was lowered by rope. The rabbi said the prayers. Then each member of the family shoveled in a spadeful of dirt. Marvin, Ellen, Ira, Sharon, Jill. Gladys wore a long coat and an orthopedic shoe. You could see her toes. Two goony guys from the factory took her under each arm. They helped her up the incline. As one steadied her, the other put the shovel into her crippled hands and helped her hoist and toss some dirt into the grave. Hitting the coffin—and Betty was in there, cold and jewel-bedecked and staring into the void—it sounded like buckshot.

Epilogue

Several years earlier, while Ben was recovering from his allergic reaction
to the antibiotics, my parents scheduled their return flight to East Hamp-
ton Airport. They asked if I wanted a seat on the flight. My brother and
sister would be going. The girl I had been dating that summer was scheduled to fly to Chicago that same morning. I decided I would drop her at
her flight, then meet my family. I had broken up with her the night before. She expressed no emotion when I did this, simply turned over and
went to sleep. I carried her bags through the terminal. When we reached
Security, she started to cry. The tears hung at the end of her lashes. But
they did not touch me. *Now is the time when your girlfriend cries at the airport*. A security guard turned me back. Never before had I been so happy
to be pushed aside by the law.

I waited at the curb for the shuttle bus. The wind was really blowing.
It was that end-of-summer wind that is crisp and already carries the smell
of the coming autumn, and the happiness wells up inside you because it's
all starting again. I stood on the bus, watching the terminals drift past, the

people coming and going. I got off at the Marine Air Terminal, where you catch the charters. I went into the coffee shop and bought a Diet Coke. The building was empty, a few pilots sitting around drinking coffee. I had two hours to kill. I went out the side door and stood on the blacktop. Carts loaded with luggage went by. I walked across the road and climbed a retaining wall and found myself on a strip of grass that dropped off into Flushing Bay. The city was across the water. I could see the Whitestone Bridge and the Throgs Neck Bridge and the Fifty-ninth Street Bridge and the Triborough Bridge and the World Trade Center and the Empire State Building and the Citicorp building spread beneath crystalline skies.

I lay down on the grass. I fell asleep. When I woke, the city was dazzling. It was as if it had been protecting me as I slept. I climbed over the wall and ran across the road to the terminal. My family was waiting. We walked to the runway and got onto the plane, a six-seat Cessna. The pilot threw some switches. The copilot said, "Here we go." We raced down the runway and the nose went up and then the city was far below. We climbed into the clouds. The plane started to shake. The turbulence went from bad to worse. We were being tossed. It seemed as if the engines would tear off and the wings fall away and the fuselage cartwheel across the sky. This is the story of the family, I thought. This is the only family you have. This is the family in its mischief and its turbulence. This is the family until the family shatters and the pieces assemble themselves into other families. The pilot said, *Roger,* and we started to ascend. The plane banked hard to the east and was gone into the redness of the morning sun.

ACKNOWLEDGMENTS

Thanks to Burke Hilsabeck for help with the research; to Cynthia Cotts for the fact-checking; to Jeremy Medoff for taking the photographs; to Jean Brown for transcribing tapes of the various interviews; to Andrew Wylie and Jeff Posternak at the Wylie Agency; to everyone at FSG, especially my editor, Jonathan Galassi; to my sister, Sharon, to my brother, Steven, and to my parents, Herb and Ellen; to Marvin Eisenstadt and Gladys Eisenstadt for telling me some of their stories; to my friends and family, those who think a lot of me and those who don't; to my wife, Jessica; and special thanks to Francis Albert Sinatra.